WHAT IS BETTER THAN A GOOD WOMAN?

What is Better than a Good Woman?

Alice Chaucer, Commoner
and
Yorkist Matriarch

Michèle Schindler

For my sister Nina,
knowing of her love for Alice Chaucer.

First published 2024
Amberley Publishing
The Hill, Stroud
Gloucestershire, GL5 4EP

www.amberley-books.com

Copyright © Michèle Schindler, 2024

The right of Michèle Schindler to be identified
as the Author of this work has been asserted
in accordance with the Copyright, Designs and
Patents Act 1988.

ISBN 978 1 3981 0969 8 (hardback)
ISBN 978 1 3981 0970 4 (ebook)

All rights reserved. No part of this book may
be reprinted or reproduced or utilised in any
form or by any electronic, mechanical or other
means, now known or hereafter invented,
including photocopying and recording, or in any
information storage or retrieval system, without
the permission in writing from the Publishers.

British Library Cataloguing in Publication Data.
A catalogue record for this book is available
from the British Library.

1 2 3 4 5 6 7 8 9 10

Typesetting by SJmagic DESIGN SERVICES, India.
Printed in the UK.

CONTENTS

Introduction	7
1 The Chaucer Family	8
Thomas Chaucer	9
Matilda Burghersh	10
2 Alice's Childhood	12
Her first years	14
Her first engagement	18
3 Marriage to Sir John Phelip	22
Sir John's death	25
4 Alice's First Widowhood	28
Alice's adolescence	29
5 Marriage to Sir Thomas Montacute, Earl of Salisbury	33
The wedding	34
Married life	38
Life in England and France	41
Alice's standing as Countess of Salisbury	46
Alice's second widowhood	50
Pregnancy and motherhood	57
6 William, Earl of Suffolk	64
Marriage to William, Earl of Suffolk	72
First years of marriage	74

What is Better than a Good Woman?

	Rise to power	84
	Contemporary opinion of Alice in the 1430s	96
	Alice's position at Henry VI's court	118
	Motherhood	129
	Combination of motherhood and political power	132
7	Alice's Relationship with Margaret of Anjou	145
	Gaining more political power	154
8	Alice as a Duchess	165
	Fall from grace	169
9	Suffolk's Murder	178
	Suffolk's trial for treason and Alice's reaction	179
	Suffolk's murder and Alice's reaction	189
	Widowhood once more	191
10	The Jack Cade Rebellion	201
	Charges against Alice	203
11	A Woman Alone	207
	Alice's changing relationship with Margaret of Anjou	215
	The beginning of the Wars of the Roses	217
	Arranging a marriage for her son	219
12	As *Mater Familias*	239
13	Alice's Death	253
14	The Aftermath	258
	Endnotes	260
	Bibliography	299
	Index	313

INTRODUCTION

She died a dowager duchess, a dowager countess, mother-in-law to a king's sister and grandmother to children who were in line to the throne. Her oldest grandson would be king by law for several months, ten years after Alice died. Her reputation would long survive her, the effigy on her tomb used as an exemplar of dress etiquette by Queen Victoria.

Alice Chaucer was to become a legend, but none of this could have been predicted when she was born to parents who were wealthy but untitled. Her ancestry was illustrious not because of any nobility of blood, but simply because of her grandfather, Geoffrey Chaucer, famous even in the fifteenth century and in later years revered as 'the father of the English language'.

This relation might have been a proud one, but not one that promised a glittering future for Alice in itself. Born to Geoffrey's oldest son Thomas and his wife Matilda Burghersh, member of the gentry, the future expected for Alice when she was born might have been nothing more and nothing less than marriage to a rich, if not noble, man, secured by her own father's wealth, and a calm, unexciting but hopefully happy life as a wife and mother. Presumably, such a future would have seemed suitable and desirable to her parents.

But fate was to have different plans for Alice.

I

THE CHAUCER FAMILY

The story of Alice's most famous ancestor, her grandfather Geoffrey Chaucer, has already been told often, most recently in Marion Turner's book, *Chaucer: A European Life*.[1] Though his reputation has, to a certain extent, become larger than life, the bare facts are readily available. Born in approximately 1343[2] to a wealthy vintner's family, he was given a position as a favoured servant in noble households, and due to his own charm and merits[3] rose in the ranks of those households. He married Philippa de Roet,[4] a knight's daughter, a marriage sometimes thought to have been arranged by the Queen of England herself. It was a presentable, perfectly suitable match. At the time he made it, it cannot have seemed very remarkable to anyone but Geoffrey and Philippa themselves; but in due time, this match would make Geoffrey come close to royalty.

Geoffrey and Philippa appear to have had a perfectly normal marriage for the time, but despite attempts by scholars to gauge anything about it from Geoffrey's works, more cannot be said. They had several children together, the oldest of whom was a son born in 1367,[5] whom they called Thomas. Interestingly, very little is known about Thomas's early life despite the fact Geoffrey's star rose in the 1370s. Being closely acquainted with Edward III,[6] Geoffrey came into royal favour. Edward was already an old man by then, but the

Chaucers' connection to royalty did not end with his death. Philippa and Geoffrey appeared to lead a respectable life as husband and wife, Philippa's sister Katherine was less conventional. Originally married to a man called Hugh Swynford, after his death Katherine became the mistress of one of Edward III's sons, John of Gaunt, and bore him four children. The relationship caused a scandal, especially when after the death of his second wife, Constance of Castile, John married Katherine, making their children legitimate by applying for and being granted a papal dispensation.

Thomas Chaucer

Scandalous though it was, through this marriage Geoffrey and Philippa became closely related to royalty, and their children had an actual prince as their uncle by marriage. The fact that despite this very little is known about their oldest son Thomas Chaucer's early life has led some scholars to theorise that there was some secret or mystery connected with him. Specifically, the scarcity of evidence has been taken as pointing towards a question mark hanging over his paternity: it has become an often-repeated theory that Geoffrey was not Thomas's biological father, John of Gaunt himself was[7].

Despite this theory's growing popularity, though, it does not have much to support it, merely the fact very little is known about Thomas's life for the first 25 years or so, and that John of Gaunt occasionally granted something to him and to his sister, Elizabeth.[8] This is, of course, is easily explained by the very fact they were his niece and nephew by marriage to a woman John obviously loved, and any attempt to see more in it veers into conspiracy theory territory.

However, while the most bruited, it is not the only theory about Thomas's parentage that excludes Geoffrey. Another theory, proposed by some Chaucer scholars but not widely known or supported, is that he was an illegitimate son of Philippa Chaucer's who went by the name of Reginald Curteys, until at the age of nearly 30 he adopted his stepfather's last name of Chaucer.[9]

What is Better than a Good Woman?

Why he should have changed his baptismal name in the process is not explained. Like the theory that assigns Thomas's paternity to John of Gaunt, it is not supported by much evidence. The only indication is a somewhat strangely worded grant to Thomas for something to be given to Reginald Curteys, obviously a different person.[10]

Even those scholars who reject both the theories have pointed out how strange it is that neither Thomas's grave, nor that of his daughter Alice's, carry the Chaucer arms.[11] This, too, is easily explained by the comparatively low birth of the Chaucers. By the time Thomas's tomb was erected, his daughter was a countess and a Lady of the Garter; by the time her own tomb was made, she was a dowager duchess. It is not particularly notable or surprising that she wanted to stress the more noble parts of her and her father's ancestry – de Roet, Burghersh.

Moreover, the theories fail to take into account that Thomas Chaucer was a popular and widely known man in his own right during his lifetime. Had there been even so much as a whisper of doubt about his parentage, it surely would at the very least been alluded to in the extensive written record about him that has survived concerning the second half of his life. The most simple and easy explanation is almost definitely the correct one: that not much is known about the first 25 or 30 years of Thomas's life because records were lost and because, despite his connection to royalty, he was not considered important enough to bother writing about before he became notable in his own right. What is known is that when he was in his mid- to late twenties, John of Gaunt purchased the right of marriage to an heiress for him. This heiress was called Matilda, or Maud, Burghersh.

Matilda Burghersh
Matilda's parentage was not exactly illustrious by the strict standards of fourteenth- and fifteenth-century nobility, but it was

The Chaucer Family

more noble than her husband's. Though the Burghersh family was not then part of the nobility, they were rich and wealthy members of the gentry and descended from nobles. Matilda's great-grandfather had been Baron Burghersh, her great-uncle Henry had been Bishop of Lincoln and Chancellor of England. Though Matilda's father, John Burghersh, Knight, Lord Kerdeston, did not occupy the same kind of high position as his ancestors, he was certainly still well-connected, though the details of this are hazy in contemporary sources. Of Matilda's mother, we only know that her name was Emma and that she died on 25 September 1419;[12] any more details about her, her husband and their marriage has been lost to history. All that we do know is that they had no son, or at least no son who survived childhood. Matilda was their second daughter, and upon his death in September 1391 she and her older sister Margaret became co-heiresses to his land and considerable wealth.[13] Margaret was already of age, meaning over fourteen years old, when her father died, but Matilda was not, and so became a ward of her aunt Joan de Mohun, Lady of Dunster. Only a year later,[14] Joan sold Matilda's wardship to John, Duke of Lancaster, who purchased it to arrange a marriage for his nephew Thomas Chaucer, doubtlessly considering her a good match for him. Some thirteen or so years younger than Thomas, Matilda's riches and connections alone must have made her seem a suitable bride for Thomas. Doubtless, she also brought a considerable dowry to the marriage, though sadly, this is speculation as details do not survive. Even if she did not, the facts mentioned above and the fact that though she was not herself noble, she was related to nobility, must have made her a great marriage prospect for the grandson of a vintner and a knight.

When exactly their marriage took place is sadly not known, though 1397 has been suggested as the year they started living together. If so, Matilda was around seventeen years old, while Thomas was approximately thirty years old when they married.

2

ALICE'S CHILDHOOD

The fact that records are so scarce about Thomas before his father's death in 1400 sadly means that we know nothing about the early years of his and Matilda's marriage. Though later records suggest nothing more but that theirs was a functional, if perhaps not affectionate, marriage, for the first years, even that cannot be said. It is known that Thomas tried and succeeded in making several claims to possessions in her name, most notably to her ancestral manor of Ewelme,[1] in which the couple was to spend a lot of time during the course of their marriage, and that in the early years of the marriage, he was often in France. In fact, one of the earliest records we have is of his receipt of a grant while in France, a few years before his father died, shortly after his wedding to Matilda must have taken place. In 1399, just before Richard II's overthrow, he was appointed Chief Butler,[2] and he was one of the few royal officials to survive Henry IV's usurpation without being stripped of any rights or positions. In fact, perhaps as a reward for his support, Henry IV was very generous to Thomas, not only keeping him in his position as Chief Butler and confirming him in the position for life in late 1402,[3] but also making him other grants. One of those was the constableship of Wallingford Castle, something that was to remain in the family even after Thomas's death.

Alice's Childhood

Possibly, this generosity was not only the result of Thomas's support of the new king. The relationship went deeper, due to Thomas's connection to John of Gaunt, Henry IV's father. Though Henry was John's son by his first wife, and thus not actually related to Thomas himself, four of Henry's younger half-siblings were Thomas's first cousins, and John, as discussed above, had shown an interest in Thomas. Since Henry IV and Thomas were the same age, both having been born in 1367,[4] it is very possible they knew each other well since their adolescence, long before Henry IV seized the throne. Though this is speculation and there is no indication of any sort of friendship between the two men, it is certainly notable that Thomas's career only truly started after Henry IV's usurpation. Whether correlation in this case equals causation is up for debate; perhaps, as is suggested by him becoming Chief Butler in 1399, he would have risen to prominence and power under Richard II as much as he did under Henry IV.

In 1400, Thomas's father Geoffrey died[5] leaving the wealth he had accumulated to Thomas. This, too, might have played a part in his rise, though sadly, the scant documentation of any details about Geoffrey's and Thomas's financial circumstances makes this hard to know. In 1400, Thomas became Speaker of the House of Commons,[6] a position to which he was elected four more times in later years. In the early 1400s, he also took over many of his late father's positions, which probably meant that he stayed in England more often than he had in the years before Geoffrey's death.

It may have been because of this that in 1403 or early 1404, Matilda became pregnant with their only (known) child. Matilda appears to have been around 24 then, and she had lived with Thomas for around six to seven years, but there are no records of her having any other pregnancies, or of her having lost children in infancy or childhood. Naturally, this does not necessarily mean it did not happen, in the light of the very scant evidence about the marriage.

What is Better than a Good Woman?

It is known that Thomas fulfilled all his duties for his positions during 1403 and 1404, as well as early 1405, but this would have been expected of him regardless, so no conclusions can be drawn from this about the pregnancy and whether or not he was worried about his wife and unborn child. Whatever happened during the pregnancy, it was to conclude happily when Matilda gave birth to a healthy baby girl.

Her first years

Though so little is known, it is almost certain the baby was born in Matilda's ancestral manor of Ewelme, probably between 28 April and 17 November 1404. When her father died on 18 November 1434, his Inquisitions Post Mortem put his only daughter and heir at the age of 30,[7] while upon Matilda's death on 27 April 1437, she was stated to be '32 and more'.[8] Though such inquisitions were frequently wrong, a reasonable accuracy is suggested by all but one, which made her a year younger, agreeing on her age.

Thomas and Matilda chose to name their newborn daughter Alice. It was a perfectly normal, common name, but despite this, their motivation for making this choice has been questioned by some historians. Due to the fame the new baby's grandfather won in the centuries since, an effort has been made to connect his granddaughter with him and his work. The fact that one of the best-known characters from his most famous work, *The Canterbury Tales*, shared her name has made this connection easy for those inclined to seek one, but there is no reason to assume that Thomas and Matilda deliberately named their child after The Wife of Bath. Most likely, little Alice was called after a godmother, or her name was chosen in honour of the Virgin Mary. She would have been baptised on the day of her birth, or a day later at the very latest, as was common then.

Though not a noble baby, as the child of a rich and influential man, it is possible her baptism was a spectacle for the village of Ewelme, as we know some baptisms were. Thomas and Matilda would have made sure it was a suitable occasion to welcome their daughter into the world, and, very importantly in the fifteenth century, into the church. As was custom then, Alice would have had two godmothers and one godfather,[9] though we can only guess who was chosen for the task. Though technically, the godparents were not supposed to be related to the baby by birth or marriage, this was a rule more honoured in breach than in observance, and it is possible that aunts or uncles were chosen to fulfil the role for Alice. Usually, baptisms for babies of the rich and noble included gifts of money for the child and their caretakers, and this would also have been the case for Alice's baptism.

Once she was baptised, she would have got her own staff, tasked solely with taking care of her and seeing to her well-being. Mothers of the nobility, and even well-off commoners usually did not breastfeed their babies but employed wetnurses. It stands to reason that Matilda chose to follow this custom, though in the absence of evidence, it cannot be said with complete certainty.

Alice's own staff would also have had so-called 'nurses', who were, in modern terms, nannies, and at least one 'rocker' or 'rockster'. This was usually a young woman, who was employed to rock the baby's cradle to help calm her and make her sleep. Despite the name suggesting this was their singular task, Nicholas Orme points out in his book *Medieval Children* that most likely, they would also have performed other menial tasks, such as changing the baby.[10]

Details about the everyday life of babies and young children are rare, and the few that exist are for royalty and therefore do not reflect what Alice's early life would have been like. Once more, as for so much of her early life, all we can do is make guesses, more or less informed ones, from customs such as we know they were, and from her surroundings, such as her mother's and father's life in the first years after Alice's birth and all we know about it.

When his daughter, who was to be his only child, or at least his only child to survive infancy and childhood, was born, Thomas

What is Better than a Good Woman?

Chaucer had already established himself as a political power to be reckoned with. In 1404, he was made Speaker of the House of Commons for a second time,[11] something he obviously took very seriously. Alice would, therefore, have grown up as the daughter of an important man. Not just politically, however, did Thomas Chaucer make a name for himself. He was obviously trusted, being tasked with arresting wrongdoers by the king,[12] and obviously important for the smooth running of the royal court. He was employed to inquire into treasons, arrest those who had spoken against the king, worked as escheator in Oxford and Berkshire[13] and performed a lot of other similarly low-key but important tasks.

Not only was Thomas important at court, he also steadily became wealthier, to the point of making loans to the king himself[14]. This engendered a certain closeness to the king, but it was an intimacy that could be fraught both for the king himself, unhappy with having to owe a subject, and for Thomas with regard to nobles and the general population, who could be angry the king was indebted to someone and thus by necessity giving him power. In short, it was both an honour and a danger, but despite this, Thomas managed to remain popular. This was due to his very special standing in society, neither too high nor too low. He had no noble blood, but through his mother he was a gentleman, and he was married to a woman related to nobility. Through marriage, he was the nephew of a prince. This meant he could not be accused of rising above his station by being close enough to the king to be so trusted. Nor was he high-born enough to be considered a likely threat to the nobility. He could profit from the position his wealth brought him without being considered a potential danger to anyone. It may be that his own charm helped him with this, as it is on record Thomas's household at Ewelme was a centre of social life, a much visited and admired place.

In the book *Thomas Chaucer*, published in 1926, the author Martin B. Rudd[15] details Thomas Chaucer's life and his social

Alice's Childhood

and political situation, and despite its age this book is still a well of information and has not been surpassed. For our subject, however, Thomas's daughter Alice, it is only relevant to know that Alice, who appears to have grown up in her father's household at Ewelme, would have grown up in a place of societal importance, surrounded by the trappings of wealth, by important people and, notably, by learning. Thomas Chaucer was a patron of the arts, which, given who his father was, should not be too surprising. He especially favoured the poet John Lydgate,[16] whose poetry was much in fashion in the early part of the fifteenth century.

Alice would have been shaped by this. Most likely, her parents would have taken pains to see her well educated. It is a bit of a myth about the Middle Ages that women were not properly educated, or not educated in scholarly pursuits. While certainly such cases existed, they cannot be said to have been the rule. We know nothing about Matilda's own education, or her opinion about it, but from what we know about Alice's own point of view on these matters, it can be concluded her mother supported her in receiving a good and thorough education. Definitely, we know that this is what Alice received, and that as an adult she could write as well as read English, French and Latin. Most likely, she spoke French fluently.[17]

Whatever Alice herself thought of her education at the time, it certainly would come to benefit her, though perhaps Thomas had her marriage prospects in mind when arranging for her to be so educated. Being married (to advantage) would have been the only choice for her future that would have seemed feasible to her parents, and most likely to Alice herself. For women of her standing, it was either that or joining a convent, with exceptions who did neither extremely rare. With Alice being an only child, and thus her father's sole heir, joining a convent would have been out of the question. As she grew up, and it would have slowly become clear that she would have no more siblings, she would have been raised in the knowledge of one day being a very rich woman. Again,

What is Better than a Good Woman?

we do not know if her mother had miscarriages or even short-lived children after Alice's birth, but if so, we have no indication of it. As Alice grew up, her parents may have slowly given up, their hopes and expectations all resting on their only daughter. They gave her all they could to make sure she would have as good a future as possible. They educated her well, perhaps partly in the hopes of raising her value as a marriage prospect, and as was expected of them, they searched for a suitable husband for her.

Her first engagement

Despite her undoubted advantages in the marriage market – her good education, the wealth she was due to inherit one day and the connections she would bring – Alice would not have ever been considered likely to marry a nobleman. Her father was a good negotiator and someone who took his chances, having dared in 1411 to contradict the king in Parliament and survive unpunished,[18] but even so, it is unlikely that the idea of matching his daughter with a nobleman ever occurred to him as more than a passing fancy.

It was not at all unusual for parents of very young children to arrange their marriage, but there is no evidence of Thomas making any enquiries or trying to come to an arrangement with anyone during his daughter's babyhood or early childhood. It is possible that such indications simply have not survived, but it is also possible that he waited for the best possible moment to find a husband suitable for his daughter, an advantageous match both for her and for himself. If that was his intention, it might explain why he did not do so until after Henry IV died, in 1413. Though always popular, Thomas's steep rise seemed to come to a sudden halt in 1411. Already in 1407, he had openly reminded the king that he still owed him money, and when he repeated this in 1411,[19] he was told that his having lent the king money did not mean he held any special privileges. After this, Thomas decided to make his excuses instead of attending the rest of Parliament, an outcome that was probably inevitable.

Alice's Childhood

This did not mean he was out of favour; almost immediately afterwards, the queen granted Thomas the manor of Woodstock during her lifetime, with the king shortly afterwards confirming it for after her death as well. This had been arranged as a way for both parties to have a satisfactory outcome from the situation, but the very fact Thomas was only prepared to be elected Speaker of the House of Commons again in 1414, when Henry IV was dead, suggests that despite all pretences at cordiality and the fact that a compromise was reached, his relationship to the king had cooled. Possibly, 1411 was a difficult year for him, and even if he already intended to find a husband for his then seven-year-old daughter he would have found it difficult, the low-key conflict with the king notwithstanding.

There is a suggestion that in 1411 Thomas had a serious relationship with a mistress called Ellen or Elena. Certainly, a woman of that name – obviously of some standing, as she had an annual income – was recorded to be 'residing with' him in one of his London properties in that year[20]. In itself, this does not have to mean anything untoward; she might have been a relative living with him. However, that is not likely, as if so, it does not seem consistent she would have her own income, making her rich enough to support herself. In such a case, she would have been more likely to live with him at his main manor in Ewelme. If she was his mistress, however, it is logical she would not have lived in the same household as his wife.

Such an arrangement, with his mistress openly living with him, could potentially have caused a bit of a scandal, and therefore be another explanation for Thomas's quiet removal from the king's closest circle. While it was far from uncommon that men had mistresses, and the idea of women never having lovers is ridiculous, to openly flaunt adultery was not the done thing. Henry IV's father and Thomas's uncle had learnt that when a scandal erupted about his relationship with Thomas's aunt, Katherine Swynford. It is conceivable that Henry IV wanted to avoid being connected with

What is Better than a Good Woman?

that sort of behaviour, and hence Thomas was removed from Parliament, while Thomas's comparatively low standing avoided it causing a huge scandal and being widely known and talked about. Again, of course, this is all speculation. The hard facts that are known are that Thomas spent the time between 1411 and 1414 somewhat disconnected from politics, unlike the decade before, and that it must have been for reasons more weighty than him reminding the king he owed him money, as such a reminder had not caused a similar reaction in 1407.

Probably, it was Henry IV's death in 1413 that helped Thomas to begin once more to rise in status. In the years between his gentle dismissal and the king's death there is no more evidence of his activities beyond his being mentioned in some fairly standard grants, such as being involved in conveying property. In 1414, however, within a short time of Henry IV's death, Thomas was on the rise again. For Henry V's Parliament, he was once more elected Speaker of the House of Commons,[21] and it seems he was in favour with the king and a much respected member of society once more. If Thomas's possible adultery had anything to do with his distance from king, court and power in the last years of Henry IV's reign, his relationship to the mysterious Elena may have ended by 1413, or Henry V was simply more tolerant of it. It is equally possible that he had no opinion on the matter and simply needed Thomas's support for what he had planned. Whatever the reason for his return to prominence, by 1414 Thomas was busy arranging for the future of his family.

This, of course, primarily meant arranging a marriage for Alice, who he must have known by that time would remain his only (legitimate) child, and his sole heiress. This would have made her a good marriage prospect, and Thomas surely did not forget to stress the connections to nobility she had, despite being a commoner by birth. Alice was only ten years old in 1414, so that any merits of her own, such as the intelligence and beauty for which she was famed as an adult woman, would not have played a part in any arrangements

Alice's Childhood

made for her marriage. This was far from unusual; personality and looks very rarely played a part in the arrangement of marriages. However, it is worth noting in this case that the two subsequent marriages Alice would go on to make were at least partly influenced by her personal attributes. Of course, because she was still a child in 1414, this would not have been the case with the first marriage.

The man Thomas Chaucer eventually chose for his daughter was John Phelip,[22] brother of William Phelip, who would go on to become Baron Bardolf in his wife's name. John Phelip, a gentleman, was closer in age to Thomas than he was to Alice, having been born in or around 1384. He had been married twice before, to gentlewomen. He himself was a member of the gentry, though one with excellent connections. His brother William, due to having been their father's heir, is generally stated in history books to have been his older brother, though several contemporary sources put them at the same age[23] so he is more likely to have been his twin. William was married to a noblewoman called Joan Bardolf, and John himself was described as a close friend of the king by Henry V himself.[24]

Thomas Chaucer was therefore arranging a marriage of equals; John and Alice were both not particularly high-born but had connections to those who were, and both were wealthy. Like Thomas, John had lent money to the king on several occasions, and it was quite obvious that for John to marry Alice was a business arrangement between Thomas and John. This was perfectly normal and is indicated by Thomas lending money to John once he was his son-in-law; but John was ready to share all of his belongings with his youthful wife, prepared not just to take but to give as well.

The marriage date is unknown, but it must have taken place in summer 1414, when Alice was ten, or shortly to turn ten, and her new husband was thirty, or shortly to turn thirty. It is then that she was first mentioned as his wife; his second wife, Matilda, having died in late 1413.[25]

3

MARRIAGE TO SIR JOHN PHELIP

As Alice was still so young, it is impossible the marriage was consummated – something that would have been illegal. In fact, her extreme youth has caused some later commenters to conclude that she was only engaged to John,[1] never actually married. However, both Thomas and John referred to Alice being John's wife, not his intended wife, or future wife.

It is possible that after her wedding Alice moved into her new husband's household, and it has sometimes been assumed that this is what happened. Even despite her extreme youth, it would not have been uncommon. However, given what happened later, and the military campaigns John was doubtlessly already planning for in summer 1414, this seems unlikely. The most likely version, which is supported by what scant evidence there is, is that Alice stayed in her father's household and little changed in her life despite being married.

John was very generous to her, unusually so. After the wedding, he made arrangements for her and for himself, very clearly having her future in mind. While it would naturally have been expected of him to take care of her, even in her extreme youth, he went above and beyond such expectations. Rather than settling some of his lands and possessions on her, as was common, he settled his entire estates on her alongside himself.[2] This was something that was very rarely done,

Marriage to Sir John Phelip

and which would have secured her future no matter what. Quite possibly, John chose to do this out of care for the child who was to be his wife, without any compulsion or pressure, though the fact that we know that Alice's third husband agreed to a fairly strict marriage settlement also makes it possible that these arrangements were part of the marriage agreement between him and Thomas Chaucer.

It seems unlikely the marriage or the arrangements made by her new husband meant much to Alice at the time. She was still a child, and even though, as Rowena Archer has pointed out, she 'became in many ways the son he never had'[3] and was treated by her father as such, she would still have been too young to understand the ramifications of it all. As her husband did, so her father gave her all she needed to make the marriage a success, purchasing the rich manor of Donnington[4] and settling it on Alice and John not too long after their wedding. This has sometimes been taken as evidence Alice lived with John from the moment of their wedding, and it is sometimes postulated that Thomas purchased it as a marital home for his daughter and her new husband.[5] However, while it is possible that this was on his mind, he did not buy the manor in 1414 but only in 1415. If it was a wedding present, it was therefore not intended to immediately serve as a home. It seems just as possible that, with war looming in early 1415, Thomas wanted to make sure his daughter was well taken care of whatever happened. Whether he made any similar arrangements for his wife Matilda, then in her thirties, we do not know.

John Phelip definitely did make arrangements for the event of his death when it became clear that war was unavoidable. Presumably, this realisation had already been dawning on most when the warlike Henry V became king in late 1413, and preparations had been made since that time, but by summer 1415, almost all was ready for his army to go to France, where Henry intended to take up his ancestor Edward III's claim to the throne of France, a claim that had already led to a lot of battles and suffering in Edward's time.

What is Better than a Good Woman?

Edward's claim was through his mother Isabella, daughter and sister of successive kings of France, but was of course disputed by the French kings. Richard II, who succeeded after his grandfather, had had no interest in continuing this claim, and Henry IV had, due to his usurpation, been too busy with establishing his claim in England itself and beating down rebellions there to entertain any ideas of conquest in France. Henry V was in a different position. Though his claim to the English throne was still not universally accepted by his subjects, the stain of usurpation clung to him far less than it had to his father. Able to unite more Englishmen behind him than Henry IV, he could make his desire to conquer France his main policy. This also had the convenient side effect of deflecting the problems still facing him in England by putting focus on France.

By early summer 1415, Henry had begun gathering men for the campaign to win the French throne, and by June, Alice's husband John would have known he was heading to war, together with his (twin?) brother William and many other Englishmen. Whether Thomas Chaucer was among the number of men gathered to fight is unknown, but unlikely. The claims that he was do not seem to be based on any contemporary source, and while there are hints he was in France in 1415, there is nothing to connect such a visit with Henry V's army. John, however, must have known he would be a soldier and would fight, and he prepared himself for it. In June 1415, while in London, he wrote his will.[6] Written partly in Latin and partly in French, it is an interesting but not particularly remarkable document. John gave bequests to his brother, who was to be his executor, to his stepdaughters by his second marriage, as well as to his new wife and her family. Again, he proved generous: despite Alice standing to hold a lot of his lands and estate for her lifetime because of the arrangements he had made shortly after their wedding, he did not stint in his will, either, and passed on some tokens to her, whom he described simply as '*ma femme*', my wife, in the document. Among these tokens were a gold cup and a gold ewer, as well as the

Marriage to Sir John Phelip

furniture of one room of his London home.[7] While the first two items were valuable but impersonal tokens, the last bequest is somewhat harder to guess at. Possibly, it was a room John had arranged for her use when she was old enough to live with him, or he simply thought the furniture it contained would appeal to a little girl.

John did not just think of Alice herself but also of her family when he made his will. He left the sizable sum of 20 pounds to her parents, as well as items valued at another 20 pounds.[8] This gives a pretty good insight into how wealthy John was. The exact annual revenue of his lands and estates is not quite certain, though his Inquisitions Post Mortem put it as £404, 20 marks 168 shillings and 16 pennies.[9]

John's will is another indicator that, despite claims to the contrary, Alice did not in fact live in John's household. Nothing of the sort is alluded to in it, and no arrangements are made for her whereabouts in the event of John's death. The bequests left to her are both generous and impersonal. This is to be expected, and John can hardly be faulted for not having a lot of interest in a barely eleven-year-old girl and her interests, but if had she lived in his household, he would have been able to gauge a bit more of her personality. The will shows he did know his stepdaughters better. All in all, it seems most likely Alice was only supposed to live with John once she was fourteen or sixteen, the former often being the age at which girls were considered old enough to run their own household, while the latter was the commonly accepted age for marriages to be consummated. Exceptions existed, but all the evidence points towards Alice's case not being one of them. Presumably, John hoped that by the time Alice was either fourteen or sixteen, the war in France would be over, successful for the English forces, and he could start a family with her in peace. It was not to be.

Sir John's death

The beginning of the French wars should have been an indicator in itself that not everything would go as smoothly as the king and

What is Better than a Good Woman?

his supporters hoped for. Henry V's policies were not popular everywhere, and in fact, many popular men rebelled against them in August 1415, while Henry's army was already getting ready for war. Richard, Earl of Cambridge, was the most famous rebel, and Henry V, never a merciful man, was not inclined to be understanding. His friend John, Alice's husband, was on the jury to judge Cambridge and his less famous fellow rebels. The verdict that was returned cannot have come as a surprise and was presumably certain before the trial began: Cambridge and his fellow rebels were found guilty of treason and would be punished accordingly. In early August 1415, they lost their heads.[10] Henry V was merciful about one thing, though, perhaps because of Cambridge's close relation to him: he did not attaint Cambridge but allowed his four-year-old son Richard to inherit his estate.[11]

Once the rebellion was dealt with, in early September Henry V and his army made their way to France. Once landed, the soldiers started marching on the important town of Harfleur, John and his brother William among them. Harfleur, however, had prepared for the arrival of the English forces and was ready for it. They did not yield, as Henry V seems to have expected, but closed the city gates and prepared for a siege.[12] This was not a particularly new or shocking strategy, and on paper, the strong English forces should have had no difficulties starving or otherwise besieging the town into submission. In this case, their very strength proved their weakness: the English army had too many men. One of the preparations for the siege done by the people of Harfleur was flooding large parts of the lands surrounding their town[13] making it impossible for the soldiers to stand in, much less to camp in. The parts the camp could be erected in were muddy and carried diseases. So many soldiers sharing so little space meant that those diseases were transmitted from one soldier to the next easily, spreading quickly.

Even as the siege and the bombardment of Harfleur was kept up day and night, the most common and most dreaded disease

Marriage to Sir John Phelip

of warfare was starting to spread with alarming speed: dysentery, then called 'the bloody flux'. Within two weeks of the English forces starting the siege, men were dying rapidly of it, and not just the lower ranks, usually forced to camp in conditions even worse than the gentry and nobility. The lack of space for the army and the extreme contagion of the disease meant that no one was exempt; Michael de la Pole, Earl of Suffolk, died of dysentery on either 14 or 17 September.[14]

Despite the fact that within four weeks more men were dying of disease than of warfare, the siege went on, and eventually, despite the extreme conditions, it was successful. On 22 September, the town surrendered.[15] In a move that was not at all characteristic, Henry V ordered his men that they were not to be cruel to the population of the town.[16] Presumably, this was because capturing Harfleur was only a means to an end, and the army soon marched on. However, the siege's consequences were still weakening the force weeks later. Despite their living conditions no longer being so cramped, dysentery was still decimating the army, and towards the end of September John Phelip contracted the disease.

It was not always fatal, but even though John presumably had fairly comfortable quarters, more so than the common soldiers, in the annexed town, he was to be one of the unlucky ones. Within days of becoming ill, on 2 October 1415, he died, at the age of about 31.[17] It seems that his brother was with him when he died, and he was probably the one who sent word back to England, to Thomas Chaucer and possibly also to the then ten- or eleven-year-old Alice, to inform them that John was dead and that Alice was a widow.

William himself, who had a daughter Alice's age, did not leave France and the army to deal with the fall-out of his brother's death until a month later, after the Battle of Agincourt. It could therefore be that Alice only received news of her husband's death a while after it happened. But sometime that autumn, Alice was informed that at the age of barely eleven, she was a widow.

4

ALICE'S FIRST WIDOWHOOD

Presumably, becoming a widow would not have changed Alice's life much immediately. Despite the fact her husband's death made her a rich landowner, she would have been much too young to act on that, and her father and later her brother-in-law William Phelip would at first have done all that needed doing for her. As discussed above, Alice barely knew John personally, so that his death, while sad, would not have been a personal blow for her.

Even so, it meant that her future, as secure as it could get before John's death, was once more rather uncertain. If, contrary to what evidence suggests, she lived in John's household she would have returned to her parents after his death. Despite the marriage never having been consummated, it was still regarded as valid, and Alice was known by her marital name, Lady Alice Phelip, from then on. Her brother-in-law William, who would go on to become Baron Bardolf later in his life, never disputed the marriage as invalid due to the lack of consummation and was never involved in any conflict with her over the many lands his brother had left her, which would otherwise have fallen to him. In fact, until his death decades later, Alice and William were on good terms. Presumably, with William in France, it would have fallen to Alice and thus to her parents by proxy to arrange John's funeral. His body was sent back from

Alice's First Widowhood

France, probably in alcohol to preserve it. As he had requested in his will, he was buried in Kidderminster. Whether Alice, as his widow, was present, we once more do not know. Henry V himself was later to commission a headstone for him, stating he had been a good fighter and a friend of his.[1] It is possible that though John was buried at the side of his second wife, he made arrangements for Alice's eventual grave to be at his side, the way her second husband did, but since this is not mentioned in his will it seems unlikely.

Alice, now a rich widow, knew that another marriage was most likely in her future, but after John's death her parents did not seem in a rush to arrange another one. Perhaps they would have liked to, but no suitable match presented itself. Alice was not only heiress to a rich man but rich in her own right after John's death, and any future match needed to reflect that.

Alice's adolescence

Alice spent the next years in her father's household, and she became a better marriage prospect still over time. She grew up to be a very beautiful, very intelligent and witty woman. While such attributes did not figure in the usually monetary arrangement of marriage, they doubtless would have been a welcome boon for any man interested in marrying her.

Little is known about Alice during her first widowhood, just as little is known about her childhood. She would have continued her education, which cannot have been finished by the time she was married for the first time. We do have some hints as to what her education must have entailed. As is pointed out in Henry Alfred Napier's book *Historical Notices of the Parishes of Swyncombe and Ewelme in the County of Oxford* she clearly could write,[2] and it is obvious she was far better educated than just that, though possibly not as much as is sometimes claimed. It is often stated that her library was huge, but there might be a slight misunderstanding about this; though she did have many

What is Better than a Good Woman?

books, several of those usually assumed to have been hers are in fact likely to have been her son's or daughter-in-law's. However, we can make assumptions based on the education Alice gave her only son. John, Duke of Suffolk, was a highly educated man, for whom Alice commissioned at least one book to be translated into Latin. It seems likely, therefore, that Alice herself read Latin and could write it, too. It seems like languages were a big part of her education, as is only fitting for Geoffrey Chaucer's granddaughter. She would also have learned basic mathematics. The second major of her education would have been social graces. These would have included dancing, making polite conversation, and knowing how to run a household.[3] As it would have been clear by 1415 that she was to be Thomas's sole heiress, she would have also learned to handle the issues that arose from the possession of lands by the example of father, who was managing the lands she held from her late husband for her.

Learning how to socialise would have been made easier by her being closely connected to some of the highest in the realm. Not only would her late husband's friendship with the king have given her an in with him, but she was also closely related to Henry V's Beaufort uncles, who had achieved high position in the realm. We know that Cardinal Henry Beaufort later helped Alice with some of her lands, so perhaps he already helped Thomas Chaucer with the same, protecting them from the claims of others. This sort of help from the cardinal shows that he and the Chaucers were well acquainted, and it is therefore likely he helped in Alice's upbringing by introducing her to several high-born and important persons. It is possible that it was through him that Alice, or initially more likely Thomas, first came into contact with the man who would be Alice's second husband. Though Thomas's importance did not wane, after 1415 he was no longer Speaker of the House of Commons, and while he was still employed by the king for tasks such as missions to France, he might not have met quite so many important nobles as he had in the first eleven years of Alice's life.

One such task given to him was an envoy to France, two years after Alice had become a widow. At that time, England had the upper hand in the war with France. Less than a month after John Phelip's death, the English forces had met the French army at Agincourt, and engaged in a battle that has become famous over the centuries. Though outnumbered since the recent outbreak of dysentery had decimated their forces, the English won against the French forces. Due to Henry V's ruthless decision not to hold prisoners taken during the battle for ransom but to kill them, the French nobility lost several very important men,[4] while the English losses were few.

Of the nobility, only the Duke of York and the youthful Earl of Suffolk – son of the man who had died of dysentery during the siege of Harfleur – died. Both these deaths would become significant for Alice later in her life, but if she heard of them at all in 1415 it would have not meant anything more to her than sad losses in the pursuit of England's glory.

Most likely, she did not even think that far, though as she became older, and especially as her father was sent to France on an embassy to discuss peace, the fact that England was winning battles between 1415 and 1417 and seemed on the way to succeeding in Henry V's aim of conquering France must have become important to her, too.

Even if she was starting to become interested in affairs of state, it is doubtful she really knew more than the fact that her father was leaving for France to discuss peace, and that this was important for the future of England and France, when Thomas was sent France in 1417.[5] We know much about this visit because of a poem by John Lydgate. The poem's intention is obviously to flatter Thomas, who was one of his rich sponsors, but even taking this into account the poem still is a testament to how respected and important

What is Better than a Good Woman?

Thomas was, a pillar of social life in the 1410s, his home a centre of culture in Oxfordshire.

The poem, which details the anguish Thomas's friends and admirers would suffer during his absence, intriguingly mentions a 'tender creature'[6] who would miss Thomas most, urging her to dry her tears. Though technically, this mention could refer to either Matilda or Alice, the sort of poem it is, and the language used suggests it was Matilda, though Alice would have missed her father as much, if not more, than her mother. During one of his expeditions to France, of which the one in 1417 was only the most famous, perhaps Thomas Chaucer came across a man he considered a suitable match as Alice's second husband, though as mentioned above, it is also possible his cousin Cardinal Beaufort introduced them.

5

MARRIAGE TO SIR THOMAS MONTACUTE, EARL OF SALISBURY

As a widow, Alice technically had the right to choose her own second husband, but even had she insisted on that right in her teens, which seems unlikely, it is hard to see why she should not have been pleased when Thomas chose Thomas Montacute, Earl of Salisbury. Having a noble and titled husband was a huge step upwards in society for Alice. In fact, even barons' daughters often married untitled men, though usually those men were members of the nobility, younger sons. For Alice to be married to someone higher in standing than a baron, an earl, was a step no one could have considered likely when she was born.

Her second husband was some sixteen years older than her,[1] four years younger than her first husband. He had been married before, like John Phelip, but unlike John he had a child. Called Alice like his new wife, Salisbury's daughter was born between 1404 and 1407.[2] Contemporary sources such as her father's Inquisitions Post Mortem do not agree on her age, so that it is guesswork, but it is clear that if she was not exactly her new stepmother's age, she was definitely close to it. Being Eleanor Holland's daughter and therefore a great-niece to the deposed

What is Better than a Good Woman?

Richard II, Alice Montacute was already married by the time her father married Alice Chaucer. Her husband was Richard Neville, the oldest son of Joan Beaufort and Ralph Neville, and therefore related to the king by marriage as well as by blood.[3] By marrying Thomas Montacute, Alice would therefore not only have gained a titled husband and become a countess herself, but also some very distinguished relations. For his part, Thomas Montacute gained a very wealthy father-in-law.

It was normal at the time that upon marriage a husband gained access to most, if not all, of his wife's wealth, so that Montacute could have hoped that he would have control over all of Thomas Chaucer's many possessions once his new father-in-law died. However, in this case, it seems likely that this would not have happened. Though nothing is known about the arrangements Thomas Montacute and Thomas Chaucer made for the marriage, it is known that when Alice married her third husband, William de la Pole, Earl of Suffolk, she arranged for a fairly strict marriage settlement whereby she kept control over all possessions she had and would still gain.[4] Logic dictates the situation was the same for Montacute, but we cannot say so for certain. However, even if her new husband would not get complete access to Alice's wealth and that of her father after he died, he would have been richer than before the wedding, as well as gaining new connections through the marriage. Alice was a young woman, and probably Thomas hoped she would be able to give him many more children.

The wedding

Eleanor Holland, Thomas Montacute's first wife, was still alive in April 1421.[5] She appears to have died within the next two years. Assuming Alice married Thomas not long after Eleanor's death, she was eighteen or nineteen years old when she married the Earl and became a countess. At that age, she was naturally old

Marriage to Sir Thomas Montacute, Earl of Salisbury

enough to be his wife not only in name. Where the marriage took place is as little known as when, but presumably it happened in England, either in one of the new husband's manors or in one of Thomas Chaucer's, such as Ewelme. It would have been too dangerous to allow a young woman, the betrothed of one of the most important men in the English army, to travel to France for her wedding.

After the wedding was over, Alice would have left her parents' household and gone to live with her new husband. If all customs were followed, the marriage was consummated immediately, and possibly, husband and wife shared a household afterwards. This was not always the case; often noble spouses had different households, which fused when they were living under the same roof, not necessarily that often. Perhaps such an arrangement was what Alice and Thomas agreed on.

Thomas was not only an earl; first and foremost he was known at the time, and would be remembered by history, as a warrior for Henry V and Henry VI in the Hundred Years' War. He was famous for it even in his own lifetime and much respected even in France, despite fighting against French forces. Not only English, but Burgundian and French contemporary sources were fulsome in their praise.[6]

Being close to the king means that in 1420 and 1421, before he ever became a widower and free to marry Alice, his thoughts, like those of many in England and especially those close to the king, were geared towards marriage – King Henry V's marriage. It took place in 1420[7] and was a great match, designed to be the pinnacle of Henry V's achievements. After several years of peace talks, like the one in 1417 in which Thomas Chaucer was involved, a treaty was made, with Henry V in the enviable situation of being able to more or less dictate the terms. It was agreed he would marry the French king's daughter, Katherine of Valois, and the Dauphin, heir to the French throne and brother of Katherine's, was to be disinherited in favour of Henry V, heir to the French throne from then on. His and

· What is Better than a Good Woman?

Katherine's children were one day to be considered rightful kings of both England and France.[8] This of course was not accepted by the disinherited Dauphin, who had been accused of 'frightful and astounding crimes and misdeeds committed against the kingdom of France'[9] in the treaty to justify his demotion, and over the years the treaty came to cause more war than it did peace. At the time, though, it was a huge coup for Henry V. He married Katherine in June 1420 and went to England with her, where she was crowned.

Despite the marriage being such a triumph for him, Henry V's focus was not on his young wife. He did not see a lot of her, spending most of his time in France battling her brother and his supporters and overseeing the parts of France belonging to the English crown by conquest. These were parts of France that Thomas Chaucer also often visited.

Despite the fact he did not often see Katherine, by early 1421 she was pregnant, and on 6 December 1421[10] she gave birth to a son who was destined to become king of both England and France one day, after the death of his father and maternal grandfather respectively. The little boy was named Henry, after his father, but he was never to meet him. Within eight months of little Prince Henry's birth, Henry V was dead of dysentery, caught during the siege of Meaux, a town holding firm for the Dauphin.[11]

Only a few weeks later, the French king also died. At the time of Eleanor Holland dying and Thomas Montacute becoming a widower, he and other royal advisors therefore had to deal with an infant who was not only their king but also heir to the contested throne of France, before he was old enough to walk or talk. The baby king's French uncle did not accept the fact he was to be disinherited for an infant. Seeing in Henry V's death a chance to take what he considered his birthright, hostilities between English and French forces started again.

It was in this charged climate that Alice and Thomas Montacute married. The fact her groom was a renowned warrior naturally

Marriage to Sir Thomas Montacute, Earl of Salisbury

meant that for Alice the war would be rather more immediate than for many of her country's people. Wives of warriors did not have much to do with France and the war there personally, their connection being their husbands' involvement and the fact that their own future, for better or worse, was connected to their wellbeing. Perhaps Alice, Thomas or both originally assumed that the same would be the case for her, but it did not turn out like that.

Looking at what is known of not only Montacute's movements and those of Thomas Chaucer, a reasonable deduction can be made about when the wedding took place. Both of them would have been in England, and Thomas would not have left immediately after the wedding, leaving his young wife behind. Similarly, Alice would not have been able, or, it is likely, willing to drop everything to accompany him. If Alice and Thomas had a honeymoon phase after their wedding in mind, it is unlikely they would have wanted to spend it in war-torn France and would have spent it in England, in one of the Earl's's manors, one of Alice's manors or one of Thomas Chaucer's, or possibly all three. Therefore, the wedding is all but certain to have taken place during a longer stay by Thomas Montacute in England. As a famous man his movements are well recorded, and we know when such visits happened. There were not very many, so that when he married Alice can be narrowed down.

It seems most likely that it was around the time of Henry V's funeral, which took place on 7 November 1422.[12] This, of course, would indicate that it had been arranged beforehand, as it seems impossible that an arrangement for a marriage would have been made at such an occasion, and would have been made with such speed. Thomas, as one of the leading warriors of the English forces, would have been very busy with the arrangement of how things were to go on under these drastically changed circumstances, and would not have had time during his stay in England for the funeral to put his feelers out for a new wife, make arrangements for the marriage, arrange a wedding and celebrate it. We know he was almost certainly not in England in October 1422, when the first Parliament in the reign of the baby king was held, but only arrived for the funeral.

His and Alice's marriage being arranged before November 1422 would mean only a few months after the death of his first wife Eleanor, or even within a month, Thomas was looking for a new wife, which even for the time seems rather callous. However, it was far from unheard of, and though Thomas had a daughter he appeared close to, he presumably hoped for a son who could inherit his earldom. Though Alice Montacute, already married to Richard Neville by then, was his only legitimate child, Thomas had an illegitimate son called John,[13] who was most likely born during his first marriage. Thomas knew he could have sons, and considered it important to try and have a legitimate one as soon as possible, regardless of his feelings towards Eleanor. Alice, still only in her late teens, seemed likely to be able to give him lots of children, in addition to the other perks of marrying her. Of course, Thomas hoping to have a legitimate son meant that not only did he need to marry Alice, but also that they needed to be together as much as possible.

Alice would have been aware of this from before the wedding took place, and there is no reason to assume she would not have hoped herself to become a mother soon. She may have been happy not only at that prospect but also generally at being married. This union made her a countess. With the marriage, she was a member of the nobility.

She travelled with her husband a lot after their wedding, but this does not have to be only because she wished to conceive. Alice and Thomas's marriage appears to have been a very successful one, husband and wife fond of each other.

Married life

Both man and wife are known to have had strong personalities. Thomas, born in around 1488, had soon gained prominence by marrying Eleanor Holland in his mid-teens at the latest, before

Marriage to Sir Thomas Montacute, Earl of Salisbury

Richard II was usurped and he thereby became a nephew by marriage to the king. It is unlikely that he was happy when John of Gaunt's oldest son Henry took the throne as Henry IV in 1399, but he never acted against him. As soon as he was old enough to be politically involved, Thomas was loyal to Henry IV, unlike some of his relatives, most notably his father.

In fact, Thomas's father John Montacute was killed while committing treason against the new king when Thomas was twelve years old.[14] Perhaps it was the fact that though his father's treason meant forfeiture of his lands and titles, Henry IV allowed him to assume at least some of his forfeited inheritance upon coming of age in 1409[15] that made Thomas so loyal to him and his son. Perhaps it was an attempt to prove his worth and be granted the entirety of his father's lands. Whichever it was, when Henry V came to the throne Thomas proved an enthusiastic supporter of his claim to the French throne.

When warfare started in 1415, he soon became known as an enthusiastic fighter and a good one, which was why, as time passed, he became more and more important to the English forces. He would not have got to where he was without being a nobleman, but since there were so many noblemen involved in these conflicts, it was at least partially through his own merits that he rose in the ranks of Henry V's army. This seems to indicate he was intelligent, a good fighter and organiser, and a successful tactician. It would have also needed a certain toughness, if not barbarism, to reach the position he had when he married Alice. For all Thomas's good qualities, so praised by his contemporaries in chronicles in several countries, he also had a streak of cruelty. For example, it seems that at least once he mistreated prisoners of war. After having successfully besieged and captured the Castle of Orsay in 1422, which had been held by supporters of the French Dauphin, Thomas forced several of the castle's defenders he had captured to be led into Paris as examples, wearing ropes around their necks.[16]

What is Better than a Good Woman?

This would fit well with what is known about Thomas, though his behaviour cannot be judged by modern standards. Such behaviour towards prisoners of war was hardly unheard of, and was, in fact, considered evidence that someone was suited to the often grim job of leading an army. Thomas was suited to the task, and he was respected not only by chroniclers but also by the men he led. Interestingly, he not only led, but was in fact close to, Alice's eventual third husband, William de la Pole, Earl of Suffolk,[17] How well Alice knew him then is unknown.

There is every reason to assume she was happy with his personality and considered it very suitable for a man of his standing and her husband. Maybe she was also attracted to his looks, but we have no pictures clear enough to give more than a passing idea of what he looked like. The only indication found in both contemporary and later depictions of him is that he had wildly curly hair, even in a soldier's cut.

For his part, there is every indication he would have been attracted to both Alice's looks and her personality. We are lucky to have a fairly good, if idealised, depiction of what Alice looked like in the effigy on top of her tomb at Ewelme. Made during her lifetime,[18] this effigy at the very least suggests how Alice wanted to be seen; and though it shows her as a young woman, and therefore would not have been worked directly from life when it was made in the 1460s and late 1470s, it must at least bear a passing resemblance to Alice. Her son's effigy, made nearly twenty years later by a different stonemason, shows him as closely resembling Alice, thus indicating that this was what they actually looked like, or at least close to it. If so, it seems that Alice was a tall woman with a long, thin face, a thin nose, big eyes and a mischievous smile – an attractive woman, at least by modern standards. Regardless of how close the effigy is to the truth, and how much of its depiction was flattery or deception, that Alice was an attractive woman, or was considered to be so by her contemporaries, is

Marriage to Sir Thomas Montacute, Earl of Salisbury

amply supported by other evidence. Some sources state it outright. For example, the French chronicler Pierre de Fenin repeated twice within two sentences that she was 'molto belle',[19] very beautiful. Alice was not just a physically beautiful woman. Pierre de Fenin also indicates that Alice was self-confident and spirited. This will be discussed in more depth below. Obviously, his testimony is that of someone admiring a woman sure of herself. This is reflected in all other evidence we have about her – she was confident, ambitious, charming when she wanted to be, and fierce. It seems that this, together with her beauty, attracted Thomas to her, making the marriage a success for him in all ways.

Life in England and France

By November 1424, the couple had gone abroad together to the wedding of the Burgundian noble Jean de la Trimoulle and the Lord of Amboise's sister.[20] Pierre de Fenin reported this wedding, and stated that Philip, Duke of Burgundy, was 'much in love with the ladies', and

> ... during that celebration, became enamoured with the Countess of Salisbury, who is very beautiful, as was said before, and there were many attempts of conversation towards her by the duke, but they did not come together. And when the Earl of Salisbury was told the news, he was very angry due to the duke Philip.[21]

Though de Fenin does not actually name the 'Countess of Salisbury', there can be no doubt it was Alice. Though some authors have thrown doubt on this, Eleanor Holland's Inquisition Post Mortem was issued in 1422, so that the Countess of Salisbury in 1424 cannot have been her.

The episode related by de Fenin paints a very vivid picture of Alice. Though often, the take-away has been solely that she was very beautiful, this might be the least interesting titbit from this chronicler.

What is Better than a Good Woman?

More interesting is what her reaction to Duke Philip's rather inept flirting reveals about her. At a celebration with some of the highest and mightiest nobles in Europe, she was not cowed. Rather than accepting the duke's passes at her or finding a low-key way to escape them, she was confident enough of herself to openly reject them.

Curiously, this has caused some modern commenters to accuse her of showing her lack of noble upbringing, insisting she should have found another, less disruptive way of rejecting the duke's approaches. However, no trace of that sentiment is found in de Fenin's report of the incident. On the contrary, he clearly seemed to consider it Alice's right to tell a man who was intrusive to stop in whatever way she wished, even a man who was much higher in standing than her.

Though it was doubtlessly an unpleasant experience for Alice, once she had thoroughly and openly rejected the duke, she might have thought it was over with. This was not to be the case. As de Fenin notes, her new husband, Thomas, was clearly enraged by the duke's behaviour. Very notably, he did not in any way blame Alice. However, his relationship to the Burgundian duke notably cooled from then on, something that was to have significant consequences some years later.

Though the battles and the conflict between France and England went on after 1424, with Burgundy often suggesting different paths to winning against the French than the ones England pursued, Thomas appeared to try his best to be with Alice as often as he could. Again, how much of this desire for each other's company was actual joy found in being together, and how much was born out of a sense of duty, a wish to conceive the male heir Thomas must have wished for, cannot be calculated.

By 1426, we have evidence for Thomas making arrangements so that no other obligations but those as the head of Henry V's army interfered with his time with Alice. For 1425, there is little evidence, but it is nice to imagine Alice and him getting to know each other better and finding a lot to like about each other.

Marriage to Sir Thomas Montacute, Earl of Salisbury

This is suggested by two grants to him found in the papal calendars, dating from 1426. Both these grants absolve him of oaths he had previously made. The first one, from March 1426, stated:

> The members of the great royal council at Paris have set forth to the pope that Thomas de Monteacuto, earl of Salisbury, when formerly on his way back to England from a visit to the Lord's Sepulchre, fell grievously ill and made a vow to revisit, if cured, the said sepulchre, without saying when; that afterwards, when restored to health and being in a certain battle [? Crevant, July, 1423], he confirmed and repeated the said vow; that although he made two attempts to fulfil his vow, nevertheless, being a vassal of Henry, king of England, he has been prevented by authority of the said king; and that when recently he made a third attempt to fulfil his said vows and, rejecting the persuasions of the said chancellor and other members of the said great council, would have set out, they repeated to him the oaths of fealty which he had taken to the said king, asserting that he could and ought not to absent himself from the service of the king without the king's express leave. The pope therefore grants faculty to the above archbishop to commute the said oaths into other works of piety.[22]

In itself, there is nothing unusual about either the vow Thomas took at some point before July 1423, and most likely before he married Alice, or about the grant absolving him of it. There are many such grants recorded in the papal calendars, but the one absolving him from a vow made to visit the Lord's Sepulchre if he survived an illness was not the only one made to him. On the same day in March 1426 that this indult was issued to him, the pope issued another, very similar one, '[t]o Thomas de Monteacuto, earl of Salisbury. Indult that the archbishop of Rouen may commute into other works of piety his vow of pilgrimage to the Holy Land

43

What is Better than a Good Woman?

(votum ultramarinum), which he cannot fulfil on account of the dangers of the ways and personal risk.'[23]

The explanation offered for dispensing with this oath is wafer-thin. It is unlikely that when making the oath to visit the Holy Land, Thomas had not been aware of such a pilgrimage being dangerous. Obviously, he either had made this vow in the heat of the moment at some point, or the circumstances of his life had changed so much between him making the vow and late 1425, when he must have made the arrangements to apply to the pope, that fulfilling it no longer seemed feasible. From what we know, his life did not change much after he married Alice, so it seems it was probably his marriage to her that made him feel unable to honour his oaths.

At least some of his desire to stay in her presence must have been motivated by her own merits, not just the hope she would fall pregnant. Though it doubtlessly was a concern, it was not one that had stopped Thomas from making such oaths when married to his first wife. Since Eleanor Holland died in 1421 at the age of approximately thirty-five, it cannot be that Thomas took the oath while thinking his wife would be unable to have more children and he therefore did not need to be in her presence to try.

Whichever his motivations were, it is clear that Alice's marriage was a good one. There seemed to be affection between her and Thomas, which was not marred by the hoped-for heir not appearing soon after the wedding. There never seemed to be any problem about it between husband and wife. They did not have the hoped-for children in the first years of marriage, Alice seemed to lead a happy life as Countess of Salisbury, enjoying her status as a noblewoman, while at the same time slowly coming into her own as landowner. Though the evidence about her is significantly scarcer than it is for her time as Countess, Duchess and dowager duchess of Suffolk, we can still tell a lot about her and her life in the mid-1420s from what evidence there is.

Marriage to Sir Thomas Montacute, Earl of Salisbury

Most of that evidence takes the form of grants and mentions in property disputes, as well as other legal proceedings. One of those proceedings was a Proof of Age for Eleanor Moleyns, daughter of William Moleyns, held in 1440.[24] One of the jurors called to testify to Eleanor's age, a man named William Langeley, '50 and more', spoke about remembering her baptism in June 1426, mentioning that he was 'in the church when Alice, countess of Salisbury, one of Eleanor's godmothers, gave her a [silver?] goblet with a gold cover, and gave 40s. to her nurse'.[25] Another man, 'William Coterell, 36 and more', reported that he was 'in the church and saw the countess, Eleanor's godmother, dressed in cloth of gold'.[26]

It is interesting to note that Alice clearly wished to stress her status, and rather than being 'dressed in blue damask' like 'Elizabeth, Lady Say, Eleanor's other godmother' to match with her and 'Thomas, Lord Scales, knight, Eleanor's godfather … dressed in blue velvet',[27] she instead wore a dress of cloth of gold. William Langley does not mention colour, so that it is possible she chose to match with them in her own way and did not try and stand apart and above them completely, but clearly, the superior fabric of her dress was what stuck in Langley's mind, and probably in that of everyone else present. Though Alice is not the main person of interest in this statement, and nothing more is said about her, it is not hard to hear a certain disapproval in the dry words. Though it is not spelled out, at least some people regarded Alice as rather vain and getting above herself once she had married Thomas – an accusation that would be levelled against her explicitly some twenty-five years later.

It is also a sign that Alice was slowly becoming a sought-after ally (or someone to be wary of) concerning social and political issues, having the ear of important men. Even if some did regard her as vain and full of self-importance – a charge which cannot be dismissed outright, as will be discussed later – such failings usually mattered less than a person's wealth and social standing.

What is Better than a Good Woman?

Alice's standing as Countess of Salisbury

Alice had wealth in addition to social standing after marrying Thomas, and it was not all dependent on her father and husband either. Though her becoming Eleanor Moleyns' godmother is often claimed to have been due to her father's influence with William Moleyns, and not because of who she was, this cannot be said for other aspects of her life. Many grants made in the 1420s reference her great wealth inherited from John Phelip in all parts of the country. There are some from Dorset and Suffolk,[28] and had she so wished, she could have very well established herself as a power to be reckoned with not only in Oxfordshire but in those counties.

For all that, it does not seem that she had very much of an interest in becoming a magnate when she was in her early twenties, and this is reflected in the language used in many of those grants. The grant of the 'manor of Newton Montagu'[29] for example, shows that Alice was regarded as 'Lady Alice Phelip', a landowner by right of her late husband, something true elsewhere. Technically speaking, this is correct. Alice's ownership of those lands was because of her marriage to John Phelip, and if not for that, she would have had no right to them. This was not a very unusual situation. Many women, wives and widows, held lands by right of their late husbands, often remarrying while they did so. It was more common for these women to be addressed by the name of their current husband, even if they held the lands in their own right rather than that of their late husband, especially if the current husband was of higher standing. That Alice retained the name of Phelip, a gentleman, in those grants, rather than being addressed by her new title by marriage as a member of the nobility, is telling. Her ownership was respected, but she herself was not adjudged to be of much importance. The fact that many of those grants included her father supports this picture. Perhaps due to lack of interest, or because Alice was busy at her husband's side, sharing in his concerns, she did not seem to show very much involvement

Marriage to Sir Thomas Montacute, Earl of Salisbury

in her lands by her first marriage, leaving their management to her father and his cousin Cardinal Henry Beaufort.

This was a common arrangement, one that is often associated with the Middle Ages: of a woman's father and/or husband running her estates for her, and in some cases, actually taking ownership; but it is not one that Alice would prefer in her later years, even when making what seemed a match of affection with William de la Pole, Earl of Suffolk, making sure she retained all rights over her own possessions. She was very clearly not happy with her lands being used without her input; so that it seems likely that in the 1420s, she simply did not have the time to give the attention to the management of these lands they might need in her eyes. She also trusted her father and his cousin to manage in her interest and not to do so without running decisions past her and asking for her consent. This would certainly have been a sensible arrangement.

For all that, we do not know what it was that kept Alice so busy and her attention focused elsewhere. Though it is very possible she spent all the time she could with Thomas and hence very often abroad, this cannot have been the only reason. We know from Eleanor Moleyn's Proof of Age that Alice was in England in June 1426, the context suggesting that she had been there for a while, enough to prepare for the occasion of a goddaughter's baptism. The timing of Thomas's papal grants suggests that they planned to be in England together by early 1426.

This might have been due to an expected lull in fighting, though obviously there was still no peace. In fact, there is some suggestion that Thomas was involved in warfare in France at least for the early part of 1426. Alice did not accompany him there. Despite knowing that warfare would almost certainly continue in France, Thomas made sure he was free to go to England at some point in 1426, and possibly also stay there. We do not know if he managed to do so, though if he did, he appears to have left for France again

What is Better than a Good Woman?

by the end of the year. Alice seems to have accompanied him then, but she returned to England before he did.

Why Thomas decided in late 1426 or early 1427 that returning home to England was urgent, after having stayed in France except for sporadic visits home since marrying Alice, we do not know. Again, the answer may be completely prosaic, Thomas hoping to conceive a child with Alice and Alice having no interest in being in war-torn France, preferring to establish herself as Countess of Salisbury in England. Her efforts to do so and find an in with the nobility may have taken her attention so completely that the management of her lands seemed dull and less important by comparison.

It is, however, also possible that there is another explanation, an answer that has not been considered before: she might in fact have conceived a child by Thomas and been pregnant in late 1426 and early 1427. This would explain her own preoccupation, her obvious pride in her position – the wife of the Earl of Salisbury, and soon to be the mother of his heir – and also Thomas's wish to be in England. Unlike Henry V, he might very well have wished to see his son once he was born. Though Henry V's own apparent disinterest in his newborn son is often presented as normal for the time, it was in fact not so, men were pardoned from Parliament and even went home from war to see their newborn children, especially if they were expecting a son and heir. Thomas, who was noted to be a good and doting father to his only legitimate daughter Alice, and who, as his will would make clear even if his actions did not, also doted on his young wife Alice, seems very likely to have wanted to be there when his new child was born, or at the very least meet the child soon after its birth.

If that was the case, then they suffered a blow at some point. Though not all children even of the nobility are recorded if they died in infancy, it is extremely unlikely, verging on the impossible, that a man of Thomas's standing would have had a son and heir, even a very short-lived one, without this being noted. It is, however, possible

Marriage to Sir Thomas Montacute, Earl of Salisbury

that Alice gave birth to a short-lived daughter who predeceased her father. A girl would not be her father's heir, that position being filled by her older half-sister, so it could be that her birth would not excite the sort of comment that survives centuries. There is no evidence of it, and on the whole it seems less likely than Alice suffering a miscarriage, if indeed she ever was pregnant in 1426-7.

Of course, this is speculation, but speculation that makes sense of other rather inexplicable facts. It seems more likely than Alice actually giving birth, because it is recorded that Alice did have difficulties with carrying children to term. There is concrete evidence for at least two miscarriages she suffered later, which will be discussed below. Her suffering a miscarriage in 1426 is therefore, given her later history, medically plausible.

Such a blow would also explain why she had little interest in becoming involved in managing her lands left to her by John Phelip, as doubtless it would have been not only an emotionally difficult blow, but also something that would have made it necessary for her to rest for a long while to recover physically. A miscarriage is one way to explain Alice's and Thomas's actions and movements as the scant evidence shows it. Whether the prosaic or the more dramatic and tragic version is true is sadly unknowable.

Such a loss was far from uncommon at the time, and life had to go on, which it did. Though there is as little record of Alice in late 1427 and 1428 as there is for her childhood, less than for any other period in her adult life, for Thomas we know more. This evidence indicates that theirs continued to be a very happy marriage, based on mutual affection. It seems that he showered Alice with gifts; at least one such gift of his is known, a fine jewel that once belonged to him that he gave her, perhaps as a wedding or anniversary gift. This gift is described in the will of Richard Beauchamp, Earl of Warwick, 'a great paytren',[30] after Alice gave it away after Thomas's death. Traditionally, the jewel has been considered as a bequest to her by her second husband in his will, but we do have

What is Better than a Good Woman?

the entire text of his will and the jewel is not mentioned. It stands to reason, therefore, that it was a gift. Such gifts were common among the rich and landed nobility, and it can be assumed that Alice would have made Thomas similarly beautiful and valuable gifts, though sadly, no records of such survive. Whatever happened during their marriage, they remained on very good terms.

The time they could spend together became more and more limited by the demands on Thomas as leader of the English forces. The French were slowly starting to gain the upper hand in the late 1420s, meaning there was more and more fighting. Added to that was the fact that the English ally, Duke Philip of Burgundy, was following a strategy against France that did not engender the support of many English fighters.

Thomas was one of the English fighters who did not agree with Duke Philip's strategy. Though it is recorded that he was far from the only one, as the leader, it is often presented as if he was. Thomas was the one who ultimately made the decisions. but he was not in a position simply to decide by his own instinct, he would have had to discuss them with others who had a say, the king's uncles and other important nobles. While his opinion was the most important one on English strategy, it was not the only one. His opinion certainly carried a lot of weight, and ever since 1424 it seems Thomas had very much turned against the Duke of Burgundy.[31] This might at least partially have been because of the duke's apparent attempt to seduce Alice, but it was mostly because of his new strategies, which also turned others against the Duke. In the mid-1420s, these had even led to a short-term rift. However, by the late 1420s, the two were allied again, and Thomas chose to go along with him. It was a decision that was to prove fatal for him, and a blow for English ambitions.

Alice's second widowhood
In 1427 the French had gained a new weapon in the person of Joan of Arc, a teenage girl who would go down in legend. Henry VI's

Marriage to Sir Thomas Montacute, Earl of Salisbury

uncle, the Dauphin, who had become disinherited by the treaty of Troyes, had support from a young woman who would turn out not only to be a good strategist but also, perhaps more importantly, offered hope to his beleaguered forces,[32] Joan turned out to be very good at what she did, with army leaders listening to her, but Thomas could not know that yet, before she had ever been tested in battle. As far as he knew, he was simply fighting against the same French forces he had been fighting for years, and he agreed when John, Duke of Bedford, his nephew Henry VI's regent, decided to attack Orléans and fulfil his late brother Henry V's dream of conquering the city. It was claimed that Henry V had once said he would own all of France if he could only conquer Orléans. Thomas, who had been in England since mid-1427, arrived back in France at the head of a contingent of new troops in July. After a series of attacks on French towns, he arrived at Orléans in October to besiege the town.

The siege began on 12 October 1428 with rather better omens than the siege of Harfleur had. Though some soldiers still became sick, as was normal on any military expedition, it was nowhere near the desperate situation at Harfleur. The city held out, but it seemed like the English would be able to keep up the siege at minimal cost to themselves until it had to surrender. When the siege began, the English had every reason to believe they would eventually win it. It would have been a major victory, more important than when Harfleur fell, at least symbolically; the city had great historic significance for the French, and the English thought gaining possession of it would break French spirit enough to make the Dauphin's forces surrender.

It might be the knowledge of his old king's statement of Orléans being the key to holding the whole of France and the importance many French people attached to the city that made Thomas decide to besiege it, but curiously, French and Burgundian chroniclers do not attach this motivation to his choice.[33] English chroniclers generally preferred not to dwell on a decision that would turn out to be disastrous, and so do

51

What is Better than a Good Woman?

not assign any motive to Thomas's choice at all. Though it is unlikely that Thomas's thoughts were so simple, all contemporaries insisted that it had been the insult to Alice that made him turn against the duke of Burgundy,[34] who had not agreed with the tactic, and his antipathy against the duke made him decide to mount the siege.

If this was true, Alice would indirectly be the cause of this most famous of sieges in European history. and the way the Hundred Years War went after 1428. But whatever Thomas's feelings were, he had been a commander for too long – and had proved too smart – to formulate strategy based on an insult. The connection to Alice and the way contemporary chroniclers assigned the siege to Thomas's feelings is simply something that should be noted.

What Alice thought of her husband's decision is unknowable. There is no evidence she had any interest in the details of military actions, beyond the immediate effect they had on her and her loved ones. All we know is that after thirteen years, Alice was once more faced with the reality of her husband being involved in a siege in France, trying to secure the French throne for an English king. Whatever she thought, the situation would turn out just as tragically. John Phelip had died of dysentery shortly after Harfleur fell. Thomas Montacute, Earl of Salisbury, would not live to see the end of the siege he had started at Orléans, or to see the extraordinary rise of Joan of Arc.

In fact, he barely even saw the first part of the siege. Only sixteen days after the siege started and three weeks after he arrived at Orléans, on 28 October[35] Thomas made the fateful decision to watch the forces from a watchtower a small distance from the city, to get a more complete picture of the situation. With him were several other important men, such as his second-in-command William de la Pole, Earl of Suffolk. There was nothing out of the ordinary about this decision. To better see his army besieging Orléans and some of the defences the city had, Thomas was standing by the window of the tower when a French cannonball

Marriage to Sir Thomas Montacute, Earl of Salisbury

crashed into it, ripping the window frame apart. According to the chronicler Enguerrand de Monstrelet,

> [t]he earl, on the third day after his arrival before Orléans, entered the tower on the bridge, and ascended to the second story, whence from a window that overlooked the town he was observing what was passing within, and was considering the best mode of reducing it to obedience. While thus occupied, a stone from a veuglaire struck the window, whence the earl, hearing the report, had withdrawn, for the shot carried away part of his face and killed a gentleman behind him on the spot.[36]

Others reporting Thomas's death concur. Having lost one eye and being horrifically injured, surely those who were in the ruined tower with him knew that he had no chance of survival. It was probably the Earl of Suffolk, now acting commander, who gave orders for him to be carried to Meaux, there to be given the best possible care in what time he had left.

Presumably, they also sent word to Alice, but since we do not know where she was at the time, we do not know if word of her husband's injury reached her before his death. If she was in England, it almost certainly did not; and even if she was in France, it is unlikely it reached her quickly enough for her to arrive at his side in time, had she wanted to do so.

On 3 November 1428,[37] eight days after being injured, Thomas died. Presumably, given the nature of his injuries, it was a mercy for him, we hope a mercy of which he was unaware, having been sedated in some way so as to not suffer from the horrible pain the injuries doubtless brought. He was forty years old, leaving behind Alice, his legitimate daughter, a granddaughter and an illegitimate son.

At the age of twenty-six, Alice was a widow again. There is no evidence when she found out about her husband's death, though given his importance, someone would have been dispatched to tell

What is Better than a Good Woman?

her and her stepdaughter immediately after his death. Even if she was in England, it is unlikely she learned of it more than a week after the fact. How she reacted to it is also not known, though every indication is that she would be sad to lose a husband with whom she had enjoyed a close marriage and mutual affection. If grief threatened to engulf her, however, she did not have time for that: preparations following her husband's death had to be made.

Like John Phelip, Thomas had made arrangements for Alice in the event of his death. He had been even more generous than John; though his title perforce passed to his daughter and her husband, Thomas had left all his other possessions equally to Alice and to his daughter. Half of his lands fell to her as well as half of his plate and other possessions, allowing for a few bequests to others, such as his illegitimate son. Just how much half of his possessions was worth is not easy to say, but according to his Inquisitions Post Mortem, it was definitely more than £500 annually.[38] Added to the wealth Alice already held from John, it meant she was one of the richest women in England, and richer than many noblemen.

The practical aspects of coping with his death included seeing to it that his body was transported home, which was done presumably in the same rather gruesome way John Phelip had been transported home, his body preserved in alcohol. Thomas had made exact provisions in his will for his funeral and the prayers for the good of his soul he wanted read:

Thomas Montacate, Earl of Salisbury, Perch, and Lord Monthermer. I will that in whatever part of the world I may chance to die that my body be buried at Bustlesham, in England, and that neither my wife … nor my executors make any great entertainment, or have a solemn hearse for me at my funeral, or that any large or sumptuous lights for worldly pomp be then provided; but when my body is carried through any city or town in my native country, I desire that four torches

Marriage to Sir Thomas Montacute, Earl of Salisbury

only be lighted at its entrance therein and borne therewith. Also I will that upon the day of my trental twenty-four torches be provided, and four other lights to be about my corpse at the solemnizing the exequies and masses there to be celebrated for my soul, and to be borne by twenty-four poor men all clothed alike. To every poor person coming to my trental pence for the health of my soul, fifty poor people being first chosen out of the whole number there present, to each of whom I desire my most beloved wife to give xxd. with her own hand; to the Monastery at Bustlesham cl. sterling out of my moveable goods, that the Prior and whole Convent there shall specially ordain one mass to be celebrated every day for my soul, in a particular place appointed for that purpose, with this collect, 'Deus cui proprium', etc; and I desire that two canons of that house, immediately after the mass of the blessed Virgin be ended before my tomb, shall for ever say the psalm of De Profundis, with the Lord's Prayer, the Angelical Salutation, and this prayer: 'Deus, cui proprium est miserere semper et parcere, propitia ani ma famuli tui Thoma, et omnia ejus peccata dimitta, ut mortis vinculis absolutus transire mereatur ad vitam' With these prayers also: 'Inclina' and 'Fidelium Deus, pro animabus parentum et progenitorum nostrorum inibi sepultorum, etc.' Also I will that my most beloved wife, so soon as possible after my death, cause one thousand masses to be specially celebrated for my soul, and the souls of all the faithful deceased; and I charge her and my executors that they cause three masses to be daily celebrated for my soul during the term of her life in such places as they may think fit within the realm of England, and if possible in her presence; likewise I desire that three poor people be every day brought, by the care of my executors, to my wife, that is to say, severally, if they can be found, to the end that she may serve each of them with one mess of meat, one loaf, and one quart of drink, and that

What is Better than a Good Woman?

she and my executors, within one year after my decease cause m marks to be distributed amongst poor people be every day brought, by the care of my executors, to my wife, that is to say, severally, if they can be found, to the end that she may serve each of them with one mess of meat, one loaf, and one quart of drink, and that she and my executors, within one year after my decease cause m marks to be distributed amongst poor people, partly in money, and partly in raiment, both linen and woollen; also I will that my said wife and my executors shall, with all good speed, cause three thousand masses to be celebrated for the souls of all the Companions of the Order of St. George of the Garter, in recompense of those masses which have been by me forgotten; to my uncle Sir Richard de Montacute, Knight cl sterling; to John, my bastard son, L marks.

IN A CODICIL. I desire that 500 marks be raised out of my lands to erect a chauntry to the honour of the Blessed Virgin, above the high altar in the east part of the Conventual Church at Bustlesham, forty feet in length, twenty feet in breadth, and the height of the walls twenty feet; and also that a tomb four feet in height be raised in the midst thereof, containing three distinct places, the middlemost higher than the other two by half a foot, in which I will that my own body be laid; and the body of the Lady Alianore, sometime my wife, on the one side, with the body of the Lady Alice my present wife, now living, on the other side, if she will, which tomb I desire be made of marble, with portraitures of each in brass, and epitaphs; as also a chapel of timber surrounding it, with an altar for masses to be daily celebrated thereat, for the health of my soul.[39]

Alice and her stepdaughter would normally have shared the duties of making certain his wishes were fulfilled, busying themselves with organising everything; but Alice's stepdaughter, Alice Montacute,

Marriage to Sir Thomas Montacute, Earl of Salisbury

was nine months pregnant when her father died, and if she was not already in the confinement noble women went into before giving birth at the time of his death, she doubtless would have been by the time her father's body arrived back in England. Though we have few details of the funeral itself, there is no suggestion it did not go exactly as Thomas wanted. Certainly, he was buried next to his first wife, Eleanor Holland, as he wished.

Once this was done, Alice presumably focused on managing her new possessions, making sure the transition went smoothly. As she did so, there was another development that soon must have occupied her mind.

Pregnancy and motherhood

Alice and Thomas had seen each other shortly before he died, and so Alice might have hoped, if not already suspected, she was pregnant by him after his death. This would have been a comfort for her in her grief, but there was something else, less high-minded behind the hope to be expecting a child many widows expressed. In case of the deceased having no male heir, a new baby might still inherit his father's riches. It was therefore common in such cases for the widow to be watched for a while for signs of pregnancy, and it is quite possible that this is what happened in this case.

In the event of a daughter or a sister being sole heir to her father, her lands should have passed to her immediately. However, as long as her mother or stepmother still thought she might be carrying an heir, these lands would be held by the stepmother, and in the event of such an heir actually being born, the mother would often hold the lands until the son and heir attained his majority. If that did not happen, then the lands were in the hands of the king, who had the right to grant them and the wardship of the heir to whomever he pleased. This was preferable not only for the mother of the heir but also for the king, who retained control over the lands in this way far longer than he would if an adult daughter assumed ownership.

What is Better than a Good Woman?

The system was sometimes abused, with widows claiming to be pregnant, especially if the heiress of her late husband was a sister or a daughter not her own, to keep control of the lands for a while longer, and the king supporting them for his own benefit. An example is Matilda de Clare, widow of Edward II's nephew Gilbert de Clare.[40] Upon Gilbert's death at the Battle of Bannockburn, the childless Matilda claimed for two years to be pregnant with her late husband's posthumous heir, thus delaying Gilbert's three sisters' inheritance. Edward II according to his biographer Kathryn Warner did not trust Gilbert's brothers-in-law, who, upon their wives entering their inheritance would become very rich men, supported Matilda's impossible claims for as long as he could. It is therefore conceivable that Alice might have stressed the possibility of being pregnant, or even pretended to be pregnant, after Thomas's death. It seems that she did not have to: she was apparently actually pregnant.

The first hint is the fact that despite Thomas's will clearly splitting his possessions between his wife and daughter,[41] Alice was given control of all of his lands However, there are some oddities about this. For one, when Thomas's Inquisitions Post Mortem were made, some of which were in fact only done in summer 1429,[42] all of them stated his daughter Alice was his heir, with no mention made of the possibility of the impending birth of a half-sibling taking this position from her. While it is possible that seven-and-a-half months after Thomas's death Alice was still pregnant and had not given birth, it would have been widely known by that time she was about to give birth, and the jurors of the Inquisition Post Mortem would have made a note of it. Of course, this would not have been the case if Alice was not actually pregnant, the claim having been made to keep Thomas's daughter – and perhaps more importantly his son-in-law Richard Neville – from entering their inheritance for as long as possible. However, in such a case, one would expect to see some resentment from her stepdaughter and

Marriage to Sir Thomas Montacute, Earl of Salisbury

from Richard. On the contrary, Alice and her stepdaughter always seemed on good terms.

If those were the only facts we had, it would seem the only sensible conclusion that Alice did in fact fall pregnant shortly before Thomas's death and carried the pregnancy to term but had a stillbirth or a child who died in infancy. There is no evidence for any such birth, but there is more evidence about the partition of Thomas's lands, which only serves to further confuse matters.

Upon Alice Montacute and her husband Richard Neville finally asking, as late as December 1436, to be given the lands owed to them by inheritance, the agreement stated that the lands and possessions were given 'to William [de la Pole, Earl of Suffolk]',[43] Alice's third husband. However, Alice married William two years after Thomas's death, and while he would have been entitled to hold any lands his wife held, he had absolutely no claim to lands Alice would have had a right to hold, had she had Thomas's son. It makes very little sense for William to be granted them two years after Thomas's death.

Fraudulent claims to lands and possessions were extremely common, and a king's favourite, as William was rapidly becoming in the 1430s, had better chances than most of getting away with it. There are nevertheless some problems with the idea of William's ownership of Thomas's lands being a particularly insolent landgrab. For one, not only would it be a particularly audacious claim to make, even at the time, but there is no record of William ever making such a claim; it seems he was simply given them, as if they were a rightful part of his wife's inheritance. Secondly, if this had been the case, it would have been logical for Richard and Alice Neville to be angry at Alice and William, to try and argue against it. This did not happen. There is no record of any proceedings Richard Neville started in his wife's name to gain possession of what was rightfully hers. Since neither Richard nor Alice were the type to simply accept being defrauded, both powerful personalities

What is Better than a Good Woman?

who could, and did, argue for their rights when they considered they were being infringed upon, it stands to reason that they acquiesced in the lands being given to Alice and William.

Evidence survives that shows Alice and her stepdaughter and stepson-in-law remaining on perfectly good, even affectionate, terms after Thomas's death, with no evidence of the resentment that would surely have been normal had Alice so blatantly conned them out of her stepdaughter's inheritance. The only way the evidence would really make sense would be if Alice had actually given birth to Thomas's heir, and the boy survived long enough to see his mother marrying William de la Pole, Earl of Suffolk.

This is almost certainly not the case. Thomas's son-in-law Richard Neville was provisionally confirmed as Earl of Salisbury in his wife's name as early as May 1429,[44] when any pregnancy of Alice's would have been known, and such an action delayed until it was known whether she had a girl, or a boy who would be entitled to the earldom over his brother-in-law. Even if Richard had been given the grant despite this, he would have lost it upon the birth of Alice's son, of which there is no evidence, and he is consistently referred to as 'Earl of Salisbury'. Any boy Alice had would have been of quite some importance, and it is inconceivable that his birth and William, Earl of Suffolk, becoming his stepfather would not have been recorded.

The only way to make any sense of the situation is if Alice did have a posthumous baby by Thomas, but not the presumably hoped for heir, a baby girl. Though a legitimate child, this girl would not have been entitled to inherit anything in the stead of her older half-sister. But in such a case, Alice Montacute and her husband might have accepted Alice holding Thomas's lands for the benefit of the baby girl, with an agreement being made to make sure that they also received a fair share.

Of course, such an agreement would be heavily in favour of Alice, but it seems likely that this would not have much upset her stepdaughter, who would always have known that regardless of other

Marriage to Sir Thomas Montacute, Earl of Salisbury

circumstances, half of Thomas's possessions would go to his widow. The other half would have been for her, and as the older daughter, the one in a more powerful situation by birth and marriage, she would not have needed to give anything to her younger sister, but she could do it regardless. She was in a position in which she could afford to be generous, and this seems to have been what happened.

In fact, there is more evidence for Alice having Thomas's posthumous daughter than it being the most likely solution to the riddle posed by the strange partition of his lands after his death. In the few surviving records of William de la Pole's household, a little girl is mentioned until the mid-1430s.[45] Though usually this little girl is ignored, or sometimes claimed to have been a daughter of Alice and William's, this is very unlikely, as the context suggests a birth before autumn 1431, which would be impossible. Her being Alice's daughter and an earl's daughter, if not heiress, would account for it. Therefore, it seems that in early autumn 1429, Alice became a mother for the first time.

If Alice did not yet know when Thomas died that she was pregnant, she must have realised it soon afterwards. One can hope that she found out early enough to tell Thomas. All we can say is that Alice's daughter would have been born before May 1429,[46] when Richard Neville was granted the earldom of Salisbury by right of his wife, suggesting, as mentioned above, knowledge that no later-born son of Thomas's would be able to challenge it. It could be that the actual grant to him was only done in May, because before that he and others were awaiting the birth of Alice's child, to see if it would be Thomas's posthumous heir. If Alice actually was pregnant, Richard would have needed to wait and see if she carried the pregnancy to term, and it is unlikely that he would have received the earldom before that even if she was not, as such matters usually took time.

Since the evidence suggests that Alice was pregnant in the months after Thomas's death, presumably that would have taken most of her

What is Better than a Good Woman?

attention. We know that once more Thomas Chaucer manages her lands.[47] These lands included those his late son-in-law Thomas had held, which he presumably hoped would stay in the family with the birth of a grandson. Though Alice had been getting more involved with the management of her lands in recent years,[48] she seemed to withdraw from doing so in the months after Thomas's death. Of course, this could simply have been because she felt it overwhelming and needed her father's guidance for it, or because she felt unable to do so because of grief. In the light of the other evidence, the most likely reason is that she wanted to focus on her pregnancy.

The news for the English in France was not good, and as winter passed into spring, it became worse. After Thomas's death, his second-in-command and friend William de la Pole, Earl of Suffolk, had taken over as leader of the army besieging the city of Orléans.[49] William continued the siege as it had been when Thomas had been fatally injured. According to contemporary English chroniclers, this seemed a good idea, and in the height of winter, the hardest time for the besieged as well as the besiegers, it looked likely that the English forces would win the city. But they did not. Orléans held out against all odds, and in spring Dauphin Charles sent Joan of Arc with forces to relieve the city.[50] This was a resounding success; within only two weeks, the English forces were defeated, the siege broken. Orléans had not been won and the English forces were on the retreat. The siege officially ended on 8 May 1429, which was coincidentally around the time that Alice must have given birth to Thomas's posthumous daughter.

When exactly this child was born, we can no longer say, though we can calculate a timespan. Richard Neville was officially granted his father-in-law's earldom by right of his wife on 3 May 1429,[51] so it was known by then that no child would be born who could take the title from him. Since Thomas did not make a new will before entering the Siege of Orléans, in expectation of another legitimate child, it also seems logical that he was not yet aware, or at least

Marriage to Sir Thomas Montacute, Earl of Salisbury

not yet certain, of his wife's pregnancy before the siege started in mid-October, which he almost certainly would have done had Alice been pregnant for more than three months by then. Therefore, the conception must have fallen between July and September, and the birth between late March and early May. Perhaps the former is more likely; we know that Thomas and Alice were together in England until July, while we do not know where Alice was after that time, or if she was with her husband at any point.

Another fact to take into account is that Richard Neville and his wife would have lost no time in making sure to secure the earldom of Salisbury as soon as possible. Since it was issued on 4 May, it must have been requested at least two weeks before that. If Alice's baby was born in early April, the timeline makes sense.

Sadly, we do not know any of Alice's feelings about her daughter's birth and can only make assumptions. Whether she would have preferred to have a son, to be the mother of the Earl of Salisbury and keep the belongings in the family, or if she was actually happier having a daughter is impossible to say. Even if she was disappointed that she did not have a son, she would have been happy at the birth of an apparently healthy daughter.

We can assume that Alice saw to it her daughter was as well taken care of as she herself had been as a baby and followed the same conventions her parents had followed; but at the end of 1429 she started involving herself again in more mundane, everyday work. She took an interest in her lands and once more took up at least some of their management, though still, as she had while married to Thomas, relying on her father. She also appeared to turn her attention once more to what was happening in France. By the end of 1429, Alice Chaucer, twice-widowed mother of an approximately 7-month-old daughter, started to look to the future again.

6

WILLIAM, EARL OF SUFFOLK

The situation in France had not improved for the English forces since May 1429, when Alice's life had changed so drastically by the birth of her baby. On the contrary, it had become significantly worse. If the fall of Orléans to the English would have meant that the rest of France would be so weakened it could be conquered, as Henry V had supposedly claimed so confidently, then the failure to take it meant the opposite. The English hegemony in France was broken, and one failure chased the next. William, Earl of Suffolk, who had lost his brother Alexander when the siege broke, signalled a strategic retreat to the nearby Jargeau to his troops.[1] Probably, his plan was to regroup, but that did not happen. The French forces, bolstered by their success at Orléans and not spent from several months of exhausting siege warfare, chased them there. The result was a pitched battle on 12 June at Jargeau,[2] which was another catastrophic loss for the English forces. Several important men died, including another brother of the army commander, John de la Pole.[3] William, Earl of Suffolk himself surrendered and was taken prisoner. According to legend, he refused to surrender to anyone but Joan of Arc herself, saying that she was the bravest woman alive. This is probably only a legend, but it proves how

William, Earl of Suffolk

quickly legends grew not only about Joan herself, but also about the failure and retreat of the English forces.

This loss had two important consequences that were not of a military nature: coronations. With the English forces, at least for the moment, defeated, Dauphin Charles decided to be crowned King of France in Reims, a well-attended affair on 17 July 1429,[4] which most Frenchmen accepted as the coronation of their king. Naturally, the English did not agree, and with their forces in disarray they decided that the nearly eight-year-old Henry VI of England, who, according to the treaty of Troyes was both King of England and of France, had to be crowned King of France as well. The problem was that due to his age he had not yet even been crowned King of England. Plans were quickly laid and Henry VI was crowned in Westminster Abbey on 6 November 1429,[5] and a coronation in France was intended to happen soon afterwards, though everyone involved must have known that the actual plans would have to wait to see if they could be realised, depending on how the situation developed.

Alice must have followed what happened in France, and especially William's actions, with interest. Though this would have been expected of her as the widow of such an important warrior, it must have soon become clear to those close to her that her interest in William exceeded mere curiosity about what happened to the English forces, and also more than a simple affection for him as the long-time friend and brother-in-arms of her late husband. By early 1430, she and William must have first started to make plans to marry.

It is not known when Alice first made contact with William or if it was actually her who initiated that contact. William, though he had been imprisoned after the Battle of Jargeau and was still the Bastard of Orléans's prisoner in 1430, was treated like many noble prisoners, so he could write letters and quite possibly even receive visitors. It was not William's first relatively comfortable incarceration, he had been taken prisoner by the French forces

What is Better than a Good Woman?

before, in 1424,[6] and might therefore have been used to the customs of it. It is therefore possible that it was he who first contacted Alice, though she was in a better position to do so and he had no way of knowing that she even wished such a contact, and of checking if any messages he sent actually reached her.

Such contact may not have immediately been with marriage in mind; in fact, it seems unlikely that it was. Alice and William had known each other at least since the Burgundian marriage of 1424, during which Duke Philip of Burgundy made passes at Alice. As has been seen above, Pierre de Fenin, who reported this scene, named William among the guests at the celebration,[7] as does Enguerrand de Monstrelet.[8] It is the only time they were noted to be together in the same place before they married, so that it does not hint at anything more than a passing acquaintance, but it does prove that they had met and known each other during most of Alice's marriage to Thomas.

Since Thomas and William were often in the same place when fighting,[9] it is quite possible that William and Alice also knew each other far better than the mention of them being guests at the same marriage implies. Alice might have been interested simply in knowing that her late husband's friend, who had taken over as commander once her husband died, was healthy and had everything he needed in his honourable imprisonment with the Bastard of Orléans. Noble prisoners were approached by family and friends like this, to provide them with money or other necessities, even treats, so perhaps Alice simply considered herself in the best situation to offer help to William should he need it. Conversely, it is also possible Alice did it for her own sake, having at some point in their acquaintance grown fond of William.

If it was William who first made contact, the same holds true. Though in his case, wanting to make sure she was not in need cannot have been a motive for establishing contact. His motive could still have been nothing to do with a possible relationship. He might

William, Earl of Suffolk

simply have wanted to make sure she was healthy and in good spirits and enquire if his friend's posthumous baby was doing well.

Though these are the perhaps most likely motives, simply judging by human nature, another motive cannot be discounted: it is perfectly possible that if Alice contacted William she had marriage in mind. The same could be said for William, but it is less likely he would have been confident enough to contact her with such an offer. She had less reason to marry than he did; though he had not shown any interest in marrying since becoming Earl of Suffolk in 1415, he had lost two of his brothers in 1429. His last remaining brother, Thomas, was a priest, so that the survival of his family line depended on him marrying and having legitimate children. Alice would have been aware of this. Though her birth was not noble, she was an earl's widow, a very rich heiress, and with the birth of her daughter had proved herself fertile and thus able to give William the heir he would presumably be looking for if he married. William, despite being an earl, did not boast very distinguished noble ancestors himself. His great-grandfather had been a wool merchant,[10] his family rising in the ranks more through merit than birth. All in all, he was a perfectly suitable husband for Alice, should she have considered remarriage in late 1429.

Though William would not have been ignorant of such considerations, he had little reason to believe Alice was interested in marriage to him unless she told him. Being already a dowager countess, marriage to him would not have offered her a rise in status. Nor could he offer a significant increase in wealth; Alice herself was already richer than him and would, once her father died, be even richer. If contact between Alice and William was established in early 1430 with the intention of marriage, it almost certainly came from Alice.

If the proposal of marriage was not a motive for establishing this contact, it soon occurred to them. Messages between France and England would have taken at least two weeks, so that any

What is Better than a Good Woman?

conversations could not have progressed very quickly. Despite this, by mid-1430, marriage between them was very clearly not only on the table but already considered in detail by both of them. Alice was making preparations for the details of such a match, perhaps helped by her father and possibly Cardinal Beaufort, while William set his mind on wooing her as best he could from prison.

We are very lucky that we have details of this wooing in the poetry of Charles of Orléans. Charles, half-brother of William's jailer the Bastard of Orléans, was a talented poet and was closely connected with William. In the manuscripts alongside Charles's poems there are also several stated to have been those of 'an English friend'.[11] As has been pointed out by scholars such as Pierre Champion[12] and Henry Noble MacCracken, this friend must have been William. Since several of these poems can be dated with reasonable accuracy to William's time in prison, we can be confident they are his. Though Alice is not actually named in any of the poems, the circumstances surrounding their being written make it all but certain they were written for her.

These poems for Alice show an earnest effort by William to woo Alice as romantically as possible under the circumstances. Written in either French or English, they sometimes speak of the difficulty of love, such as this one:

What displeasure, what ruin, what distress,
What grief, what ills go through loves.
What anguishes here found all the days
Certainly I believe what I say here
I really believe to choose a mistress
One needs to be joyous, but I am full of tears
I say no more, I see my youth
When breathing in, thinking of my pain
Then when I see it, when I see all the past,
Of my pleasures, I am no longer as sad.[13]

68

William, Earl of Suffolk

Others were more upbeat, more geared to the future, such as one probably written earlier:

From this moment to all days
From all and more to nothing
I am yours and remain yours
My love, my joy, and my only good,
My comfort, my desire, my peace
My will, my desires, my deeds
Are for you and will stay so always
That's the lesson I remember
Where I am, where I go
What I say, what I do
You have the heart that was mine
If we maintain it, it will be good
And surround us with perfect pleasures.[14]

At the risk of slipping into literary criticism, it seems clear from these poems that William wished to focus on the romantic aspect of the marriage, personal feelings more than anything else, trying to incorporate the difficult and sad situations they both found themselves in, as well as hope for the future. Perhaps he was writing what he actually felt, if exaggerated for poetic effect, or he was actively trying to create a favourable impression as a romantic and empathetic man. William was trying to woo Alice in as romantic a way as he could. In all, there were sixteen poems[15] written over eight or nine months. Alice herself, meanwhile, was rather more concerned with the more practical aspects of marriage, and what their marriage would look like. By September 1430 at the latest, Alice and William had agreed to marry.

Most likely, they did not actually see each other in person during all their negotiations for marriage, or if they did, not more than once. Though many noble prisoners in the same situation as

What is Better than a Good Woman?

William were allowed to receive visitors, and nothing of the Bastard of Orléans's behaviour towards William suggests any hostility or that he would not have agreed to letting Alice visit him, it would have been an arduous journey for Alice, and a dangerous one. Though the idea of her not wanting to leave her daughter alone is a very modern one, since the baby would have had a staff of her own and her mother would not have been in charge of her everyday care, the thought of leaving the child an orphan at the mercy of the king and his regents might have stopped her from making such a fraught journey at a time when the English forces were no longer as powerful in France as they had been two years before.

Even if she chose to make such a journey once, most of Alice and William's discussions about their future and their marriage must have taken place remotely, through messengers. This would have made matters more difficult than face-to-face discussions would have, but remote communication concerning marriages were not only a matter of course for royalty but also common for nobles, who could not always afford the time to travel far to participate in such dialogue.

However challenging it may have proved, clearly Alice and William came to an agreement that suited them both, and Alice set about making arrangements. Very significantly, she chose to draw up a marriage settlement for her and William. The fact she used a lawyer who worked for her father has made William's sole biographer, Susan Curran, suggest that it had been Thomas Chaucer's idea to make this settlement,[16] but nothing in the settlement can confirm or dismiss this. It does show, however, that whoever was the mastermind behind it was driving a hard bargain for Alice.

It is a settlement which is notable in several ways, as it established not only what Alice's jointure would be, but also that she was to keep control of her own lands and that William needed her consent if he wished to use funds from them. This shows that despite Alice having no reason to remarry but her own personal happiness, she did not enter this third marriage with any illusions. Whatever her feelings towards William were, she was determined to protect her own interests no matter what. It also makes clear she was perfectly aware of her own worth. Moreover, more abstractly, this stern settlement also proves a myth about the Middle Ages wrong: that women had no control over their own possessions once married, and that the husband automatically owned everything his wife did. Obviously, this was not the case, and, like today, a marriage contract could prevent overreach by a spouse.

There is something else notable about this marriage settlement: William agreed to it, as far as we know, without trying to debate it and win better terms for himself. As it stood, he would not have any access to Alice's money without her agreement and would simply be a rich woman's husband. This would have been less than perfect for him, as the earldom of Suffolk was not a notably rich one. Moreover, his imprisonment meant he needed money: as was usual for that sort of imprisonment, the Bastard of Orléans was demanding a steep price for his release, 20,000 pounds.[17] This would have meant that William would have been all but penniless after paying it, and even if Alice agreed to pay part of it, he would be dependent on her.

Despite this, he neither protested against the settlement nor tried to secure another match before agreeing to marry Alice. He was determined to marry Alice, even if it meant little in the way of financial improvement. Though William's pedigree was less than perfect, he was still an earl and probably could have found a match that would make him much richer, but he never showed an interest in this, which suggests real feelings for Alice.

Though motives are always hard to guess at after five centuries, what evidence we have suggests that practical considerations may have played a part in Alice and William's decision to get married, but it was at least partially motivated by affection. Alice had absolutely no reason to get married to William if she did not want to, neither financial, nor for status, nor even motherhood. It is possible that she, twenty-six years of age in 1430, did not want to stay alone for the rest of her life and considered William the best match she was likely to secure, but even so, it is unlikely she would have chosen to marry him if she was not fond of him at least. William may have been attracted by her connections and the fact that, even if she retained control over her money, she was very rich and this could make his life easier, but he could have presumably found a more advantageous match in those terms. So it seems that he, too, was at least partially motivated by fondness, or at the very least, attraction to his friend's widow – who had been repeatedly described as very beautiful.

Marriage to William, Earl of Suffolk

Once the marriage settlement had been agreed upon, both Alice and William had to turn to other practical arrangements before they could actually wed. William, of course, had been imprisoned throughout his discussions with and wooing of Alice and he was still, when all details about the marriage had been agreed upon. The most obvious problem facing him once all this was done was just that: he could not marry Alice as a prisoner.

This, too, was not a new problem, one that other honourable prisoners had faced before, and it was solved in the time-honoured way: a prisoner exchange. Because William could not raise the sort of money needed for his release from prison in a short time, and because he could not marry while in prison, the Bastard of Orléans agreed to let him go if he found someone else to be his prisoner for him. This was agreed upon, and William's younger brother, the last surviving, Thomas de la Pole, a man of the cloth, agreed to be Orléans' prisoner in his stead until William had raised the money for his release.

Such arrangements would have taken at least a month, for the agreement to be made between William, Orléans and Thomas, for

William, Earl of Suffolk

Thomas to come to Orléans's castle, for William to be released and travel to England. In the meantime, Alice was not idle, but made what agreements she could for the marriage to be able to go ahead. This would have included mundane arrangements such as having a dress fitted for the wedding and giving orders for the celebration, but there was something more important and probably also more time-sensitive: applying for a licence to marry.

It is not known when exactly Alice did this, only when it was issued, on 11 November 1430.[18] Since it was rare for such bureaucracy to be rapid, Alice must have applied for it as soon as the marriage settlement was drawn up and agreed upon. There appears to have been no difficulties with being issued the licence; as was common then, Alice paid a fairly hefty sum for it: £40, which is about £25,000 today.[19]

Once it was issued, all was set for the marriage. An advantage of both Alice and William's comparatively unimpressive pedigree was that they were not at all related, the way so many nobles at the time were, and therefore did not need to apply to the pope for a dispensation. Once Alice had paid for and been issued the licence to marry William, all that was needed was for William to return to England.

It is not known when exactly Alice married William, just as the dates of her first two weddings are unknown. Neither of them would have wanted to wait long after the difficult arrangements had been made, but even if they really wished to marry as soon as possible, they may not actually have been able to marry immediately upon William returning to England after around one-and-a-half years as a prisoner. Since we have no way of knowing when exactly this return happened, only that it must have been in late 1430, it is possible his return happened during the season of advent, when weddings were forbidden.

Even if that was so, it seems likely one of William's first actions upon returning home would be to meet with his intended, possibly for the first time not only since they had agreed to marry but since

What is Better than a Good Woman?

the death of Thomas Montacute. He would have met his future stepdaughter for the first time then. While it is possible that during the discussions about their upcoming marriage Alice came to see him William once as a prisoner, she would not have brought a baby who was not yet two years old.

The details of any such meeting are not recorded, of course, but there is no reason not to assume it went perfectly well. Alice and William's marriage was to be a notably happy one from all evidence we have, and, as discussed above, must have been at least partially made because of affection or attraction. Perhaps, to modern minds, the meeting with his baby stepdaughter could have been difficult, but it seems unlikely it was a problem for William. It was more common than today for widows and widowers to remarry, bringing children from a previous marriage with them, and it rarely caused difficulties. Moreover, William himself had an illegitimate daughter to introduce to Alice, so that even had he been minded to, he would have hardly been able to complain about her also having a child. Actually, given the circumstances, William meeting Alice's daughter could very well have been a happy occasion. Not only did he obviously at least like her mother, he had also been friends with her father, and might very well have been happy to become her stepfather, seen her as a joy rather than a burden.

Soon after they married, William and Alice settled into a happy family, with his own illegitimate daughter at one point becoming a part of it, and – though we have so very little evidence about her – a companion for Alice's toddler daughter.

First years of marriage

Alice and William must have been married by February 1431. Again, we can only assume what the first weeks and months of their marriage looked like, as we can only assume what it was like for Alice and her second husband, Thomas. There would have been a honeymoon phase, but of course, with Alice being a mother,

William, Earl of Suffolk

it would have been different. She had been a teenager when she married Thomas, when she married William she was a grown woman with responsibilities. The most important of these was the care of her daughter, but there were also her riches, which, unlike at the beginning of her second marriage, she was very involved in overseeing.

For all that, it might still have been a romantic honeymoon, but as was so often the case, politics and social responsibilities would have prevented them from becoming too lost in each other. William needed to re-establish himself as an earl, after over a decade of absence from England fighting in France, something he would later clearly view as a sacrifice in the name of the king. In fact, William had barely been to England at all since becoming an earl after his older brother died at the Battle of Agincourt in 1415, so that once he was home and respectably married, he had to not so much to re-establish himself as Earl of Suffolk and manager of his corresponding lands, but first to establish himself.

It was not as if he was a complete unknown to those who had to do business with him: while he had not been able to do most of the business connected with the management of his lands and the earldom of Suffolk in general over the years of fighting in France after attaining his majority, he had seen to it that qualified men did it in his name and in his best interest. Again, this was the norm, it was what Thomas Montacute had done while he was with the army in France and could not personally take care of his possessions and his earldom.

William was in a somewhat more unusual situation because he had not had an extended period of stay in his lands, making sure all his dependants as well as all those working for him got to know him as an earl, before he was forced to hand over these concerns to others. From the time he unexpectedly became Earl of Suffolk in 1415 to the time he married Alice in very late 1430, around the same time Henry VI was crowned in Paris as king of France,

What is Better than a Good Woman?

or very early 1431, he had been a warrior first and foremost, his earldom coming second.

Despite this, William's lands were well taken care of in that time, and his earldom was held in high regard. Without a doubt, his service to the king in France helped in this, as several contemporary sources and even sources from later in the fifteenth century, such as the *Croyland Chronicle*,[20] show the English population was very much in support of the French wars and the king's claim to the French throne. William's long service and his personal sacrifices, his loss of family and imprisonments were likely to endear him to the population and make those concerned more likely to forgive any mismanagement of his lands that happened while he was at war.

Homecoming and finding his place as Earl of Suffolk was not, therefore, as difficult for William as it might have been, but it would not have been easy. As he began to re-establish his position, he would not only be grateful to have Alice for personal reasons, to have a wife to help and comfort him, but also for the connections she brought, and the help he could get through them. Thomas Chaucer, to whom Alice had remained extremely close through the last years, became close to William.[21] He helped him with the management of his lands in those first years.

Though the relationship of the two men was a good one, Thomas would not have done this just for William. Alice, too, profited from William being accepted as earl and as manager of his lands. It had been over ten years since William's mother, the last Dowager Countess of Suffolk had died,[22] and since then there had of course not been a countess. This meant that William also had to set up his new wife as his countess, a very active and involved countess at that. Though these tasks sound rather daunting, there is no evidence this was in any way contentious or that any difficulties arose.

William had not just married a woman who was to be a countess. He had married a widow of two rich and one very important man, the mother of a little girl who had a claim to be the co-heiress of that rich and famous man. There would have been very little time for a honeymoon phase, or at least not the sort of comparatively carefree one that she might have enjoyed with Thomas.

William lost no time in trying to do all he could to make sure he could meet these challenges, with energetic help from Alice. Again, this was not from pure selflessness, though it has sometimes been portrayed as that, especially in older books. Since Alice Chaucer was a popular subject for Victorian authors, though never the central figure, it makes sense that the image of a helpful wife who was eventually corrupted by ambition took hold at the time as a sort of morality tale. A good example of this is Henry Napier's book, *Historical Notices of the Parishes of Swyncombe and Ewelme in the County of Oxford.* This was not focused on Alice herself and did not bother to illuminate her own interests, of which she had many.

Alice as we know was significantly richer than William, and though for a long time her father had done the bulk of estate management for her, she still had more experience of it than William. Therefore, it made sense for her to help him with it, initially at least. Alice's lands, due to the marriage settlement she and William had agreed on, were not under William's control but were often managed by the same people, their assets in this way combined. It was therefore not only for William's benefit that Alice did the best she could and helped William, it was also in her own interests and in the interests of her daughter.

There was something else William had to do, something he would soon show he was very skilled at: socialising and making important connections with powerful people. Unlike the management of his lands, it was something he could work at during his time in France. There, he not only encountered some of the highest nobility of England but also of France and Burgundy. However, while these men were important and had a lot of influence, the fact that the king was still very young in 1431, turning ten at the end of the year, meant that those who were closest to him personally were not

What is Better than a Good Woman?

fighting in France. William was shrewd enough to see very early on that it would pay to become close to the king and those he valued, in addition to the noble warriors with whom he had spent most of time in France and to whom he had become close.

His marriage to Alice helped him with this, as her and her father's connections were significant in England. Perhaps the most important of Alice's connections was to her stepdaughter from her second marriage and her stepson-in-law, Richard Neville. The eldest of the large family of Joan Beaufort and Ralph Neville, Richard was related to Thomas Chaucer and therefore to Alice without the marriage. More importantly, he was also related to the king and to men like Cardinal Henry Beaufort and John Beaufort, Earl of Somerset, who was close to the youthful king and would have his ear as he grew up. Cultivating Richard's friendship was therefore worthwhile for William, and through Alice he had the perfect in, but despite clearly having an interest in rising in the king's favour, he did not seem to use it. Alice was on good terms with her stepdaughter and with Richard Neville, but though never antagonistic, there was no discernible warmth between William and Richard. Even so, they came to an agreement concerning the partition of Thomas Montacute's lands. As mentioned earlier, they were held by Alice and by William, either through an informal agreement or a formal one evidence for which was lost. Alice Montacute would get all the money owed to her from her quarter of the lands.

Presumably, once Alice Chaucer's daughter came of age, a different agreement would have been reached, as she had a right to be recognised formally as her father's co-heir, while Alice Montacute would not have been happy to see any of her lands in the hands of any man her half-sister eventually married, where she could never be sure if he would give her what was her due. Interestingly, she never seems to have had any worries of that nature concerning William. From the surviving documents there was no argument taken to court, suggesting an agreement of some

William, Earl of Suffolk

sort was in place. In a document dated 10 December 1436,[23] William promised to detail exactly how much of the income of the lands and possessions his wife's stepdaughter was owed. The lack of abrasiveness in the document is striking; it was simply a document detailing in writing an agreement that had long since been reached and kept to.

Though this was a sensitive subject, and its calm and peaceable solution suggests that Alice and her husband became close to her stepdaughter and stepson-in-law, this never seemed to be the case. Alice was closer to them than William, but even for her, it never seemed to go particularly deep. Despite the fact that this was a missed opportunity that could have enabled the couple to have an in at court, other connections gave them the same chance, one they took. Alice's brother-in-law by her first marriage, William Phelip, rose in young Henry VI's favour in the 1430s, and Alice's connection to him meant that she could profit from it.

Most of all, however, it seems that Alice's and William's own personalities boosted their standing with the king. In 1421 William had been made a Knight of the Order of the Garter,[24] a distinguished position that only 24 people were ever allowed at the same time. This was most likely not because of the strength of Henry V's affection for him, but on the strength of his military service. Even so, it gave him an opening to work himself up, which he soon did after the wedding, receiving a position in Henry VI's household as early as 1432.[25]

Alice was doubtless pleased by this, but shortly after she and William married she must have feared that it could never happen, that their happiness would only be short-lived and that William never would get the chance to achieve any of the things she was hoping he would: he became critically ill. In April 1431, William should have been there for his first Garter festivities, which were celebrated in England and which he therefore could not have attended in the previous years. He also could not attend the

What is Better than a Good Woman?

festivities in 1431 because he was 'seized with the plague'.[26] This does not have to mean that William actually had the plague. It is not impossible, as the survival rate of the plague was up to 40 per cent, not the instant death sentence that is often associated with the plague today, but it is not very likely. For one, the plague was extremely contagious and yet none of those close to William became ill, an improbability had he truly been sick with the plague. In medieval chronicles, 'plague' was often used as a generic word for illness in general, and it seems likely that this is what had happened in his case. Whatever he was suffering from, Alice must have feared that she was about to become a widow again. The best physicians would have been summoned to take care of him, but sadly, though we have several documents about physicians in the fifteenth century and in fact even some referring to the Suffolk family, nothing survives that could throw a light on William's 1431 illness.

The illness passed and he returned to full health. His sickness means that in all likelihood he was not, as is often assumed, back in France by May 1431, for one of the most significant and tragic events in the history of France: the execution of Joan of Arc.

While William had been imprisoned, then busy with his marital arrangements and finally sick, there had been significant developments among the French, the Burgundian and the English forces in France. The wheel of fate had once more turned, this time against the previously so successful Joan of Arc. It is often claimed that she became too confident, too sure of her own abilities,[27] something that has happened to many great commanders both before and after her. Certainly, she was keen on continuing the war against the English, while the newly crowned King Charles, who had previously supported her, started to be bored by her suggestions, and once crowned was more interested in making treaties and less in making war.

Though it is understandable that Charles had less interest in fighting once he had gained what he had fought for – his coronation

William, Earl of Suffolk

and acceptance as French king by most of his country – he acted shamefully in this instance. Though more and more lukewarm towards Joan's ideas of continued warfare, he still nominally supported them and gave her men and weapons. It has sometimes been suggested that he hoped that she would fall in battle, thus freeing him of her presence that had clearly become irksome to him, while at the same time not going against someone many believed was chosen by God to help free France from the English forces, and who had helped him greatly in winning the throne.

He was to get his wish, though perhaps not in the way he might have envisioned. Joan did not fall in battle, but her luck did not hold out. While fighting against the Burgundians in 1430, who despite the difficulties in the late 1420s were still nominally allied to England[28] and disliked France and its policies towards their territories, Joan's forces lost and she was taken prisoner. Initially, it may not have worried her too much, as it seems that her imprisonment was first intended to be like William's two imprisonments had been – an honourable stay in a comfortable prison, Joan assessed as a valuable warrior to be freed for payment of a hefty sum of money.

King Charles had no interest in paying for Joan's release, though he did not actually say so, he simply did not react to the demands by Duke Philip of Burgundy for ransom. Things were to become even worse. Though the French king did not want to pay, there was someone else interested in having her in custody: the English forces. Though they had to pay the huge price of 10,000 livres,[29] the English commanders decided it was worth it. The English would treat her as they would treat other commanders of the French army they managed to capture: dispose of her by execution.

With a woman, this looked more difficult. No matter what Joan had done or not done, once she had led the French army to victory against the English forces, they would have found a reason to execute her once she fell into their hands, and the circumstances of Joan's actions gave them a way.

What is Better than a Good Woman?

It was heresy that she was charged with by the English court she found herself faced with after the English forces had paid her ransom and Duke Philip had handed her over. This tribunal, which started in February 1431, was technically led by a churchman, Pierre Cauchon, Bishop of Beauvais, but obviously influenced by the English. It is often assumed, or simply stated as fact, that William was one of those manning the tribunal, but this is definitely untrue, as he cannot have been present in France in a trial lasting from February to May while at the same time being critically ill in England in April at the same time. And he was not mentioned by Guillaume Manchon,[30] who took notes on the trial.

As everyone must have expected, Joan was eventually condemned to death, though reaching that charge was not as easy as the English tribunal originally expected. Despite theological trick questions, trying to make Joan commit blasphemy, Joan acted so cleverly at the trial this was impossible for them, so that her English would-be executioners had to resort to trickery: using her wearing men's clothes against her. Her 'pretending' to be a man could be construed as an affront against God, and if she was caught doing it again she could be executed for it, as it could be said to be heresy. Joan was clearly aware of this and wore a dress for her trial, but her English jailors put her in a man's jail. Wearing a dress, she was at risk from the criminals there, and Joan appears to have been afraid of drawing attention and possibly being raped – a justified fear. This was accepted by the English forces, so long as she did not do it again. Joan swore on 24 May not to do it, but once again, she was put in a man's jail so that she decided to stop wearing her dress and wore trousers and men's clothes her English jailors had ready for just that reaction. With this relapse, an affront against God, she could legally be burned for heresy, the sentence carried out on 31 May 1431.[31]

Of course, it was clear to everyone that the heresy charge was a pretext, that Joan's real 'crime' had been fighting against the English, but despite what is claimed in some more recent books,

William, Earl of Suffolk

it is unlikely many, including women, saw it as a punishment for being a woman doing a man's work. Certainly, Alice would not have considered it to be so; in fact, she might have very well seen it as justice being served.

Many books place her, together with William, at Joan's execution, but again, this seems unlikely. While it is less impossible than William being part of the tribunal, and he might well have been healthy enough by the end of May to travel to France, there is no indication he did so or was present, nor for Alice. There is no evidence at all they went to France that year, though it is often claimed as fact.

There would have been little reason for them to do so. William might have wanted to visit his brother Thomas, still imprisoned with the Bastard of Orléans in his stead, but such a visit meant little. The only thing William could do for his brother was to raise the £20,000 Orléans demanded as quickly as possible, and the best way to do this was by staying in England; and leaving for France within months of returning to England would have been counterproductive in his efforts to secure his position at home. The analysis of whether William and Alice went to France is centred on William, as we know little of Alice's movements at the time, but what little evidence there is also places her in England. For one, there are several grants of lands mentioning her, which required her attention and were concerned with the changed circumstances she found herself in, newly remarried. Several of these grants are still on record and clearly refer to lands and possessions being solely hers.

This ignores any personal reasons Alice might have had for staying in England, such as her little daughter. Unlike the management of her lands, this is guesswork. While managing her lands required her presence unless she handed it to someone else, as she had done before but did not seem to do in 1431, her daughter would not necessarily need her presence. Whatever her, and William's, motives were, what evidence there is suggests that they did not go to France, were not present for Joan of Arc's trial

What is Better than a Good Woman?

or her execution or later, to see everyone deal with the aftermath, but instead stayed in England, to set up their life together there.

Rise to power

They were quickly very successful in this. In 1432, William received a position in the king's household,[32] and as Alice's husband received custody of several of Thomas Montacute's lands, to be held by him and managed for both Alice[33] her daughter and Thomas's older daughter, as documented in the agreement between him and Richard Neville of 10 December 1436.

Alice herself became more and more important. On 21 May 1432 she was made a Lady of the Order of the Garter,[34] an honour given to even fewer women than men. It is unlikely that this was done simply because she was married to William, or even on the strength of being Thomas Monatcute's widow. Usually, women had to be in some way related to the king to become a Lady of the Garter. For Alice to be given entry into this most prestigious of orders therefore means that she must have been very high in Henry VI's esteem, or the esteem of his regents, approbation she was held in on her own account, not because of some connection to powerful men.

The grant making her a lady of the Garter still exists, but sadly, such dry mentions in record books is all we know about Alice and William's life at that time. From snippets years later, it seems like the 1430s in general, and especially the first years after their wedding were the happiest, and definitely the calmest of their entire marriage. Though they made frequent visits to court, they spent more time in their own manors than they did in later years. The old adage holds true of happiness not making much of a story or, in this case, leaving a lot of traces on records. We can assume that they worked together on the management of their lands, socialised and built connections and, at least initially, worked to raise money to free William's brother.

William, Earl of Suffolk

It would never happen. At some point in 1432, Thomas de la Pole died while still imprisoned by the Bastard of Orléans.[35] There is no evidence to indicate that his death was anything but natural, or that it had anything at all to do with him being a prisoner. William would later claim that he had lost all his brothers in France, though Thomas's death there was only indirectly due to the war. There is nothing to suggest that he would not have died in England at the same time as he did in France.

No doubt, his brother's death would have been a blow for William, and the fact that nearly twenty years later, he mentioned Thomas as a casualty of war suggests he might have also felt guilty for being responsible for him being in France. Interestingly, it has been suggested that when Thomas died, the Bastard of Orléans agreed not to ask for the money he was owed,[36] though William claimed otherwise.[37] Even so, the Bastard of Orléans was very obliging and courteous about the whole affair. Though according to all customs, he would have been entitled to ask for another hostage, he did not.[38] Perhaps this turn of events was instrumental in slowly forming William's resolve to be for peace with France, against the continuing war, an attitude for which he would later be famous – and for which he eventually became hated.

It is also possible that Alice influenced him. Her attitude to the war in France is not known, but it would be only too understandable if she, after losing two husbands, was against the conflict continuing, fearful of also losing William because of it, even if she was generally in favour of Henry's claim to the throne.

Another possibility is that spending more time at Henry's court, William and Alice came more into contact with people who were against war, as Henry himself would eventually grow up to be. In this case, it might be that the usually accepted version is the right one: that Henry VI was more influenced by William's opinion of the continuing war in France and his antipathy towards it than the other way around. This seems more logical, since in the early

What is Better than a Good Woman?

1430s Henry VI was still only a child, unlikely to have any in-depth knowledge of warfare and would have been incapable of forming a grounded opinion on it. Though he was surrounded by adults who could have had such an opinion and been vocal about it, in later years, when Henry was an adult and himself opposed to war, William was noted to be the leader of the anti-war faction, the most vocal member of it. He was the one working most towards ending the wars, so it does not seem particularly likely that he was converted by more convinced members, and more likely that it was William who convinced others, including the king. William's conviction that peace with France was the best policy to follow may simply have come from his long years of fighting and the many losses he had sustained while doing so. At the age of thirty-five in 1431, he was a seasoned warrior and probably saw the war with clearer and more disillusioned eyes than most men in Henry's government.

If so, he was surely more sympathetic to the French warriors he had spent so long fighting against than most others. This sympathy, along with his knowledge of France, made him an obvious candidate for an honour – and an obligation – he worked on receiving together with Alice in the summer of 1432: the custody of Charles, Duke of Orléans,[39] half-brother to the Bastard of Orléans, whose prisoner William had been.

As William had been, Charles was a prisoner of war, captured by the English forces after the Battle of Agincourt in 1415[40] – the battle in which William's older brother Michael had perished, making William unexpectedly the Earl of Suffolk. Charles had been one of the lucky French fighters: famously, after the battle Henry V had given the order to kill all French prisoners. It seems to have been Charles's very high standing that saved him from this fate, and possibly the hope of him being worth a hefty ransom.[41] If that was the hope of the man who captured him, he was to be disappointed. Henry V decided that due to Charles's extremely high birth and claim to the French throne he could be a focal point of rebellion against him, and that therefore he was never to be released.

This was kept to even long after Henry V's death, with the same reasoning he had given. For all that Charles was a prisoner, he was treated very well, much like William had been in his half-brother's care, allowed to keep up his lordly lifestyle. This meant that those lords who had custody of him were often faced with onerous expenses, even if Charles had access in some way to his own wealth. Being his custodian nevertheless signified a great deal of trust on the part of the government, as it showed that the man granted custody was thought capable of keeping a potentially dangerous enemy secure, and in such a way that it would not enrage the French unnecessarily.

In some ways, Alice and William's household was the ideal place for Charles. As the widow of one of the most famous English fighters and mother of his child, she could be expected not to side with any French plots against the English throne. William, too, was thought trustworthy because of his long service in the king's army, though perhaps even then, his time as the prisoner of Charles's half-brother made him suspect to some. It certainly was brought up against him in later years when he was accused of being a French agent,[42] but there is no indication that anyone had any such thoughts in the early 1430s. If some people were suspicious of him then, it was not noted down.

Charles's custody being granted to William and Alice was probably not considered very interesting when it happened. It was a financially significant decision for both, which means that Alice, as the significantly richer of the two, must have been involved. Famously, the offer William made meant that he would earn nothing from Charles being in his custody but would actually have to pay his expenses.[43] This, too, was why the grant was accepted without much trouble, with no one else being very keen on bearing the associated costs.

What is Better than a Good Woman?

Even if the costs did not matter to Alice, custodianship would have meant a change for her and those in her household. Interestingly, she and William appeared to have households together most of the time, more so than was common for people of their status, which meant that Charles would have lived with them both for most of the time. From all we know, Charles became quite close to Alice and her husband, and though this was something that was used against them later by political enemies, at the time it must have been a newly budding friendship that gave them pleasure.

There is a lot known about William and Charles's friendship, and though not quite as much is known about the relationship between Alice and her distinguished prisoner houseguest, this has not stopped historians from speculating. One theory that is often mentioned, though it is considered as debunked by now, is that Charles fell in love with Alice and, like William had done before they were married, wrote poems to her.

This theory was advanced by the French historian Pierre Champion,[44] but it can safely be considered as faulty. For one, it is of course a fallacy to make conclusions about an author's actual feeling from poetry that could very well be simply an exercise in writing. Moreover, while there is actually evidence to support Charles falling in love during his long honourable imprisonment in England, there is nothing to suggest that Alice was the subject of his feelings. On the contrary, it is by now usually accepted that there were two successive women Charles was interested in,[45] but neither of them sound anything like Alice. The fact that had convinced Pierre Champion of it being Alice was simply that in some poems, Charles was speaking about being in love with a lady who was someone else's lady. This, of course, could have referred to Alice, but it was hardly unique to her and could refer to any number of other women. Nor was Charles, as Champion seemed to think,[46] in a situation where he was unlikely to meet any women but the wife and possibly sisters and daughters of his custodian. This pre-supposes that Charles was held like a modern prisoner. As described, this was not the case: while Charles would not have been able to go anywhere unwatched, or travel wherever he wished, he was perfectly able, even encouraged, to take part in the social life of his custodians and could have met any number of women who were not unattached but to whom he felt attracted.

Whoever these women were must remain a mystery, probably forever. We know that Charles was an important figure in Alice and William's life, part of their social circle. Charles, who was a poetic soul, might in fact have felt quite comfortable in their milieu, which included Alice's father Thomas, who was not only an extremely famous poet's son but, as discussed above, had actually been a champion of literature and poetry for several decades before his daughter Alice ever married William, let alone before Charles started living with them.

It might have been because of this shared interest that the Suffolks seemed to have an interest in Charles as a person from the first.[47] The very fact that they were ready to pay for the privilege of having Charles as their houseguest has usually been taken as a sign that they, or at least William, were at the very least sympathetic to Charles, if not already friends with him, and this might actually be true. After all, at that point, William had himself been released from prison less than two years ago, and hence might very well have felt sympathetic to Charles's plight, all personal feelings notwithstanding. It is equally possible that in the years since his release, he had met Charles and got along very well with him, as they would become friends and clearly their personalities mixed well.

It seems that no one has yet noted the coincidence of William's brother dying in the same year as William chose to take Charles's custody in a way that was almost injurious to his finances. The exact date of Thomas de la Pole's death is not known, just the year, and it is also known that the Bastard of Orléans was in contact with William then, to inform him of his brother's death and agree

What is Better than a Good Woman?

not to ask for another hostage. Quite possibly, the two men agreed on this with the stipulation being that William was to make sure the Bastard's half-brother Charles had all he needed and was well taken care of. It is even possible that such a stipulation outright said that William should take Charles's custody, and William attempted – and succeeded in – achieving this goal by doing it in such a way that nobody could possibly make a better offer.

This would hardly have been a strange stipulation. The Bastard of Orléans and William had struck up a cordial relationship during the time William was his prisoner, and Orléans had treated his brother very well when he had been his hostage. It would not be surprising if Orléans demanded that William do the same for his brother, in a similar situation, and in view of the £20,000 ransom, by comparison it would be a cheap demand.

It would have been best, if England wanted to continue the wars in France, to keep Charles imprisoned; or it would have been best to allow him his freedom if England wanted to make peace with France, something that William was very invested in, something the nearly 19-year-old king was inclined to agree with. That William, and possibly Alice, also had a personal motive in wanting what was best for their friend Charles was another factor, but there is no reason to believe that this would have been more important to them than service to their king.

Whatever Charles's, or in fact Alice's or William's feelings originally were, they soon seemed to start a sort of chivalrous poetry competition. These poems are still in existence, a valuable survival. In them, Charles talks about love, but also about his life as a prisoner,[48] whereas the sixteen or so that survive of William's are mostly concerned with love and almost all seem to be geared towards Alice.[49] It is tempting to imagine her as being the judge in such competitions, of her husband flattering her, her houseguest prisoner earnestly trying to convince her of the superior quality of his poems. Such an image has fired the imagination of several authors, such as Pierre Champion,[50] but of course, that is all it is: imagination. A sort of competition certainly took place; this is agreed upon by scholars. What form it took and what, if any, part Alice played in it is unknowable. She had an interest in literature, which was encouraged by her father and husbands. Her father's favourite poet John Lydgate dedicated his book *The Virtues of the Mass* to her.[51] Maybe Alice, despite an obvious appreciation for poetry and literature, simply had no talent for dabbling in it herself, or thought she did not.

These first years, with Charles being in their custody, were arguably the happiest years of William and Alice's marriage. Though they appeared to be very happy together all their married life, in later years many obligations swallowed up their time and left them with less opportunities to enjoy each other's presence, as well as that of friends, and to devote time to things they simply enjoyed.

There is a lot of evidence of them doing so during the whole of the 1430s, but for a number of reasons the early part of this decade was a particularly happy one, and although their focus seemed very much on personal, domestic arrangements, it was not just on them. Their efforts were more concentrated on their rise at court later, but the task was not forgotten at that time. They saw to it that their social circle included many important men, and they rose steadily in favour, if not as steeply as they later would. William's rise is widely documented. By 1433, he held several important posts.[52] Alice's part is less illuminated, but her star was also in the ascendant. As mentioned above, as early as 1432 she became a Lady of the Garter, and she was forming important relationships through this appointment, such as with Isabelle, lady Despenser, who became a member of the Garter at the same time as Alice.[53]

In November 1434, Alice suffered a loss that must have come as a terrible blow to her: her father, Thomas Chaucer, died at the age of sixty-seven[54]. The cause is unknown, though since he was nearly seventy, it is he probably simply died of old age, or some illness

What is Better than a Good Woman?

he no longer had the energy to fight. Though life expectancy was nowhere near as bad in the fifteenth century as is often assumed, sixty-seven was still considered quite an age. Thomas's will does not survive, if indeed he ever wrote one, so that we don't know what he left his daughter or his granddaughter, or the value of his estate. It can be said with certainty that with Thomas's death, Alice was an even richer woman. As Rowena Archer points out,[55] we cannot put a figure on her wealth, but it can be assumed that it was impressive. Inquisitions Post Mortem[56] were only issued in counties where the deceased had property, and they were issued for Thomas in Suffolk, Cambridgeshire, Lincolnshire, Berkshire, Essex, Buckinghamshire, Hampshire and Oxfordshire[57]. Though this was not particularly impressive compared to the riches some nobles had amassed, it was extremely wealthy for a commoner, and possessions in those counties added to Alice's riches from her two earlier marriages must have made her at least as rich as most barons, and richer than some.

Thomas Chaucer's Inquisitions Post Mortem also contain another interesting piece of information: the only reference to Alice's age. As the one source we cannot be too certain of its accuracy, since these inquisitions were frequently wrong on such matters, sometimes by several years. However, all of the inquisitions put Alice's age as thirty at the time of her father's death.[58] This is not proof positive of her actually being thirty in November 1434, but if she was not, she was very close to it. The information in her mother's Inquisitions Post Mortem[59] issued after her death two-and-a-half years later confirms it. Alice must have been thirty, or a few months older or younger, when her father died.

Though his will did not survive, the Calendar of Patent Rolls[60] indicate Alice, William and Alice's mother Matilda were each to receive a third of Thomas's lands, apparently without any objections from Alice or William. This would suggest that Alice was close enough to her mother, though sadly, there is almost nothing known about their relationship. Enough is known about

William, Earl of Suffolk

Thomas and Alice's relationship to know that his death would not only have been a personal blow, but also one that had ramifications for her as a landowner. To the last, Thomas had supported his daughter in managing her lands, as he did for his son-in-law as well, and without his support things had to change. Not only did they have to manage the lands that came to them after Thomas's death, they also had to re-organise the management of Alice's and William's estates anew. Again, it seems that Alice's relations helped with this, most notably Cardinal Henry Beaufort.[61]

There was something else, a sad task that Alice undertook after her father's death: the erection of a tomb suited to his position in life, something Alice gave a lot of thought to, as well as something she was prepared to spend a lot of money on. Sadly, Thomas's tomb no longer survives in its entirety, but what we have gives a good picture of what Alice considered important and how she wished her father to be remembered in perpetuity. His tomb has a brass with a likeness of him on it,[62] but unlike Alice's own tomb and its splendid effigy, this likeness does not give much information about Thomas's looks or his personality. The face is not developed enough to be seen as anything but a generic representation of a man, wearing the armour of the early fifteenth century. Alice chose to have her father represented as a warrior, even though Thomas was not particularly noted as such in his lifetime. Ever since Alice would have been able to remember, he had not actually taken part in any military campaign, though it is possible he did so in the early part of his life, of which we know little. Alice choosing to have her father depicted in armour on his tomb therefore says more about her and her values than about Thomas Chaucer. Given that she decided against having a lifelike effigy for him, it seems as if his identity as a warrior was more important to Alice than an accurate depiction of him.

This is an aspect of Alice's personality that has not been fully explored. Though every work introducing her is at pains to stress that she was the wife and widow of three successive warriors, there

What is Better than a Good Woman?

is little analysis of Alice's own attitude towards the war in France. Most of the works going into more depth about her are from the nineteenth century and are thus deeply steeped in the prejudices of the day, most notably Henry Alfred Napier's work.[63] It has usually been assumed that Alice, while supportive of her husbands, was opposed to anything that might bring them into danger. This does not appear to have been the case; while naturally, it is likely that Alice worried about her husbands when they were engaged in battle, she considered a man being a warrior as self-evidently good.

As has mentioned in Chapter 2, the Chaucer arms are not on Thomas's tomb, which has caused several theories about his paternity to be advanced. The explanation for Alice neglecting to have her grandfather's arms on her father's tomb is simple: put in modern terms, snobbery.[64] Geoffrey Chaucer, famous and admired though he was even in the 1430s, had been a commoner, a vintner's son. It was not a connection Alice, who by that time was a countess and a dowager countess, mother of an earl's daughter, wanted to bring attention to. All the arms of Thomas's ancestors and relations that were, with a view to Alice's exalted status, acceptable, she included on her father's tomb: the de Roet arms of her grandmother, Thomas's mother and the Burghersh arms of her own mother, Matilda.[65]

It would be easy to accuse Alice of vanity because of this, but she moved in circles in which her husband William's comparatively low birth was used against him, even though he was an earl in his own right. Stressing her and her father's lowborn roots would not only have been unthinkable for a woman who wanted to move socially upwards, it would also have given her and her husband's enemies ammunition against them. This does not mean that the charge of vanity against Alice is completely unjustified, as protection of her own position came before any desire to create a faithful representation of her father. There can be no denying that Alice held her father in high regard, so that it seems unlikely it was pure selfishness. Quite possibly, Alice thought she was showing her father in the best light. Though having him presented in armour on his memorial brass may seem strange, even fraudulent, it is possible that Alice knew he would want to be presented like this, or that this was how she thought of him: as a strong warrior.

Alice chose to have her father buried in Ewelme, a manor with which his family, despite later claims, was not actually connected. Thomas's connection with the manor came solely through his wife and her family. However, sources suggest it was one of his favourite manors where he spent a lot of time, so that it was an appropriate choice. Perhaps Alice appreciated it for the same reasons Thomas had. In later Tudor times, the manor was praised for being located in such a beautiful, calm place,[66] which might have been part of the appeal when William and Alice lived there. Alice did not let her father's death ruin the manor for her. While some extremely rich family members would shun a manor in which a particularly close relative or loved one had died, it was not a custom Alice chose to follow. On the contrary, like her father before her, she was to make it her main manor with William, and after his death, as a widow as well.

Both of them were connected so much with the manor that even over a century later, in the time of Elizabeth I, the association was not forgotten. The Tudor chronicler John Leland claimed that 'Suffolk, from love of his wife, and the commodity of her lands, felt much to dwell in Oxfordshire and Berkshire, where his wife's land lay.'[67] Despite Alice being the much larger presence in these lands, not least due to her longer life span, William was also connected with them – and even long after his death, William's motivation was acknowledged to be 'love of his wife'.

Of course, it is possible to read too much into this, but it is interesting to see that such a connection was made even long after William and Alice's deaths. Whatever the chronicler actually thought or believed, it is well known that especially in the 1430s, Alice and William spent a lot of their time in Ewelme and the surrounding lands and became a local power there, before they both became a national power as well.

Contemporary opinion of Alice in the 1430s

One connection they established is worth looking at more closely, since it was one that has been of great significance to historians: to a local family of the gentry, the Stonor family. Their letters that have survived the centuries,[68] together with the those of another Oxfordshire family, the Pastons,[69] have done much to shape our understanding of everyday life in the fifteenth century. The Stonors had a close relationship with Alice's father. The relationship Alice and, through her, William, shaped with them shows how they stepped into his shoes after Thomas died.

Thomas Chaucer was already close to the Stonors by the time Alice married Thomas Monacute, and when Thomas's first son, another Thomas, was born in 1424.[70] Thomas Chaucer was one of his godfathers. Possibly, the child was named after him. We know from the Stonor papers that Thomas was a constant in the boy's life, as well as his parents'. When the older Thomas Stonor died in 1431[71] his son was seven. Thomas Chaucer was an executor of the father's will and was designated the child's guardian.[72]

Thomas Chaucer himself died only three years after receiving the wardship of his godson. In his own will, he could have left the care of Thomas to his daughter and son-in-law, we don't know. Even if he did not, they did take care of him and in fact, once the opportunity arose, connected the families forever, when Thomas Stonor married William's illegitimate daughter Jane.

The timeline of this is slightly uncertain; we cannot say definitely that it was not Thomas Chaucer who arranged the marriage between his godson Thomas Stonor and his daughter's stepdaughter Jane, but simply judging by the customs of the day, it seems somewhat unlikely, given Thomas's youth – as well as Jane's probable youth, though we can be less certain about her age than about her

William, Earl of Suffolk

husband's. Though children did marry in the fifteenth century, it was only the norm for noble families, with most others, even if wealthy, choosing to wait until both bride and groom were at least in their teens. Similar to the case of the king having a minor's wardship, it is a situation that is sometimes assumed to have been the same for the rest of society as it was for high nobility, but it was not. Thomas and Jane very probably married in later years.

When this happened is unknown, but it must have been before 1450 when they had their first son, named William after his grandfather. While the Stonors were not of high enough standing to be married as children, they were of high enough standing not to wait for marriage until their twenties, as most commoners did. It would have been typical of their class for them to marry in their adolescence. If Jane and Thomas Stonor followed that custom, they must have married in the mid- to late 1430s, so after Thomas Chaucer's death.

Though it is technically possible that it was Jane and Thomas's own decision to marry and was not an arranged match, this, too, seems unlikely. Though as a gentleman and an earl's illegitimate daughter, they were not of enough importance for their marriage to be worked out when they were barely out of their nappies, they were important enough to consider marriage a business arrangement.

What both of them gained is fairly obvious: Thomas became son-in-law to a powerful earl, forging a formal relationship that might help him with any ambitions he might have. Jane would have a rich and, though not noble, gentleman as husband, a respectable marriage for a woman of her status. Almost certainly, these considerations were behind their match, rather than love. Even had it been a love match, it would still indicate a closeness between Alice's family and her father's godson. If he and Jane chose to marry for love, that would obviously mean they knew each other well, something that could only have happened if he was often in contact with her and her family. It is much more likely that Alice and William chose to arrange the match. This is

What is Better than a Good Woman?

interesting in itself, as it means that they, even as countess and earl, used Thomas Chaucer's old connections and thought they were worthy of cultivating and retaining. This shows the respect Thomas was held in in his lifetime as well as the value of the relations he had been able to build, though born a commoner and never holding a title.

On a more personal note, it also shows the unusual closeness of the family. As mentioned above, it was common even for man and wife to have separate households that came together only occasionally, for example, for festivities. Alice and William clearly did not follow this custom, choosing instead to spend most of their time together whenever they could. William was taken into the fold of her family, so much so he was seen as the natural heir of Thomas Chaucer's position in Oxfordshire society.

This does not necessarily have to indicate any closeness between father-in-law and son-in-law. If a man of some standing did not have a male heir, it was very often his daughter's husband who stepped into his shoes wherever he could. A very good example for this is Alice's own stepdaughter, Alice Montacute, and her husband Richard Neville. Once Alice had given birth to her late husband's posthumous daughter and it had thus become clear that there was no male heir to Thomas Montacute's title and position, Richard Neville not only assumed the title by right of his wife, but also most of his positions, and tried building on his relations, though, as discussed above, his father-in-law's lands remained in Alice and William's hands for a long time.

The example of Richard Neville also shows that assuming a father-in-law's position and stepping into his shoes was not always easy. Richard Neville's career as Earl of Salisbury is discussed elsewhere, and it is not the intention of this work to go into much depth about it. The only point that is relevant a study of Alice is that Neville often struggled with the inheritance from his father-in-law, something that William de la Pole, Earl of Suffolk, very

William, Earl of Suffolk

notably did not, when he, in his position as Alice's husband, took over Thomas Chaucer's position.

Moreover, the marriage between his illegitimate daughter and Thomas Stonor was, for all that it was business, building on a personal relationship Thomas Chaucer had developed, not on a business one. Though Thomas Chaucer's position as the boy's guardian and godfather was charged with politics, it was not one he would have held if he not been close to Thomas Stonor. If it had been solely based on objective importance in the realm, Thomas Stonor would have most likely made Alice his son's godmother to profit from her connections as Countess of Salisbury, instead of choosing her father as a godparent. That he did not shows that at least to some extent personal affection and closeness had been the reason for Thomas Stonor's choice.

By taking over the child's wardship from Thomas and deciding to continue and deepen the bond between the two families through marriage, Alice and William also took over her father's personal relationships. Again, this was not uncommon, but it usually only happened if the daughter or son in question had been close to the father during his lifetime. The Stonor marriage shows that not only Alice was, which we know from other evidence as well, but so was William. Their arrangements as a married couple were sometimes quite close to modern-day arrangements, more so than the arrangements of many of their contemporaries. The fact that William's illegitimate daughter became a part of Alice's family shows that.

Sadly, we do not have a lot of information about the relationship between Alice and her stepdaughter. It can be assumed that it was at the very least cordial, but that is all that can be said. Alice would later be close, if not unusually so, to Jane's son William, and her and William's own son John was on good terms with Jane's husband, Thomas Stonor, but that is all we can discern. However, for all the lack of evidence of a personal relationship between Alice and Jane, there is no reason to assume that Alice was not

What is Better than a Good Woman?

perfectly happy to accept her stepdaughter into her family. Men, particularly noblemen, having illegitimate children was completely normal and accepted at the time, and even such children born during marriage were often accepted not only by their fathers but their stepmothers, and in many cases raised together with their legitimate siblings. William's illegitimate daughter was born at least two years before he married Alice, so that even had she been inclined to be jealous of her husband sleeping with other women, as only few wives at least openly were in the fifteenth century, there would have been no cause for her to be so in this case. In fact, Alice might have been pleased; if Jane, as is often assumed, was born *c.* 1427/8, she would have been very close in age to her own daughter, providing a natural playmate for her daughter.

It is nice to imagine this cosy family scene: Alice and her husband being close to her father, Thomas Chaucer being the proud grandfather of Thomas Montacute's daughter and William's daughter, but though cordiality is suggested by later dealings with the Stonor family, it does not go any further than that. At best, we can say Jane fitted in well, but that is it.

The next few years were hard for Alice. Most of 1435 seems to have been taken up with the business side of the fallout of her father's death, and some of his Inquisitions Post Mortem were only taken more than six months after his demise,[73] meaning that at least formally, no actions could have been taken before that. Alice included William in this work. It was a wise choice, as William proved to be a shrewd and clever manager. He did not do this himself, but as he had already proved when choosing the men to manage his lands and his earldom for him while he was fighting in France, he chose capable, honest men who did a good job for him, and in this case, his wife.

As time passed, Alice must have taken comfort in knowing she was managing his estates and his inheritance well. Her income from these lands in fact increased in comparison to what it had been in

William, Earl of Suffolk

her father's lifetime. This increase in income has, however, earned Alice some criticism from later authors; her practices were labelled greedy and her personality criticised. Some believe that when she stepped into her father's shoes, she was not very good at it and was 'not always charming'[74] to her tenants. This may be true, but it is hard to imagine a similar criticism levelled at Thomas himself, or William. Alice's own actions are under more scrutiny than her husband's and father's, for no discernible reason but sexism. Despite being a woman, Alice had neither an obligation nor, clearly, any interest in being 'always charming' to her tenants or anyone else she was in a mere business relationship with, and nobody at the time expected her to, or commented on any lack of 'charm' on her part.

William de la Pole's biographer, Susan Curran, states in her book *The English Friend* that Alice had 'not quite inherited her father's gift of likability',[75] though without giving any source for this. Again, this assessment seems to be based on the expectation that a woman must be charming and likeable even when running her estates according to her own best interests.

This, of course, does not mean Alice was exempt from criticism in her own time. The opposite is true. Especially in the 1440s and when managing her son's estates as well as her own in the 1450s, the charge of greed was very often levelled against her,[76] as discussed below. However, this was an obviously non-gendered charge levelled against men for the same reasons, with the same vitriol.

In fact, though Alice often faced legitimate criticism for her business practices,[77] none was levelled against her in the first years after her father's death. Though it is always possible that something got lost, all we have suggests that nobody had any problem with how Alice took over and managed her inheritance from her father, all seemed to regard it as perfectly acceptable and nothing more or less than what she was expected to do. If doing this and being successful at it gave Alice comfort, this must have been helpful in 1436.

What is Better than a Good Woman?

The year did not start badly, on the contrary, it started off very well and must have made Alice proud and given her hope for the future: William was once more given an important role in King Henry's government, the most important so far, as part of an embassy to France.[78] However, though this must have been pleasing, it was not an unalloyed blessing: it meant that Charles, Duke of Orléans, had to leave their custody and their household[79] after four years there as a friend more than a prisoner. That William at least considered him a friend is confirmed by what would happen in later years.[80] Just why William's part in the embassy to France meant he had to leave is not quite clear. Perhaps some of the more warlike members of Henry VI's government were becoming wary of William's obvious preference for peace with France and feared that after he had actually been in France, he might find himself inclined actually to do something to help Charles, or undermine the war efforts still going on in France.

The reasoning might have been less sinister for William, and been simple sexism, with Alice considered unable to take proper care of Charles, and to stop anything he might be plotting. Or else, the reasoning might have been perfectly prosaic: Charles had been given into the care and nominal imprisonment of several lords[81] during his 21 years as English prisoner, never staying anywhere for too long. The king or his regents may simply have considered it time for him to move on. This might have been to prevent William from becoming too friendly to him and doing something that would be to the disadvantage of the English king, but if so, it was not William alone who was so suspected, but simply a security measure applied to all of Charles's jailors.

Given the friendship that had grown between William and Charles and also between Alice and Charles[82] – though we have far less evidence for that – it must have been hard for her as well to see him leave their household. Since he was not actually freed and would stay in England, his leaving the household would not have meant Alice would never see him again. If she so wished, she could have visited him.

In fact, with William leaving and Charles leaving, Alice might have felt lonely, but this is a rather modern way of thinking. Though Alice probably missed her husband, whom she made a point of being with whenever she could, it was not as if she was alone and had nothing to do. The responsibility of running her estates and William's in his absence would have kept her busy, and her household included her own daughter and mother, meaning that she was not lonely either, even if one disregards the many servants a countess's household would have had.

William's embassy was a step to becoming an even more important man, perhaps even becoming close to the king, who was by then fourteen years old and would soon be able to choose his own advisors and rule without regents. There is little reason to assume that Alice was anything but hopeful for the future for the first part of 1436, but it is unlikely this remained so: though we only have very little evidence for her daughter by the Earl of Salisbury, it seems that at some point in mid- to end 1436, the girl died. There is only one piece of evidence for this, dated 10 December 1436, an agreement between William and Richard Neville:

Agreement by William de la Pole, earl of Suffolk, Admiral of the Sea, Master of the king's household, for himself and Alys his wife, countess of Suffolk, late the wife of Thomas de Montagu, earl of Salisbury, deceased, that they will render a good and loyal account to Richard de Nevill, earl of Salisbury, and Dame Alayce de Montagu, countess of Salisbury, his wife, sole heiress of the said Sir Thomas, of the moneys they shall receive on account of the goods and debts, etc. of the said Sir Thomas, on this side (deca) the sea in France and Normandy etc. including the moneys owed to him by the late duke of Bedford, governor and regent of France; all which goods, etc.

What is Better than a Good Woman?

have been committed to the said earl of Suffolk, on account of the said Alys, by the said Richard de Nevill and Dame Alayce; if the said William and Alys pay half the said moneys received to the said Richard and Dame Alayce, the said Richard shall pay half expenses. France. 10 December, 1436.[83]

The fact that this agreement was drawn up in France, not some months later in England, is the clearest indication that it was something they worked out between themselves after something had happened, not an agreement that had been a long time in coming. Naturally, even while Alice's daughter was still alive, the apparently informal agreement that had been in place between her and her daughter and son-in-law could not have remained like this forever, it would eventually have to be changed to be made legal and agreeable for both parties in the long run. The date suggests that it was with this in mind that the agreement was made. In that year, Alice's daughter would have turned seven, usually considered the age for children to leave the nursery, and therefore an appropriate age for coming to an agreement between her half-sister and her mother via their husbands. In that way, whenever Alice and William chose to find a husband for their (step)daughter, an agreement was in place that would simplify marriage arrangements. Alice Montacute and Richard Neville could be certain that their rights as heir to half of Thomas Montacute's lands were not in danger, even if Alice's daughter married a particularly powerful or influential man.

This could be an indication that the agreement was not made in reaction to the death of Alice's small daughter, but simply in anticipation of the future: the arrangements of marriage for their own children Richard and his wife were making at that time. Their oldest son, called Richard after his father, who would go down in history as Warwick the Kingmaker, had either recently been married to Anne Beauchamp, daughter of the extremely rich

William, Earl of Suffolk

Richard Beauchamp, Earl of Warwick, or was shortly to be so after December 1436.[84] It follows that young Richard's parents wanted to make sure that his mother's part of her inheritance, which was to be his inheritance after her death one day, was secured. It is possible that Richard Beauchamp demanded that this was secured and his daughter's future as a rich lady be in no doubt before agreeing to marry her to Richard.

Since the marriage of their heir to young Anne Beauchamp was a coup and was connected with their daughter Cecily's marriage to Beauchamp's son and heir Henry,[85] it is possible that despite having themselves been fine with the informal agreement that had been in place between them and Alice ever since the birth of her daughter, they agreed to have it put down in writing, so as to make sure the Beauchamp marriages for their children were not put in jeopardy. The agreement explicitly refers to Thomas's lands and goods in France, so it might be argued that William and Thomas had to be in France to settle these lands between them. This, however, seems unlikely, as the agreement refers to them both interacting with these lands after Thomas's death, without both of them needing to be there. In fact, it seems rather unlikely that they would both want to wait until they were sent to France by the king to make an agreement that could be extremely important to both their families.

There are two major indications contradicting the idea of the agreement being made in vague expectation of future developments, with nothing having changed, instead suggesting that Alice's child had died and it was intended to settle the consequences of her death. For one, while the timing might be explained by the two explanations above, these would not offer any reason why it could not wait until William and Richard had returned from France. Neither Alice's daughter turning seven years old and becoming too old to stay in the nursery nor the marriage of Richard and Alice Montacute's children would have happened unexpectedly. They could have been anticipated well in advance, thus making it

What is Better than a Good Woman?

unnecessary to draw up the arrangement while in France. Perhaps most important, 'the said William and Alys [were to] pay half the said moneys received to the said Richard and Dame Alayce.'[86] This would be what they were entitled to if there was no other heiress, if the estates were simply to be settled between Alice Montacute and Alice de la Pole, widow of Thomas Montacute, Earl of Salisbury. This was also the way Thomas himself had anticipated it in his will. Had Alice's daughter still been alive, her older half-sister, though the heiress of the Salisbury title, would not have been entitled to half of her father's lands. Alice's child would have been entitled to inherit just as much as her older half-sister – which during her mother's lifetime, would have meant one quarter of the entirety of Thomas's lands, with another quarter falling to her upon her mother's death.

That William, in Alice's name, agreed for one half to be given to her stepdaughter means either that she was suddenly happy to give up all her daughter's claim to her father's lands, or that with her daughter's death, Alice Montacute had a claim to a lot more of those lands, being his sole heiress.

The agreement in itself does not actually mention Alice's daughter, but there is no other reason why Alice Montacute and her husband would have been perfectly fine with Alice having custody of all her lands, and actually giving them to her and her husband.

Since the agreement, sealed by both William and Richard in the names of their wives, explicitly states that these lands not only were in Alice and William's custody but that they 'have been committed to the said earl of Suffolk, on account of the said Alys, by the said Richard de Nevill and Dame Alayce', it is hard to think of any other explanation. This wording suggests that it was only through an informal agreement that William and Alice ever received those lands. Since Alice Montacute was declared her father's only heir in all his IPMs, made before her half-sister's birth,[87] it is possible that she either wished to hold onto the lands, insisting on her rights as the older daughter to be sole heiress, or perhaps more likely, had been in possession of those lands since after her father's death; and upon Alice giving birth she reached an agreement with her that made her give these lands to her. Since such land disputes and agreements often took a while to execute, Alice might have only come into possession of these lands, or at least some of them, well after her daughter's first birthday, when she was already married to William.

All in all, the evidence taken together indicates Alice had a daughter who lived until some point in 1436, dying presumably while her stepfather was away on an embassy in France.

This must have been a massive blow for Alice. With William acting in France, she must have sent news of her daughter's death to him, but she would have been alone, without the helpmate and pillar of support for her in the nearly six years in which they had been married, and without the father who had helped her through so many other difficult times. She and her mother would have had to oversee the little girl's funeral for themselves.

Sadly, as we know nearly nothing of Thomas Montacute, Earl of Salisbury's younger daughter, her very existence having been forgotten for centuries, we also do not know where her tomb is. In this case, as in most other facts about her, we can only guess: if Alice's own preferences were any indication, she had her daughter interred in the church in Ewelme, which either she, or Thomas Chaucer himself, had chosen as a final resting place for her father. It is possible that the girl was buried in her grandfather's tomb. It is also possible that the child did not die at Ewelme but in one of Alice's other manors, and was interred there. In such a case, Alice might have had a tomb, or effigy built for her, which was destroyed in the centuries since.

A final possibility is that Alice chose to have her daughter interred not with her own family, but with her father's family, in her father's

What is Better than a Good Woman?

tomb or near it. This tomb was destroyed during the Reformation,[88] but was described as a family tomb while it still existed.[89] Alice had already shown when her father died that she, like most others of her standing at the time, valued nobility and standing even after death and might have wished for her daughter to be buried not primarily as her daughter, countess by marriage but born a commoner, but the daughter of the Earl of Salisbury, noble by birth.

In April 1437[90] Alice's mother Matilda died. As with Thomas Chaucer, there is no indication of the cause. Matilda was about fifty-seven when she died but. While it may have been unexpected, it was not an age at which it was considered unusual to die. The strain on Alice of her death, less than three years after her beloved father's death and less than a year after that of her only daughter, is hard to imagine, and must have taken its toll on her. We know less about Alice's relationship with Matilda than we do about her relationship with Thomas, but the very fact that Matilda appeared to live with Alice – and William if he was there, which he was most of the time after Thomas's death – at the very least suggests an amiability between mother and daughter.

All in all, it must have been a very sad and emotionally taxing year for Alice between summer 1436 and summer 1437. Once more she found herself faced with the sad task of organising the funeral of a loved one. Matilda was buried in Ewelme Church, next to Thomas.[91]

Perhaps prompted by the loss of both her parents and her daughter, in 1437 Alice decided to have changes made to Ewelme, a project she undertook, as she did so many, with her husband. The already comfortable manor house was worked on so that eventually it became a veritable palace.[92] They also decided to found an almshouse in Ewelme, with the aim of offering education to poor students and feeding those in need.[93]

To either found or endow almshouses was fairly common for noble men and women. This was not only an act of charity, desirable

William, Earl of Suffolk

in itself. Since these almshouses were invariably religious, it was also a way of storing up treasure in heaven for the founder. Alice's son would be involved in the re-establishment of an almshouse.

The almshouse at Ewelme was a particularly big one. There was not just the theological aspect to think about and make sure it was well done, but also the more prosaic matters of ensuring the almshouse had all it needed, that men and women were employed to take care of the foundation, that workmen as well as theological laymen involved with it were well taken care of. It would have been a very big project to undertake, perhaps something Alice figured was just the right thing for her at such a time: something to take the mind off her losses, while at the same time putting her more in God's favour.

Perhaps, it also simply gave her satisfaction: Alice seemed an organizer. Sorting things out was something she threw herself into after William's death. In that case, it might have simply been necessity, or fear that upon his death much if not all of her son's inheritance would be lost to him. Once her daughter had been born, she very clearly also focused on organisation, and her failure to do so immediately after Thomas Earl of Salisbury's death had to do with her pregnancy, not with an inclination to rest and deal with grief quietly and sedately.

The almshouse was a project that meant a lot to Alice and William, and they would be involved in its care for the rest of their lives, Alice continuing after William's death. It must have been a pleasure to them both when on 3 July 1437[94] the king granted their application for a licence to build the almshouse. It was no surprise; such applications were always answered in the affirmative. It is obvious why: there was absolutely no disadvantage for the king in granting such a licence. There was no monetary loss connected with it; on the contrary, since applying for any licence at all from the king meant fees; and such projects undertaken with his assent could only be beneficial to his soul.

What is Better than a Good Woman?

The wording of this licence was perfectly normal, with Henry VI making the licence out to his 'most beloved and faithful cousin, William De La Pole, Earl of Suffolk [and] Alice his wife' giving them his permission 'to found an Almshouse at their manor of Ewelme in Oxfordshire, to be called God's House'. According to the licence, the couple's intention was to 'support two chaplains, and thirteen poor men', who 'should be in ret nomine, corpus corporatum, and have a common seal, with the power of possessing lands, etc'.[95] This was not the only charitable work they did, and it would have been very unusual had it been so. Most noble families were involved in several charitable works, and the higher their standing was, the more charitable projects were expected of them. As a countess and earl who were quite close to the king, nothing less would have been expected from William and Alice.

In January 1437, Henry VI's mother, Catherine of Valois, died at the age of thirty-five.[96] Catherine had been in a relationship with one of her servants, Owen Tudor[97] and had several children with him. Henry became the guardian of his young half-siblings upon his mother's death. It was claimed she had secretly married Owen before having children with him,[98] but an often repeated modern assumption is that it was only a common law marriage, not an actual one. Even if Owen and Catherine secretly married, it was an illegal match by English law, since Catherine was forbidden to marry anyone without the royal council's consent, though it would have been considered as binding in the eyes of God, earthly laws notwithstanding.

In 1432, when the situation was discovered, there was nothing that could be done because Catherine could protect Owen. Even so, it caused a lot of anger with Owen, and after Catherine's death Owen was imprisoned.[99] He was released two years later, but from the first, Henry was ready and willing to accept his half-siblings as part of his family.

How many children Owen and Katherine actually had is not known, with some claiming three,[100] others four[101] and some even

William, Earl of Suffolk

claiming Henry VI had seven half-siblings. Since it is known that Catherine was definitely not married in 1429, it is hard to see how it could have been more than five.[102] What is known, though, is that they had two boys: Edmund, born in 1430, around the time Alice and William married, and Jasper, whose birth is usually guessed to have been in 1431. It also seems certain that there was another son called Owen after his father,[103] although unlike his brothers, he would not leave any traces in the historical record.

With the death of their mother, these boys were suddenly thrust into the limelight, into the disapproving glare of public opinion. Made their half-brother's wards, Henry VI did not take visit any anger he might have felt about his mother remarrying without his consent out on them. On the contrary, he seemed genuinely to want to do what was best for them, and eventually he made the decision to give them into the care of William and Alice.

This decision obviously shows what trust the teenage king had in the couple, and it might also confirm a theory that has sometimes been suggested: that Henry saw William in many ways as a substitute father, and Alice, by extension, as his substitute mother. The fact that he considered it the best course of action for his half-brothers after their mother's death and their father's imprisonment, indicates he saw the couple not only as completely trustworthy, but also able to give the boys the stability they needed after such a drastic change in their lives.

William and Alice rose to the occasion. It was usual for nobles to be given the wardship of aristocratic orphans by the king, and in many cases they became quite close to the children in their care. William and Alice's own son John would eventually find himself acting as a father to a noble ward.[104] However, the wardship of Edmund, Jasper and Owen, as well as any siblings they might have had whose names are no longer remembered, was somewhat different in that they were close relatives of the king, and of the French king as well.

What is Better than a Good Woman?

Perhaps, this French connection was another reason why Henry VI considered the then (relatively) Francophile William the best choice as their guardian. Quickly, however, it seems that looking after the Tudor children was not an honour the couple were particularly interested in. Within months of being granted the Tudor children's wardship, they had decided that the best place for the children would not be in their household but under the care of William's sister Katherine, the Abbess of Barking Abbey.[105]

Why this decision was made is lost to history, but there is no indication it was done because William or Alice in any way held their parentage against the children. It is possible that having their care so shortly after she had lost her similarly aged daughter proved too much for Alice, but that might be putting too modern a spin on it. Perhaps most likely is either that William and Alice decided they would be travelling too much to provide a stable and safe environment for children who were in the hostile glare of the public eye, or that their stay in William and Alice's household had always been planned as a short stint. In fact, most chronicles do not even mention the short time during which the couple held their wardship, simply stating that after their mother Catherine's death and their father Owen's imprisonment, they were given into the care of Katherine de la Pole, sister of William, Earl of Suffolk.[106] Since there is no indication of the relationship between Henry VI and William and Alice cooling, and in fact enough evidence for the opposite, it seems unlikely that the boys had been intended to stay with them for long. It may have been that they were to house the boys briefly and gently prepared them for their lives in Katherine's care, in which case the king would have no cause for complaint.

The boys seemed to be treated very well and according to their noble status in the abbey,[107] kept safe and out of the limelight until well after the scandal had blown over. Alice or William had no more interest in the children[108] than any other noble at court.

William, Earl of Suffolk

What occupied them most of all in 1437 was the establishment of their almshouse.

As William rose at court he had to travel a lot, more so than in the years before, and possibly more than was usual for someone of his standing. Alice tended to accompany him wherever he went. Probably, this was done at least partially for affection, but there would have been another reason: there can be little doubt about Alice and William wanting to have children together.

There is no evidence of Alice conceiving a child of William's before 1438. In fact, it is often claimed[109] that Alice only ever conceived one child, her son John, who grew up to be the second Duke of Suffolk and the husband of Edward IV's and Richard III's sister. However, if we accept that she was the mother of Thomas Montacute's daughter, this is obviously wrong. She might not have been very fertile – such things are all but impossible to say at a distance of over 500 years – but she had been fertile enough to conceive a child in the four to six years of her marriage to Thomas, and quite possibly to conceive twice, if she had a miscarriage in 1426.

Therefore, whatever their issues were, it could not have been that one of them was infertile. This does not mean Alice necessarily conceived, simply that, with her having had a daughter by a previous husband already, it is unlikely that the issue was her not being able to have any children. Presumably, if indeed she did not conceive, she and William simply considered it the will of God and prayed for conception, the way many other couples in such a situation are known to have done. There is no evidence for that. Alice might not have conceived a child, or she might have suffered miscarriages that were not recorded.

In 1438, we have a suggestion something did change, found in the Papal Calendars: a grant for them in October that year:

To William de la Pole, earl of Suffolk, and Alice his wife. Indult, at their recent petition (containing that they are often

What is Better than a Good Woman?

obliged to go to divers of their manors in the dioceses of Norwich, Salisbury and Lincoln, in each of which, during their stay, they keep a chapel wherein they have mass and other divine offices celebrated daily), to have a baptismal font erected in such chapel, and cause the children which may be born to them to be christened therein; saving the right of the parish church etc. Sincere devotionis affectus.[110]

Does this mean that Alice was pregnant? They had been married for over seven years by that point, and if they wanted to simply make sure there would never be a problem with the baptism of a child wherever they were, it seems likely they would have done it a lot earlier. Though they had to travel more by 1438, with William steadily rising in favour, this does not mean they did not have to travel before that. Even in the early years of their marriage, it would have been considered their 'obligation to go to diverse manors' in several parts of the country. In fact, the obligation cited in the grant seems to have nothing to do with work for the king. Therefore, it seems that when they made their petition Alice and William thought it was at the very least likely that she would soon be pregnant, if she was not actually already with child.

It would not have been sensible to send the petition too late, as of course it took its time until a messenger carrying it reached Rome and after arriving, it would not have immediately been addressed by the papal court. Then a return journey, so it would not have made a lot of sense to wait very long after Alice found out about her pregnancy, if indeed she was pregnant. With the grant being issued in October, their request was probably made in the summer of that year.

If Alice was indeed pregnant, she must have either lost the child or had a child who died during the birth or very soon afterwards. Again, this would have doubtlessly been a terrible blow to her, and also to William, both for personal reasons as well as a blow to his hopes for an heir.

William, Earl of Suffolk

Depending on what happened, Alice would have needed to rest after her miscarriage, or if she actually gave birth. But nothing is known about Alice's movements either in late 1438 or early 1439, nor indeed anything about William's whereabouts, so we can only make assumptions. In fact, we know very little about both their movements in most of 1439.[111] There are curiously few mentions of William in any royal chronicles, or even account books.

The same does not hold true for 1440, which proved to be a busy year for both William and his wife, and an emotional one. The perhaps most important thing for them both was to see to it that Charles, Duke of Orléans was finally released from his long imprisonment in England and allowed to return home.[112] This was something William especially had worked towards.

Charles's release was not simply their idea; Henry VI was approached with it by the Duke and Duchess of Burgundy.[113] Charles's release is supposed the duchess's pet project, but it is also known that William was highly involved in the negotiations.[114] The exact stipulations are known and suggest that William was very eager to see his friend freed. Despite this, he was not ready to have it happen at a disadvantage to England.[115]

The same things her husband would be accused of were later levelled, to a lesser extent, against Alice, but that does not mean she shared his feelings throughout. It is possible she was just associated with him and known to have the ear of king and queen, so that those who had brought about her husband's downfall did not want to run the risk of being punished if she insisted on it. However, in the specific case of Charles, Duke of Orléans, it is in fact quite likely that she agreed with her husband on every point, having become close to Charles as well.

The negotiations led by William succeeded, and Charles was freed after twenty-five years of honourable imprisonment in England.[116] He had spent most of his adult life in England, and had several friendly relationships with nobles, most notably with Alice

What is Better than a Good Woman?

and William, but even so, he was obviously happy to be released. When Charles was allowed to leave England and go to Burgundy, legend has it that upon arriving and being greeted by the Duchess of Burgundy, he declared himself her prisoner.

Alice might have had another reason to be happy in 1440, other than Charles's release: it is possible she was expecting a child. At the very least, it seems she was hopeful she would soon, if she was not actually pregnant. She made some arrangements that had in mind the birth of a child. This is stated by Dr Rachel Delman[117] when discussing the choice of decoration for the chambers in which Alice's grandchild was born twenty-six years later. It is known from an inventory existing for that year that Alice sent for some tapestries for this occasion.[118] Those tapestries belonged to her, not to her daughter-in-law Elizabeth, and Alice apparently considered them suitable for the chambers in which Elizabeth would stay during her confinement, the seclusion in which noble ladies awaited the birth of their children from around a month before the birth was expected. About these tapestries, Delman notes: 'They are believed to have been among the furnishings and textiles commissioned by William de la Pole from the London mercer, Robert Worsley, in 1440.' They are a somewhat inexplicable choice for the confinement of Alice's daughter-in-law – unless they were ones used for Alice's own confinement. However, the only known child of William and Alice, their son John, whose wife was the one going into confinement in 1466, was not born in 1440 or early 1441. There is no way that tapestries commissioned in 1440 were commissioned with Alice's pregnancy with him in mind, nearly nine years after William's and Alice's wedding, nine childless years, it would have been a strange choice to have them commissioned for a confinement simply in case one would happen in the future.

Maybe William simply commissioned them for Alice without being aware of any childbearing connection these tapestries had, but Delman throws doubt on this: 'While the commission of the tapestries is usually attributed solely to William, the couple's joint involvement in the building works at Ewelme at this time raises the possibility of Alice's input ... it is possible that the tapestries were commissioned with Alice's future confinement in mind.'[119]

The subject matter of these tapestries, famous ladies and female saints such as the thrice married St Anne,[120] mother of the Virgin Mary, also suggests Alice's input, as well as the idea that they were made for a female space, which confinement was. The 1440 date very much suggests that Alice had an impending confinement in mind when commissioning them, and that William had them made according to her wishes.

Once more, however, their hopes came to naught. There was no baby born to Alice and William in 1440 or 1441, suggesting that Alice once more had a miscarriage. Alice was thirty-six in 1440, and while it was hardly unheard of for women even seven or eight years older to still give birth to healthy children.[121] she must have feared that she would never have another baby.

At the time, if a couple did not have children, it was usually blamed on the woman, and the assumption is usually that this was so in Alice and William's case, especially since William's illegitimate daughter is well known, The effect of Alice's supposed infertility on her has been commented on. Susan Curran, even suggests that Alice might have consulted a 'witch', one her contemporary Eleanor Cobham was found to have attended, to try and conceive a child.[122]

The whole issue with 'witchcraft' was at the time only just emerging, and it was not that which eventually saw Eleanor Cobham accused and condemned of treason.[123] The very fact that a woman offering 'witchcraft' to solve problems such as a very high-born and noble woman's infertility was so readily available proves that it was a fairly widespread 'solution' to such problems. Even so, it seems rather far-fetched in the face of no evidence to assume Alice would have gone to consult with a woman offering such services.

Such speculations overlook a large part of Alice's childbearing history. The fact that she had borne a posthumous daughter to Thomas Montacute showed that she could have healthy children. As discussed above, there are indications of at least two miscarriages while Alice was married to William until she finally gave birth to John. Therefore, it seems highly unlikely that she, or anyone who knew her, thought that infertility was her problem.

This does not mean she was not worried, or in fact that she did not think that the problem lay with her in some way. If she really conceived only twice between 1431 and 1440, she might in fact have thought that something was wrong with her even though she had already given birth once. Since there is also the possibility of Alice losing a pregnancy in 1427, she may simply have been, and considered herself to be, extremely unlucky.

After her hopes were dashed once more in 1440, she must have slowly started to give up hope, and William must have as well. There is no evidence that this caused any sort of argument or even rift between them, the way it often happened, and in fact still does, when a wish to have children cannot be fulfilled. This is intriguing because it is usually claimed that William married Alice at least suspecting she would not be able to give him children, and that he did not care about this, simply wanted her for herself. The fact that he had not married, or ever tried to marry, for fifteen years after becoming an earl is often cited as evidence that he was extremely unconventional in these matters and was not actually concerned about having an heir. There is a certain truth in this; the marriage did not promise him many of the perks he might have expected from a marriage to someone else, especially of a financial nature. Quite possibly, they both saw it simply as God's will, but even so, it must have been painful to them.

Alice's position at Henry VI's court
Life had to go on, and of course it did, with William becoming ever more important at court. The king, after a long majority now finally

William, Earl of Suffolk

able to rule for himself, had shown very little inclination to do so in the four years he could. This began to arouse comment and inspired many nobles to attempt to be close to Henry to try and manipulate him into acting in their interest. Of course, others tried to prevent that and to inveigle themselves into such a position, so that by 1441 factions were forming at court. William seemed to be on the winning side in the early 1440s, which caused people, then as now, to question his motives. Those opposed to him claimed that he was only trying to get the king's ear for his own benefit, and even that his ideas were actively inimical to the English kingdom,[124] a view that has been echoed down the centuries since. Those disposed to be friendly towards William, on the other hand, chose to take his actions to mean that he did all he could to help England to prosper – a view that has become more popular in recent years.

The truth, as always, probably lies in the middle, with William doubtlessly being ambitious and hoping to profit from his position at court, while at the same time influencing Henry to do what he considered the best for him and for the country. Alice is often said to have shared William's ambition and egged him on. Alice had shown before she was ambitious, and proud of what she had achieved by marriage, while wary of drawing any attention to her commoner roots. It is reasonable to think she wanted William to become powerful at court, for his own sake as well as for the opportunities this would afford her.

For all the often scathing comments by chroniclers about William's rise and Alice's part in it, particularly after Henry VI married Margaret of Anjou, it is interesting to note that hardly any accusations of any specific personal failings were ever levelled against them by anyone who knew them. This was rare. While the political accusations were central, personal attacks were often used to buttress political accusations and illustrate that the target was not just bad for the government and not suited to their position, but a bad person per se. Personal attacks against William were

What is Better than a Good Woman?

rare, but though the list of her supposed political crimes was a long one, not a single ad hominem attack was levelled against Alice.

This is striking. At the time, few women were so overtly involved in politics as Alice was in the late 1440s, unless they were royal themselves. The few women who tried it were often slandered, and though it could be argued that men were as well, the slanders levelled against women were of a different nature. Those used against women were very often sexual; the witchcraft accusations against Eleanor Cobham claimed she wanted to make her husband king and then conceive a child to become the next king.[125]The implication was that she intended to use her sexuality to become powerful.

It would have been easy to use the same, or similar, charges against Alice. After all, before William, she had been married to a very popular and very powerful man, a man who was then known to have been so smitten with her that when the Duke of Burgundy insulted her by flirting, he turned against him. The very fact that no one used this against Alice, claiming she used sexual wiles to ensnare Thomas Montacute, who was of much higher standing than she was at the time, is rather impressive, and suggests that for all that she was becoming unpopular in the 1440s, an attack on her personal life was deemed unlikely to succeed.

There is another possible explanation. If someone had attacked her by throwing doubt on how her marriage to Thomas Montacute, Earl of Salisbury, came to be, they would have also implicitly criticised Thomas himself in the charge, as a victim of a 'cunning' woman. Since Thomas was an extremely popular and fondly remembered man even over a decade after his death,[126] this might have turned more people against those making such an attack than against Alice. Moreover, in the 1440s, Richard Neville, Earl of Salisbury was a very powerful man, and his wife Alice Montacute was extremely influential.[127] It would not have been very smart to drag her father's name into the mud in an attempt to condemn her

William, Earl of Suffolk

stepmother. In addition to that, if the marriage was considered to be somehow tainted, then that would have also reflected badly on Thomas and Alice's daughter, and Alice Montacute might very well have drawn the line on besmirching the name of her late half-sister.

Richard Neville and Alice Montacute, Earl and Countess of Salisbury, were very closely connected to the man from whom, according to all evidence, most of the attacks originated: Richard Plantagenet, Duke of York.[128] Though in modern times, his involvement in what happened to William has often been doubted, with some accounts going so far as to present him as a total innocent who was himself slandered, there is enough evidence to prove that if he did not start the attacks, he was involved in spreading them.[129] This is not in itself particularly surprising, nor does it make him any worse than most other men involved in politics at the time. However, it might very well have influenced the nature of those accusations against Alice, and even against William. Since Richard Neville was Richard, Duke of York's brother-in-law, oldest and supposedly favourite brother of his duchess, Cecily Neville, York might very well have paid attention to his wife's feelings, and not done anything that she would have disapproved of. Since Alice Montacute was on good terms with her stepmother Alice, even over a decade after her father had died, she might not have wanted to see her personally attacked, even if understanding the need to reprove her politically. Any condemnation of William's personal life would, by definition, also have been an attack on Alice's personal life, something her stepdaughter might not have been happy to see. There might not have been any need for more personal charges, so no need to risk making enemies of the Earl and Countess of Salisbury.

Slanders were starting to circulate about Alice and William in 1441, but they were not particularly notable then, nothing more than what any other influential man, or couple, in politics heard about themselves. In 1441, they might in fact have been very hopeful about

What is Better than a Good Woman?

their political future, although interestingly, given the influence Alice later had, she did not seem very involved and spent some time apart from William. With William more and more tied up with politics at court, it fell more to Alice to manage both their lands, and it may very well be that she was occupied with that for most of 1441.

They found the time to see each other occasionally, and Alice had enough energy to follow frivolous pastimes. One of these is recorded in the early 1440s – dressing up as an 'ordinary country housewife' with some servants, to 'adjourn to Lakenham Woods, to take the air and disport themselves' and being caught by one of William's men doing so. There was nothing illegal about Alice dressing in whatever way she wished, so long as she did not pretend to be of higher standing than she was. This she did not do, but pretending to be a simple commoner carried other risks, ones Alice had apparently not considered before setting off on this jaunt: of her being caught by the keeper of these woods, Thomas Ailmer,[130] not being recognised and taken for a trespasser, which was what happened. The keeper attempted to make them leave. Presumably, Alice protested that she was Earl William's wife, and the property she was found 'trespassing' on was her own, but of course, with her not being in fine clothes, this was not easy to prove. One of her men accompanying her called Tuddenham[131] took offence to Alice being quizzed and attacked Ailmer. Tuddenham was arrested and stayed in prison for a month.[132]

It would be interesting to know what Alice thought of this incident. It suggests a naivety in Alice's character she did not often show. She must have known, being manager of her own lands for so long and having known of her father doing so even longer, that trespassers were not allowed. Alice did not expect that anyone could think these rules applied to her, or simply expected to be recognised as Countess of Suffolk. For all that Alice had experienced, she was still obviously sheltered from the world in some ways.

William, Earl of Suffolk

It was recorded that she and her servants, who were named as the unlucky Tuddenham and another man called Heydon, men with whom she would be associated in later years, 'disported themselves' together. This, of course, makes the whole incident sound rather more dramatic than it was. Alice's actions when dressing up as an 'ordinary country housewife', probably intended as nothing more than some harmless fun, were seen as rather more serious than that by contemporaries.[133]

Comments exaggerating the import of the incident of course came from those hostile to her and William. Alice had unwittingly handed them ammunition. The story brings to mind Marie Antoinette, three-and-a-half centuries later, playing farmer, something seen as thoughtless but not as morally reprehensible, which was the way Alice's enemies framed it.[134]

It was in 1441 that William, and through him Alice, first took political centre stage. This was in part due to Humphrey, Duke of Gloucester's disgrace that year,[135] which moved William yet closer to the king, someone considered by him as a capable courtier and important man, someone the king could trust. Such elevation, albeit only in the king's favour, always came at a price: that of other men's jealousy. This was not something confined to the fifteenth century. While no one accused William in 1441 of having engineered the events that eventually caused the Duke of Gloucester[136] to withdraw from public life, so that nobody with opinions so opposed to William's own opinions had the king's ear, he certainly was in later years.

It is, in fact, possible that William was involved in the campaign against Humphrey, as his popularity was resented by many at court. Since the duke was a very popular man, especially with the commons, he was not attacked directly[137] but via his unpopular second wife, Eleanor Cobham. She was accused of treason, of having married Humphrey with the help of witchcraft and of having wanted the king dead. Humphrey was, in a way, presented as her

What is Better than a Good Woman?

victim, but naturally, he could not escape being tainted with her ostensible guilt. Under pressure Eleanor later confessed to some of the charges, admitting she had indeed seen a 'witch', but only to become pregnant, and this was used against Humphrey himself.

The only part of her charge that is considered by many historians to have been probably true is that she did visit a woman known as a 'witch' to get help in becoming pregnant. As discussed above, this was not at all unusual at the time, and that it was used against her was simply an attempt to break her husband's influence.

The driving force behind these absurd claims against Eleanor is no longer known. William might have been involved, but even if he was not, he would be resented for stepping into the void left by Humphrey at court and make enemies. This cannot have come as a surprise to him. His family had been through a lot of ups and downs since his grandfather Michael, a merchant's son, was made an earl due to his closeness to the king.[138] His good fortune had not lasted, many men working for his downfall from the first, outraged that a man that low-born was allowed such a high honour. Eventually, being implicated in treason, he had died in exile, declared a traitor in England. William's own father had spent many of his adult years trying to regain his father's title, and even after being successful[139] had not been able to rest, as Henry IV's usurpation meant the title, newly granted to him shortly before the usurpation by Richard II, was taken from him and he had to start working towards regaining it all over again.[140]

Eventually he did, and William must have remembered the struggle. Alice, however, while doubtlessly she knew of what had happened to William's family and was aware of the pitfalls of politics, had never actually known them first-hand. Her father had always been a very popular man, and while there were doubtlessly those who spoke against him, as is normal for any public figure, it had never affected him or his rise. Similarly, both her previous husbands had been popular men, popular with the king as well

William, Earl of Suffolk

as political figures. Both had lived in the king's and the people's favour. Though Alicer was in her late thirties by now and we can assume she had faced as much strife as any other person that age, in the fifteenth century as much as at any other time, from all we know, she had never been anything but pampered and cosseted. First as Thomas Chaucer's adored daughter, only child and heir, for whom he obviously did everything, then as John Phelip's spoiled child bride, whom he can have met only once but whom he still endowed with lands and possessions.[141] After that, she was Thomas Montacute, Earl of Salisbury's wife, obviously loved and adored, the wife he wanted to see inherit as much of his lands and possessions as his daughter. Then she had become William de la Pole, Earl of Suffolk's wife, whom he had married despite the fact he did not gain much from the union. All these men had, and, in William's case, still did, go out of their way to make sure she had whatever she wanted and was treated, in modern terms, like a princess.

It was not only these men. Though of course they were the people who loomed largest in her life, she was supported by others as well. Her stepdaughter Alice Montacute was always on the best of terms with her, from all we know, though it would hardly have been unnatural for her to be resentful towards her for not only taking half of what she might have considered her own inheritance, but also giving birth to a much younger half-sibling, thus further reducing Alice Montacute's inheritance. That the two women were on good terms despite that says a lot for both their personalities and Alice's likeability. Similarly, from the time that Alice as a small girl became John Phelip's widow, her brother-in-law William Phelip supported her in all ways he could, never once showing a single sign of annoyance that his young sister-in-law, who had been too young even to be his brother's wife in anything but name only when he died, inherited so many of his possessions, taking large swathes of what would otherwise have belonged to him. This shows a certain kind-heartedness on his part, but it also shows

What is Better than a Good Woman?

that Alice, at least as she grew up, must have been likeable. While he might have hesitated to attempt to disinherit a child, even one he considered not to be a rightful heiress, there was nothing to prevent him from trying to do so when she was an adult. Even if he did not think this very likely to succeed, he most definitely would not have been under an obligation to be on good terms with her as an adult, and help her with the management of her lands.

Until the early 1440s, Alice had usually encountered only appreciation, fondness and love. Though there had been mild criticisms, such as her being considered vain for wearing cloth of gold at the baptism of her goddaughter Eleanor Moleyns,[142], those were mild rebukes, hardly hostility. Of course, she had faced blows, most recently her daughter's and parents' death, but these was not the same sort of shocks she suddenly found herself faced with in the early 1440s: people actively disliking her and her husband, wishing them nothing but failure. Her inexperience had meant she did not think of possible consequences when dressing as an 'ordinary country housewife' with some servants. It is possible that at first the hostility frightened her, but she was not to stay frightened for long. As William rose at court, she was noted to be by his side unusually often, and to be actively involved in politics. She was not afraid of gossips and those wishing her ill. She also appeared to learn her lesson about ill-considered adventures like her dressing up; such a thing did not happen again.

Another blow would fall in 1441: the death of her brother-in-law William Phelip, Lord Bardolf, brother of her first husband John, who died on 6 June 1441 at the age of about 57. Since she had been on good terms with him ever since marrying his brother as a young girl, it can reasonably be assumed she was sad about his death. Perhaps this was also why she did not stay with William at court for much of 1441, not feeling up to it after such a blow, the loss of someone who had been supportive of her for nearly thirty years.

William, Earl of Suffolk

In December 1441, just before Christmas, William did return home to Ewelme and Alice,[143] probably wishing to spend Christmas with her. One can assume that their Christmas then was a happy one, probably attended by several nobles and important people. It must have been in late December 1441 that their son John was conceived. William and Alice obviously even after ten years of marriage were attracted to each other. As discussed above, it is possible they had even stopped thinking they could have children after Alice's miscarriage the year before, so there was no pressure. Presumably, it was simply because they wanted to sleep together.

William and Alice stayed together at Ewelme, in a peaceful haven of sorts, for nearly two months. Around February, Alice must have started suspecting she was pregnant, but she was probably not that hopeful. She had lost two babies in the previous five years, and she might very well have feared losing this one as well.

On 24 February, William was summoned back to court.[144] Maybe William did not want to leave Alice – he had certainly shown no inclination to do so until being summoned – but it shows how important he had become. He had bishops summoning him[145] so a problem could be dealt with – that must have inevitably engendered an intoxicating feeling of power.

As for Alice, we do not know what she did in the first months of 1442. The logical thing to do would have been to rest, in the hopes of not losing the pregnancy. This was a very common and sensible course of action chosen by many women who had had either difficulties conceiving or had lost one or more pregnancies before. It is possible that Alice rested in the first months of her pregnancy, but we know that she did not do so during her entire pregnancy.

A letter of 6 June reported William and Alice's movements. They had just spent several days in Alice's castle of Donnington and had then returned to Ewelme.[146] Such visits were normal and in fact expected of couples of their standing, to see to it that all their lands and possessions were well taken care of. In this particular case,

What is Better than a Good Woman?

there might have been another reason, to visit the grave of William Phelip. William's daughter Elizabeth had died in the same year,[147] only weeks after him, in childbirth. It is possible Alice had seen both their graves before, but the fact that her visit to Donnington manor, very close to where William was buried, coincides with his death date, suggests that her and her husband's visit there had been a gesture of respect. The visit shows something else: Alice did not avoid travelling, despite being six months pregnant by that time. She would want to be present for William Phelip's year's mind, but it is not reasonable to assume that she considered this more important than keeping her pregnancy. Therefore, Alice was not very worried about miscarrying. In this case, she was right. Chambers were specially prepared for the birth and the time before and after it, and Alice retired to Ewelme in late summer of the year 1442, around six weeks to a month before the expected birth date.

Sadly, we have no surviving evidence of what decorations she chose for her chambers for this occasion, what books or other entertainment she had brought and what other arrangements she made. However, we know about Alice's arrangements made for her daughter-in-law's confinement in 1466,[148] as discussed earlier, and we can make deductions from that. For example, Alice would have chosen the tapestries depicting St Anne and other famous and noble women she had made in 1440, for a confinement that was never to be.

Many women wrote their will before giving birth, as so many women died either in childbirth or shortly afterwards of childbed fever, but if Alice also did so, this will has not survived. Even if she did not, she must have prepared herself for the possibility of not surviving the birth. Perhaps, As she was thirty-eight or shortly to turn thirty-eight at the time, and it was known that the older the mother, the higher the danger of dying in childbirth, she feared it more than she had the last time she had given birth thirteen years earlier.

Whatever her fears were, if indeed she had any, they were confounded. Either late on 26 September or on the 27th, Alice went into labour. Alice would not have given birth on a bed. Instead, she would have been encouraged to walk at first while in labour, then she would have sat in a birthing chair. At the time, and for centuries afterwards, there was no pain relief. The end result was a happy one: on 27 September 1442, Alice gave birth to a little boy, without any lasting ill-effects.

Motherhood

Their little boy's birth, after eleven years of marriage and at least two miscarriages, must have seemed like a miracle to the new parents, and it is hardly possible to overstate their joy at finally having a child together, an heir to their vast wealth. They decided to name him John, probably after William's brother John, though it is also possible the child was named after a godfather, or after St John. The child was baptised either on 27 September, his actual birth day, or very shortly afterwards, as was common. Though we have absolutely no information about his baptism, it is virtually certain that his godfathers and godmother were important people, given his father and mother's status at the time of his birth. Possible candidates for his godmothers are several of his aunts, such as Abbess Katherine, or Alice Montacute, who would have been a very highborn and excellent choice.

In fact, one or both of his godfathers might have been higher born still. It is possible that King Henry VI, then nearly twenty-one years of age, was godfather to his favourite advisor's son and heir. Despite the lack of evidence for or against this, it sounds very likely: it was hardly uncommon for kings and queens to be godparents to children, and Henry VI had already shown he was fond of the Suffolks. Being godfather to their son would have been a nice gesture, without requiring much from him. He would have been expected to make the boy a small gift for his baptism, but that was as far as the duties would have gone for a royal godparent.

What is Better than a Good Woman?

Whether he or any of his other nobles were in fact little John's godparents, the baby was born with a splendid future ahead of him. It is easy to imagine Alice picturing her son's future as a man close to the king, though that she could have foreseen even in her most optimistic moments that he would marry a princess one day and be a king's brother-in-law is doubtful; as doubtful as her father ever thinking his adored daughter would one day be a duchess. Even in 1442, this must have seemed like an unreachable fantasy, not something Alice even considered. However, after the birth of her son, she must have been even more ambitious for herself and for William, as the higher they rose in the king's favour and the more privileges they got from him, the more John would also profit.

It seems that Alice was now, for the first time in their marriage, torn as to where she wanted to spend her time. Before John's birth, she had always been by William's side whenever possible, but after, while still being with her husband more often than was common for people of their standing, she was with her son for long periods. Though Alice was unusually close to her son for a lady of her standing,[149] her son had his own staff and his day-to-day life was being taken care of by those paid to do so. It was what she had known from her own childhood, though she took special care to make sure only the best of the best took care of little John. In the first years of his life, she kept a specially close eye on his staff to make sure her son was cared for in a way that met her approval. During most of John's first year, Alice was at Ewelme with him, William coming to be with them when he could. Though William seemed more distant from his son than Alice was, more the stereotypical medieval noble father, there can be no doubt he loved his son dearly, as later events would show.

William gave Alice nearly complete control of their son's education and upbringing. Though it is a common misconception about the Middle Ages that wives and mothers had little or no say in their children's upbringing, especially not their sons',[150]

William, Earl of Suffolk

few men left all decisions to be made for their oldest son and heir so completely to their wives as William did. The most logical inference from the facts we have is to assume that William and Alice agreed that Alice was to stay with their small son as often as possible during his first year of life, and that she was to make all immediate decisions for his education and upbringing, with William eventually agreeing with them or making changes as he saw fit. There is no evidence that he ever saw fit to challenge any decision Alice had made regarding their son.

It was quite normal for young children to be in the care of their mothers while they were still in the nursery, and though most noble fathers tended to be more involved with some of the more major decisions, most of the care fell to the mothers. Since John was only seven when his father died, we don't know if William would have become more involved in the decision-making process once he was out of the nursery, or if he would have continued letting Alice decide.

Whether Alice chose to be conventional in the establishment of her son's household or if she chose to do something her own way, such as breastfeeding herself, there is no way of saying. However, if we judge by Alice's actions in general, it does not seem she would have risked rumours to be spread about her parenting reputation by doing something unusual, something that could remind people that she was born a commoner and use this as ammunition against her, against William, and most importantly, against little John.

In the first year of John's life Alice did not accompany William to court as she had done in the previous years.[151] By the end of that year, something important was happening at court, which might be why Alice decided to join her husband again. Or with her son being one year old and all the decisions she had made for his care tested and working well, she decided that she had done all she could do and once more wished to be at the centre of government.

Later events throw doubt on whether Alice wanted to do this for her own sake, or for William's sake and, after 1442, for her son's

What is Better than a Good Woman?

sake. In 1443, she showed every sign of being happy to be at court, involved in what was happening. It was only in later years that she showed a disinclination to be involved in government matters, and this will be discussed later. It could have been a reaction to what happened to William or done to shelter her son, rather than a personal inclination.

Combination of motherhood and political power

In 1443, Alice threw herself into the discussions at the royal court over the marriage of the then nearly twenty-two-year-old king.[152] There were two factions at court who could not agree on who England's new queen should be.[153]

The candidate favoured by the king was the French king's niece, Margaret, daughter of the Count of Anjou.[154] Henry and the others pushing for the marriage hoped to get a peace deal through it with France, certainly sorely needed at the time.[155] Ever since William and Alice had married, things had been going steadily downhill in France, with the French king's forces winning more and more battles. Though the English population was not aware of the extent of this, and many nobles simply saw bad English leadership as the cause, others, like William, saw the writing on the wall. The wars in France had become unwinnable, but few people wanted to admit it. William was of the faction ready to do so and was eager to make peace before more lives (and treasure) were lost. He was probably also one of the very few Englishmen genuinely concerned with French loss of life. Henry VI, who was of course half-French, was in agreement with him, which was seen as a weakness by several in his court.

Despite this, the council agreed that the marriage was worth pursuing, and Henry decided that William should be the one who went to negotiate with the French king. He would be the leader of a large party of nobles, with exact instructions given by Henry VI.[156]

Despite what his enemies later claimed,[157] William was not eager to take up this duty and only agreed to go if it was agreed upon by the lords spiritual and temporal that he would not be blamed for any outcome to the negotiations, or if in fact the marriage was not as intended.[158] This was duly agreed on and sworn to.

William insistence on this shows that he was aware of how wrong the negotiations could go and what ramifications they could have for England's lands in France, Anjou and Maine. He almost certainly knew from the secret instructions given to him by Henry before he left England to secure the marriage that the surrender of Anjou and Maine to France would be part of the agreement.[159]

Henry VI must have known how well-suited William was for this task, perhaps better so than anyone else. He had lost more in the French war than perhaps anyone else of the nobility, and he was closely acquainted with French habits and customs. He was actually sympathetic to France and the French people, which meant he was most likely of all the nobility to want to make the negotiations a success. Alice, for her part, was a well-known figure even in France. Though she was not actually formally required to be part of the envoy and she could have stayed at home with their son if she wanted, her presence might have been considered a very good idea, providing a female touch and someone the 14-year-old Margaret of Anjou could trust, more so than the male negotiators. This was what happened; Margaret seems to have immediately taken to Alice. Others in this most important of envoys were Adam Moleyns, Henry VI's Keeper of the Privy Seal, one of his secretaries and one of his esquires.[160]

When they arrived in France, they were greeted with honour. The French king, though in a better bargaining situation than his English peer and nephew, was also eager for peace.[161] Quite sensibly, he would not let the English have it without a high price. This was perfectly normal behaviour, but it was also behaviour many of the English, especially English commoners, would not accept. It was for this reason that the terms William could agree to in order to clinch the marriage were to only be presented to the English population as a fait accompli.

William, Alice and the rest of the party met the French king and his young niece Margaret at Tours on 4 May 1444 and began the negotiations with King Charles and his advisors, who also included Charles, Duke of Orléans.[162] His presence might have made William more likely to agree with what was suggested by the French, or it might have been intended as such. If it worked is unknowable.

What we do know is that it was quickly decided that the marriage would be a desirable one and that Margaret was considered suitable, so that the negotiations went ahead, with William taking a leading part. After three weeks they concluded, with King Charles of France and William, in Henry VI's name, being satisfied with the terms they had agreed.[163] Those terms were not at all favourable for the English. In fact, they were worse even than Henry seems to have hoped for: they did not include a treaty of perpetual peace, only a peace treaty for slightly less than two years, with a possibility of it being extended.[164]

William must have been disappointed with that, but perhaps he was hopeful that though not an agreement to end the war for good, it would prove the beginning of the end. Though this might have been what he and Henry VI, disagreed with most, there were other terms in the marriage contract that were likely to agitate William's countrymen. There had been no agreement made on who was the rightful King of France – not a subject King Charles and King Henry were likely to agree on, but still always a point of contention – William had agreed to the English ally the Duke of Burgundy being officially called a French vassal, and that England would give back the lands of Maine and Anjou to France after the marriage.

By all standards, this was a remarkably bad treaty for England. They gained only a twenty-three-months-long peace and a bride for their king, while the French gained agreement on almost all

William, Earl of Suffolk

points and vast swathes of land, all at nearly no cost to themselves. There are two important caveats.

Firstly, William, along with some others such as Henry VI himself, believed that there was no way, with the way the war was going at the time, that England could hold Maine and Anjou forever. William's reasoning seemed to be that it was better to lose them in a treaty, with no further loss of life, rather than spent more years fighting in vain for them.

The second point is more important for a study of Alice: the charge against William, and by extension against her, that they had planned for this and made the decisions by themselves does not hold up. There is no way that William could have made such important decisions without having the go-ahead from Henry VI, and if he had tried it, not only would the treaty have been void, Henry would without a doubt have been furious with William. That he was not is discussed below.

The fact that William insisted that the lords spiritual and temporal officially declare that he was not to be blamed for the terms of the treaty made for the marriage before even setting off suggests that he had been briefed by Henry with what he was allowed to let Charles get away with, and that he had known that neither the English population nor the nobility would be happy with it. What he personally thought of these terms is not recorded, any more than Alice's reaction.

It is usually stated as a fact that William at the very least agreed with the terms, if not outright dictated them to Henry, and that Alice was in support of this. There is no evidence for this at all. Though there can be no doubt that William very much supported the idea of Henry VI marrying Margaret of Anjou and had been very vocal about wanting peace, there is no saying if he agreed with such terms or would have preferred to negotiate something more favourable for England but was under orders by Henry VI to arrange the marriage no matter what.

What is Better than a Good Woman?

When he was accused of treason for selling England out to France, he pointed out that he had lost a lot fighting in France and so of course would not act against his country's interests.[165] This cannot necessarily be taken at face value, as it was a defence against a treason charge and William was fighting for his life, but even so, it is true that he had lost much and might very well have considered the treaty a step too far, if still preferable to more war.

Similarly, Alice might not have been as happy about the treaty as she is usually assumed to have been. In her case, this agreement is usually inferred from her later closeness to Margaret, not her political opinions, but one does not necessarily follow from the other. Alice might have genuinely liked Margaret; in fact, this is suggested by the surviving evidence, which will be discussed, but still not thought that the marriage treaty was a good one. Alice, like William, had reason not to want the English sacrifice of the last decades dismissed in this way, as the treaty was seen by many. After all, she had lost two husbands in the wars in France. The opposite might also hold true. Having lost two husbands in these wars, her daughter having never met her father because of them, Alice might very well have considered any price acceptable to end them. There is no way of saying; but it is definitely not a proven fact, as is often claimed, that she and William whole-heartedly supported the treaty.

The marriage of King Henry VI and Margaret was slated to go ahead. So that this could not be simply broken by either side, on 24 May, a formal betrothal was agreed upon and Margaret went through a proxy wedding, with William standing in for Henry VI.

There was nothing particularly unusual about such a proxy wedding, but this, too, has been used against William. The ceremony was nothing more than a betrothal, a way to make sure that the two future spouses were promised to each other in the eyes of God. This was done when there might otherwise be a

William, Earl of Suffolk

danger of the bride being prevented from travelling to her future husband by someone kidnapping her and forcing her to marry him instead, or – something that happened more often the in the fifteenth century – there was a danger of one or both of the parties reneging on the marriage treaty. With them having made their promises in God's eyes, this was much harder and would require a dispensation from the pope.

All of this obviously meant that William was simply acting for Henry VI, in his interest. It did not mean that Margaret had any obligation to him. He was simply fulfilling a task for his lord as others had before him and would after him, an action that showed how important a man he was at that point, being so trusted by his king.

Conversely, it has been pointed out that it must have been strange for William, a man who was not only married but whose wife was in attendance, to go through a wedding with someone else. His biographer Susan Curran suggests 'We must hope they laughed.'[166] But there is no real reason why Alice should have been in any way jealous or considered it as a betrayal. Though for Margaret, it was of course important, as it was a binding marriage ceremony, for William it was simply another part of duty. Perhaps Alice was even proud of William, proud that her husband was important enough to go through a proxy wedding with a princess and future queen.

Once that was done, the envoy made their way back to England. Margaret stayed in France for the time being with her family, to prepare for her departure for England to her future husband a year later.

The envoy, headed by William, was greeted with delight by Henry VI.[167] According to several chroniclers, Henry was extremely happy that his marriage was secured and eager to learn all about his new bride. If he was at all disappointed with the terms attached, he did not show it. On the contrary, he showed all signs of being grateful to the men who had negotiated it, especially to William. If William had any misgivings about the treaty he had negotiated,

What is Better than a Good Woman?

he was compensated by rich rewards from his king, rewards so great he cannot possibly have expected them, and that must have pleased him and Alice immensely.

The first reward given to him was not, in fact, solely for William, or even William or Alice, but most profitable for their toddler son, not quite two years of age in May 1444: Henry VI granted his parents a wardship that they, if they were so minded, could turn into a highly profitable marriage for little John: the wardship of little Margaret Beaufort.[168]

Born most likely on 31 May 1443, but definitely not before 31 May 1441,[169] the little girl was the only child of John Beaufort, Duke of Somerset, and his wife Margaret Beauchamp. She was therefore the only heiress of John, one of the richest and, next to William, most powerful men in the realm. John had been commander of the English forces in France, with catastrophic outcomes, and shortly after returning from France with that failure hanging over his head, he died on 27 May 1444, while William and Alice were still in France or possibly on their way back to England.

The causes of the duke's death are disputed. The *Croyland Chronicle*, a contemporary source, stated that he had committed suicide,[170] possibly in shame over his catastrophic failure as army commander. Since this was a mortal sin in the fifteenth century, that not only meant that anyone who committed suicide would be damned forever, but also that he had committed a crime that would result in his family being disinherited. For that reason, suicides were often hushed up, especially if committed by a member of the nobility, which could explain the occasional vague wording of 'extreme melancholy', implying what had happened while not spelling it out. There is a theory that he died of an illness, but one that *caused* melancholy, which led the chronicler at Croyland to believe he had committed suicide. We do know that John's family was not disinherited, meaning that if he committed suicide, it was hushed up.

William, Earl of Suffolk

Whatever had happened, the grant of wardship, and by extension of marriage, of Margaret was a huge honour for William and Alice, and obviously intended to be:

> ... forasmuch as our cousin the Duke of Somerset is now late passed to God's mercy, the which hath a daughter and heir to succeed him, of full tender age called Margaret. We considering the notable services that our cousin the earl of Suffolk hath done unto us, and tendering him therefore the more specially as reason will, have of our grace and especial proper motion and mere deliberation granted unto him to have the ward and marriage of the said Margaret, without anything.[171]

This was normal wording for a grant, with the exception of the last sentence, which makes it very clear that the wardship was considered a reward for William's actions in France. The fact that it says it was Henry VI's 'mere deliberation' that made him decide on this grant could indicate that this grant went against an early one to Margaret Beauchamp, but it does not have to be so. Legal language in the fifteenth century was extremely flowery, so it would be a mistake to read too much into a single unusual turn of phrase.

Henry VI might have considered Margaret a suitable bride for his favourite advisor's son and heir. This would have been an extremely splendid match for John, and some think that it would have been beneath Margaret to marry him. Margaret's most recent biographer, Dr Nicola Tallis, stated that his ancestry was not as impressive as hers, having 'no royal blood, being descended from wool merchants'.[172] This is correct but seems to be overstating Margaret's own ancestry and importance a little. In fact, John and Margaret were related: Margaret's great-grandparents were John of Gaunt and Katherine Swynford,[173] the sister of John's

What is Better than a Good Woman?

great-grandmother, Philippa Chaucer. This connection gave Margaret royal blood and not John, but though Margaret's grandfather John Beaufort had eventually been declared legitimate by the pope, he had been born a bastard and was by many still considered so. Though it has been debated in recent years,[174] the Beaufort branch was explicitly barred from the line of succession, thus, as it were, draining Margaret's royal blood. At the time, the very suggestion of doubting this and considering Margaret close to the throne was explicitly treasonous.[175] No such supposed importance would have stood in the way of her marrying John, or made him beneath her.

While John's ancestors were doubtlessly less illustrious than Margaret's, at the time of his parents receiving her wardship his own family was much more important and much more in favour than Margaret's. Though she was the only child and daughter of a duke, the dukedom was either in the male entail, or claimed to be so, and the title did not fall to her. Her father's riches did however fall to her and were the primary reason for her importance on the marriage market. This did not make up for her father's disgrace in France and the rumours of his suicide. It might be thought that such considerations counted less than her enormous inheritance, but they did mean that her standing was much lower in 1444 than is usually assumed. John was at that time heir to an earl and son to the king's most favoured advisor, as well as to one of the politically most important and well-connected women in the realm. What he did not have in money and ancestry, he made up for in title and connections. A marriage between the two would have been perfectly suitable.

William and Alice did not seem to think so, and this reward was one they showed very little interest in. In fact, if anything, William showed some distaste for the Somerset family, and had no scruples about disadvantaging them to help his own family. It was almost definitely due to him that John Beaufort's second title, Earl of

William, Earl of Suffolk

Kendall, fell neither to little Margaret nor to John's brother, but to Jean de Foix, husband of William's niece.[176]

Nor did he and Alice show any eagerness to assume the wardship of Margaret or make any arrangements to marry her to their son. This is contrary to what is usually claimed,[177] presumably due to hindsight and the fact that the two children did eventually marry. That was still several years in the future, and all of William's actions indicate there was no point before late 1449 that he or Alice showed any interest in wanting to have anything to do with the wardship, or the little girl herself.

We only know their actions, and since these usually focus on William in chronicles, Alice's part in the decisions that led to them is rather obscured. However, we have plenty of evidence of William considering Alice's opinion as very important and consulting her on any number of topics, and of course, he left the decisions pertaining to their son almost entirely to her. Therefore, before making any decision as to whether to marry their son to Margaret Beaufort or try and find him another bride, the two surely discussed the matter extensively, and there is no reason to assume that Alice was any more eager than her husband to see the two children married.

The evidence, such as it is, suggests that though receiving the grant of Margaret's wardship and marriage, Alice and William did not act upon it. Even apart from the marriage prospect it offered for their son, it could have been of immense profit for them; Margaret being their ward meant that they could have as much or as little to do with her and her upbringing as they wished and still have complete control over her entire inheritance, lands and possessions until she either married or came of age at fourteen. Since Margaret's inheritance was vast, they could have been very rich from that alone, but it does not seem they tried bring this about.

As has been remarked by many of Margaret's biographers, there is evidence that the little girl never lived in the Suffolk household,

What is Better than a Good Woman?

and before their hurried wedding in early 1450,[178] probably never met either John or his parents. This, of course, could have been an arrangement made between Alice and William and Margaret Beauchamp, and considered to be the best for the little girl, even if they did still think of arranging a marriage in due course. However, if so, it would be logical for them to at least profit from the money they had access to from Margaret's inheritance, but while it is of course possible they used it occasionally, they never took any large amount of Margaret's money.

This was quite unusual, and in fact rather decent of them, as there would have been nothing to stop them from doing so and it would have been their right. Though technically, money taken by guardians from their wards' inheritance was meant to be spent on their behalf, this was rarely the case and in fact, handing a valuable wardship to a favourite was a cheap way for a king to reward someone. It may have also been part of why Henry VI chose to grant Margaret's wardship to William and Alice.

Margaret Beaufort would go on to be the mother of the future Henry VII, and a very important woman, which is why a lot more attention has been paid to her early years and what happened with her wardship than there has been to other little children in her position. A lot of what we 'know' about it comes from her confessor John Fisher and his speech at her funeral. It is from this speech, later published in the book *Mornyng Remembrance*, that the idea William and Alice were eager not only for her wardship and also to marry her to their son comes from. Fisher stated that William 'most diligently worked to procure her for his son and heir', a statement that, since it came from someone so close to Margaret, has often been taken as a fact. However, there are two problems: for one, there is no way that Margaret could possibly have known first-hand what William did or did not do in 1444, when she was only one year old. Secondly, Fisher's speech did not exist in a void. It was given at her funeral in front of her grandson

William, Earl of Suffolk

Henry VIII, and therefore Fisher had a vested interest in making Margaret seem more important than she actually was.

This scarcely appreciated wardship was not the only reward William and Alice received for their service in France concerning the marriage. Henry VI was either extremely pleased with the work William had done in France, despite the fact he had returned with a substandard treaty, or he just wanted to reward him for his service in general. Shortly after granting William the wardship of Margaret Beaufort, he decided to make him a marquess, a step above an earldom.[179]

William and Alice were becoming one of the most politically important couples in the realm also one of the highest titled. Alice must have been delighted with this grant, making her a marchioness. Born a commoner, in 1444 she became one of the most noble women in the realm. Her steep rise was only to continue in the next few years.

The last reward she and William received was a grant that in the event of William's death while 'his heir [was] within age, Alice and his executors shall have the keeping of the heir with his marriage and so from heir to heir'. This grant was explicitly framed as a reward, said to have been issued 'in consideration of [William's] long stay in France at his great costs for the treaty of peace between the king and his uncle of France and his realms'.[180]

The rise meant having to be more and more in Henry VI's presence and working for him, though presumably, she and William would have done that even had they remained a mere earl and countess. They turn up more and more in chronicles reporting activities at court. Their main residence from the mid-1440s onwards seemed to be at court.

In late 1444, their presence at court was hardly surprising. Most noblemen and noblewomen were there, preparing for the arrival of Henry VI's bride and his wedding. This was a monumental and very expensive effort. Though technically, being

What is Better than a Good Woman?

a queen means simply being married to a king, in practice it meant an actual job. A queen was not only meant to counsel the king and give birth to many princes and princesses, but she also held vast lands and possessions, with many tenants. Henry VI indebted himself to prepare a splendid household for his new wife. Preparations were made for her arrival, for the wedding itself, for Margaret's coronation and for the household the new queen would have after it.

It was assumed from the first that Alice would play a large part in this household. This had less to do with her own merits and more with the inherently political nature of being a chief lady-in-waiting to the queen. Though the queen could choose for herself her intimates and who she rewarded, she could not choose for herself her ladies-in-waiting, with the wives of important noblemen being entitled to the position if they so wished.

Several noble ladies did not in fact want to hold such a position, but Alice clearly did, so that she was involved in planning this household. She was also figured in as a part of the envoy that was to go to France again in early 1445, to accompany the new queen to England. This was not a straightforward travel arrangement, it would mean festivities in both France and England.

7

ALICE'S RELATIONSHIP WITH MARGARET OF ANJOU

It is often assumed that Alice was chosen to come along because even in their short acquaintance in 1444, she and Margaret had become close, but that is hindsight. When the preparations were made for the envoy in late 1444 and early 1445, it would once more have been up to Alice to decide whether she wanted to join her husband, she was not obliged in any way and there is no indication that her presence was intended for Margaret's sake.

However, unlike the year before, when her presence would not have been needed or necessarily expected, it would have been very strange for Alice not to join her husband on this formal envoy to bring the queen home. It would have also been a very exciting event and offer an opportunity to become close to the queen. Alice would have wanted to accompany William not simply for his sake, but also for her own enjoyment and possible advancement. The entourage for the new queen cost 5000 pounds and was 300 men (and women) strong, including many nobles, not only William and Alice but also Richard, Duke of York and his wife Cecily.

The journey to France probably started in late February 1445, William and Alice leaving their son behind in Ewelme. The future queen started out from her native Anjou in March. On the first leg of her journey she was accompanied by her brother Jean, but

What is Better than a Good Woman?

at St Denis she was given into the custody of Charles, Duke of Orléans. Whatever he or William and Alice thought about the treaty that had made the marriage happen, presumably all three were glad to see each other again.

They met in Pontoise to await Margaret's arrival, which was celebrated with a grand reception. What Alice did during it is not recorded, though she would have spent most of her time serving young Margaret. It may have been from that moment that Alice started to form a connection with the young woman who was to be her queen. It must have been pleasing for Margaret to see a face that was at least vaguely familiar. It is known that Alice very quickly became of importance in the entourage. After the future queen was received with all due honour in Pontoise, she bade goodbye to Charles, Duke of Orléans and the entourage travelled on to Rouen, where more festivities had been planned. Margaret was supposed to enter the city in a chariot covered with cloth of gold, waving to the masses who had come to see her arrival. However, Margaret had become ill, with some sort of stomach issue. Just what exactly her illness was is not known, but it is usually assumed to have come from nervousness – a likely explanation, since there is no evidence of her infecting anyone else.

Whatever was ailing Margaret, she was in no condition to sit decoratively in a chariot as it entered the city of Rouen and wave to the assembled masses.[1] However, since it had already been planned in detail and people had arrived for it, it would have been unthinkable to cancel. Cancelling would have signalled to everyone that Margaret was ill, possibly life-threateningly so. People may have begun to doubt her suitability as queen. To avoid this, the reception had to go ahead, and someone else had to sit in the decorated chariot, waving to all. The substitute chosen for this task was Alice[2]

This was a massive honour for the common-born Alice, as in fact it would have been even for the most high-born duchess. It meant

Alice's Relationship with Margaret of Anjou

that she was to dress like a queen and be received like a queen in Margaret's place, getting to enjoy, if only for some hours and only in the name of someone else, all the trappings of queenship.

It is not recorded why Alice was chosen for the task, leaving historians to debate the whys and wherefores. The most logical explanation, and therefore the explanation most likely to be true, is because William was the leader of the English envoy and therefore the most important task for a woman naturally fell to his wife.[3] It is also possible that William, in his capacity as head of the envoy, got to decide who was best suited and so chose his own wife. Some have argued that it was Margaret's choice, but this seems unlikely. No matter how quickly Margaret and Alice became friends, Margaret would have known the rules of queenship and would have not wanted to affront any high-ranking noblewoman simply to do a favour to a woman she liked but barely knew.

Another theory which has been suggested is that Alice and Margaret had similar physiques[4] and Alice could therefore pass for Margaret from a distance better than any of the other noblewomen in the envoy. Since the people Alice was supposed to wave to in Margaret's place were commoners, it is very unlikely they had any idea what Margaret looked like. In any case, Alice was significantly older than her. Her own daughter was a year older than Margaret. Since the assembled masses are much more likely to have known that Margaret was a fifteen-year-old girl than what she actually looked like, anyone who wished to cast her substitute as someone who could be taken for her would have been unlikely to pick a 41-year-old woman.

Whatever the reasoning, the English envoy chose Alice.[5] Finding a dress Alice could wear could not have been easy, as no matter how rich and noble she was, it is unlikely she had any clothes with her that were suited for a queen to wear during such a public task. According to the sumptuary laws, she would not even have been allowed to own such a dress. Whatever Alice thought of

What is Better than a Good Woman?

her strange task, it must have been a heady feeling to be dressed as a queen, complete with regalia such as a diadem to signify royal blood. She may have been uncomfortable with this sudden, short-lived honour thrust on her at such short notice. Royal blood and the duties and privileges that came with it were taken very seriously, regarded as God-given, so that is quite possible that instead of finding it a thrilling occasion, a short glimpse at what being queen would be like, Alice considered the whole spectacle as a potentially dangerous mockery.

Alice did her job well. There is every indication that the entry into Rouen was a success[6] and that the people who came to cheer Margaret either could not tell it was not her in the decorated chariot waving to them, or did not care. They duly cheered, and Alice waved, while the real Margaret entered Rouen in the care of one of the English nobles and was brought to a palace to recuperate.

If Alice had to substitute for Margaret somewhere else on the way to the French coast, it has not been recorded. Since the reception at Rouen was the biggest of the festivities prepared, this is not particularly surprising, and it is likely that the ailing Margaret managed some of the smaller tasks she faced as she travelled to her new home.

All in all, despite Margaret's illness, everything went well and the English envoy must have been satisfied when on 3 April 1445[7] they boarded the ships to bring them back to England. What Margaret felt is less certain, with many historians stating that she was less than happy about it.[8] This is possible, but she would have always known that she was to be in an arranged marriage one day, and being a queen was as good a marriage as any woman could hope for. Her feelings would most likely not have mattered to anyone but herself, though the noble ladies in the entourage would have done all they could to ease any of her apprehensions. It was a rough passage, with Margaret's ship, the same ship on

Alice's Relationship with Margaret of Anjou

which William and Alice travelled, being tossed around by a spring storm.

The young future queen was so ill with seasickness, and presumably still feeling weak from whatever illness she had suffered in France, that she could not walk ashore to be greeted by the people who had gathered to cheer her arrival.[9] William had to carry her ashore, and she was brought to a convent to recover.[10]

The very fact that Margaret was so ill upon arriving in England has been used by many historians as evidence she was not simply nervous and seasick but suffering from something more serious.[11] However, this is almost certainly untrue; not only is it unlikely that she would not have infected anyone else had she had a contagious illness, even one that was not actually dangerous, it also overlooks the effects of nervousness and especially seasickness. Margaret was not the only one to need several days to recover from a rough journey by ship to England; almost exactly four centuries later, the same symptoms were observed in Queen Victoria's future husband Prince Albert when he arrived in England for his wedding.[12] He, too, needed several days to recover from the rough journey, and several festivities planned to receive him as the monarch's future spouse had to be cancelled.[13].

Margaret's sickness is not the only focus of interest in this boat journey; that this illness made her unable to walk and William had to carry her ashore has caused led historians, especially in the twentieth and twenty-first century, to speculate about the nature of their relationship. In itself, William carrying his future queen was simply a gentlemanly act, seeing to it his future queen was taken care of in the best possible way. Since this was his most important task while heading the entourage to bring her to England, there is nothing very remarkable about it, and at the time, nobody thought it particularly noteworthy.

In later centuries, however, speculation began about William being romantically and sexually interested in Margaret, or else using her romantic and sexual interest in him for his own

What is Better than a Good Woman?

nefarious plans. Alice's importance to both William and Margaret is diminished by this slanderous story. Today, while the idea of any sexual or romantic relationship between William and Margaret is usually dismissed, Alice's importance still suffers from the effects of several centuries of belief in it.

Primary sources from that time indicate that Margaret did not show any sort of interest in William except as her servant. Those sources suggest that far from Margaret considering Alice as a danger to any interest she supposedly had in William, she never had any such interest in him at all. At least one modern historian considers that far from having any sexual interest in William, or simply accepting Alice into her close circle solely for his sake, Margaret considered the marquess and marquesse as substitute parents in the strange new land she found herself in, and that she trusted them to advise her without any ulterior motives.[14]

This is most likely true. Margaret was born in the same year that Alice married William; she was therefore young enough to be their daughter. Such feelings would therefore be perfectly explicable for both parties, and explain the intergenerational friendship very well. Their actions over the next years suggest that this is a very plausible reading of their relationship, much more so than anything steamier.

Even as early as April 1445, Margaret appeared to be happy that she had Alice and William to rely on. Usually, her reliance on William is stressed far more than that on Alice, partly due to the long-standing if faulty tradition of something untoward existing between them, or just developing at that time. But it was Alice, rather than William, who was Margaret's main support at that time. Acting as her lady-in-waiting, she would have counselled her about English politics, informed her of the personalities of courtiers, of cross-currents between them, and similar important but informal insights. We have no documents actually spelling this out, but we know that this is what usually happened when a new

Alice's Relationship with Margaret of Anjou

consort arrived in a country, and Margaret was soon to give Alice first presents in gratitude for her help during her first months as queen.[15] The ramifications of this have been ignored, even though they are fairly obvious: it meant that Margaret's knowledge of the English court, its courtiers and even all of what had happened in the previous years, was coloured by Alice's opinion. Even if Alice genuinely tried to inform Margaret of only the facts, without any bias, some interpretation of events would have been included.

Of course, Alice was not Margaret's only lady-in-waiting, so Margaret did not get her information about her new kingdom, her new husband and those around him solely from Alice. It is well-known, for example, that the Duchess of York, Cecily, was also quite close to the new queen in her early years,[16] and given that she and Alice were opposed on many if not most political issues, Margaret would have received a more rounded picture than she would have, had Alice been her only informant.

Even so, Margaret was particularly close to Alice, and therefore presumably gave more weight to her statements than to anyone else's. This meant that in 1445, Alice must have believed she had reached the zenith of her power, far beyond what she or anyone could have expected: a marquess, so honoured she had been allowed to substitute for a queen, and having her queen's ear. With her husband being the king's closest advisor, it must have seemed that they could rise no higher. If they did not already know that this would make them powerful enemies, more powerful than any they had had before, they would soon find out.

Still, such foreboding was not at the forefront of the couple's thinking in 1445, as they prepared for the king's and new queen's wedding. With Margaret recovered, the preparations for the wedding started in earnest.[17] Though handymen had been working on making everything ready for weeks, as had citizens who were involved in displays that were to be given on the days of the wedding and the coronation.

What is Better than a Good Woman?

In the meantime, king, future queen and those around them were involved with the traditions surrounding the meeting of the two protagonists, both intimate but structured by traditions and expectations. William helped Henry VI arrange a 'surprise' meeting with his new bride, in which the king, dressed as a squire, gave Margaret a letter from her new husband, and while she read it, got the first view of his future wife.[18] This little plan went without a hitch, all those involved playing their part well. Alice and William would not have been asked if they were interested in being involved in the wedding itself and Margaret's coronation, their presence and help in arranging it simply being accepted as a matter of course. They had been involved at court for long enough that they would not have expected anything else.

It is quite possible Alice was given an important part in Margaret's coronation, something that many nobles would have envied. If she was given such a position, it would have also suggested to everyone of importance her place in the queen's affections, as well as in her household. However, since there is only scant evidence about the coronation, this must remain guesswork. Though Alice herself seems to have been delighted with her own new-found importance in politics through her closeness to the queen, there were many people, especially nobles, who resented it. This is hardly surprising. However, for Alice, it was made worse by the fact that her husband had the ear of the king, so that many considered that William and Alice between them controlled king and queen for their own benefit.[19]

It did not help that shortly after the wedding, the extremely unfavourable terms of the marriage contract became known, especially the fact that England had to surrender Maine and Anjou and all English citizens who lived there had to return to England. Anger about this was understandable, particularly since it was kept a secret until after the marriage was done. William, being the

Alice's Relationship with Margaret of Anjou

man who had negotiated the contract, was a convenient focus for that anger.[20]

Most of the nobility would have been aware of what the marriage contract entailed, and none of them had spoken against it since it had been made,[21] though several had protested before it had been agreed. Now, no one would want to be seen as agreeing to it and being connected with what was widely seen as a disaster in the public mind. Blaming William for it was a way to damage him and attempt to curtail his power and importance. His influence on the king had already been inconvenient to many in the years leading up to the wedding, and after it had happened, it seemed likely only to increase, with the queen also being very well-disposed towards him and making his wife her closest confidante.

Public opinion was therefore already starting to turn, but in 1445 it might still have seemed a fairly unimportant development. Some rage would have been expected once the fact that England had surrendered Maine and Anjou became known, and William had, in fact, made arrangements he would not be blamed for anything before he went to negotiate the marriage contract. He and others associated with it might have therefore been unhappy with the opinion swinging against them, but considered it temporary, which at first it seemed to be.

The outrage did not seem to last very long in relation to William and Alice, but moved on. They were not personally considered particularly culpable; while William had negotiated the treaty, it was generally seen as the failure of a weak king. While it was very common at the time, and for long afterwards, to exempt this or any king from criticism aimed at him, instead deflecting it to his 'evil advisors',[22] William and Alice were not yet considered that at the time. They were seen as involved in it, but since the entourage to fetch Margaret from France had included many important nobles, no one was singled out.

What is Better than a Good Woman?

While there was ill will, it did not yet manifest itself in any violence or budding rebellion. It was not at all uncommon for any medieval government to go through periods of unpopularity, and it may not have seemed much more than that in 1445. While the people directly affected by the loss of Maine and Anjou, the people who lost their home, were naturally furious, many others considered it as a price that was to be paid for peace, and for having a new queen.

Even if what they must have initially considered their temporary unpopularity bothered William and Alice, they had more than enough favours from king and queen to comfort them. In 1445, they were the second most important couple in England, after the king and queen. For almost all of that year they were at court, Alice being busy with helping Margaret find her place as queen. Again, this means that a lot of Margaret's early queenship was based on Alice's advice and made Alice much more powerful than is usually accepted. While William's part in influencing the king is often expanded upon, and his supposed influence over Margaret is spoken about in works on Margaret's queenship, Alice is portrayed as a much less influential figure than she really was.

Gaining more political power

Alice enjoyed the same relationship with Margaret as William did with Henry. Though Margaret seemed to be a stronger personality than Henry, and therefore less likely to be influenced,[23] she was still only a teenager when she became queen. That she was therefore much more likely to be influenced than she would be in later years is not the argument usually made. Some modern works echo the sexist views of contemporary chroniclers,[24] presenting Margaret as easily influenced – but only by a succession of male advisors, starting with William, then the Duke of Somerset and after that Somerset's brother.

This makes Margaret being influenced sound rather sinister, but there was nothing at all remarkable in Margaret being advised by

Alice's Relationship with Margaret of Anjou

those close to her, any more than there was for Henry. Historically, it was a much better turn of events than a monarch or a consort acting according to their own whims, without consulting others. Moreover, neither Henry nor Margaret really had much of a choice but to rely on other people's advice. Henry had not had the time most other kings had to acquaint himself with court and courtiers before being thrust into the position of king. Even when his long minority was over, he could not simply do as he pleased, even had he been so inclined. The very fact he had needed others to govern for him while he had been a child meant that those men of power could not simply be ignored. It also meant that there were many factions at court, and that whoever Henry chose as his closest advisor, there would be those resentful of the choice.

Choosing William as his advisor was actually astute in one way, as William was not one of the men who had run the country while Henry was growing up, but someone Henry himself had chosen. This meant that his regents and those connected with them were angry, but at the same time not one of them felt more snubbed than another.

Similarly, Margaret naturally needed someone to advise her when she first arrived in England, as the courtiers about her and English politics were of course foreign to her. She needed someone who was actually involved in politics. Alice was a smart choice as advisor, as she was an experienced woman rather than an adolescent as Margaret herself was, and she had been in contact with the high and mighty of the realm since she herself had been an adolescent. She could explain to Margaret the current political situation and the personalities of the courtiers, detail how the current political situation had come to be as it was, and speak about the families of the nobility. That some bias would colour such explanations is obvious, but that does not mean Alice explicitly tried to influence Margaret to serve her own ambition. There is no evidence that Alice did anything but what she considered was best for Margaret

What is Better than a Good Woman?

and the kingdom at large, though it would only be logical if she also thought about the benefit for her own family.

Whether she and William intended it, they and their family did profit from their closeness to king and queen. There were gifts of jewels from Margaret to Alice, which are perhaps the most telling indicator of affection between the two women. While grants were often given to those in power, this was only partly to do with any personal feelings. Those close to the king and queen were more likely to receive more, but it was dangerous to hand out favours according to affection. So grants of lands or possessions did not necessarily reflect the personal feelings of the monarch and his spouse. However, jewels were seen as a personal gift. There could have been no pressure on Margaret to give such a gift to anyone she did not like. Those jewels were nevertheless extremely valuable, and as such a great indicator of what Alice's friendship was worth to the queen. Margaret started making such grants to Alice as soon as 1445 and continued until 1450.[25]

Their son also profited; first of all, when Henry Beauchamp, Duke of Warwick, died in June 1446, leaving his two-year-old daughter a ward of the crown. William decided to purchase the wardship from the king. This is recorded in 16 September 1446: 'William, marquis and earl of Suffolk, bought of late the keeping of Anne, daughter and heir of the said duke [Henry Beauchamp, Duke of Warwick].'[26] Henry, Duke of Warwick, had been one of the richest men in the realm, richer even than John, Duke of Somerset,[27] so that his daughter was one of the richest, if not actually the richest, heiress in the realm. Though the dukedom was in the male entail, and therefore little Anne only inherited an earldom, it was a prestigious one, which means that like the wardship of Margaret Beaufort, having it had multiple advantages for William and Alice, as well as for their then four-year-old son.

It could be argued that William's purchase of the wardship had nothing to do with his and Alice's position at court, since he paid money for it. We do not know how much William paid, but given how rich little Anne was and what wealth would therefore be in William and Alice's control after the purchase, we can assume that it was quite a lot. However, even if they paid a very fair price for it, it is still unlikely Henry would have agreed to them buying it if William had not been close to him, and possibly also, Alice close to his wife. He would pay close attention to who had what under his control and would have considered it dangerous if someone he did not trust completely had access to little Anne Beauchamp's wealth. Henry Beauchamp had moreover been Henry VI's closest friend.[28] They had grown up together, so the decision was not purely a political one for him, but personal as well. Though technically the wardship system was supposed to serve the children, in practice it very rarely did, and how their wealth was being managed was often completely ignored. With little Anne being his best friend's daughter, it is unlikely Henry would have been as cavalier about her well-being and the management of her lands as he might have been about any other wardship.

William and Alice would show much more interest in this wardship than in the one of little Margaret Beaufort's they had already held for two years at that point. They decided that their new ward would be brought up with their own son John, who was some two years older than his new companion.[29] Presumably, they intended for them to marry one day, when they were a little older. At least, William would later claim so, stating that he had told 'a large number of the lords that if the duke of Warwick's daughter had lived he had intended to marry his son to her'.[30] It could be argued that he was lying then, as he only said this when he was tried for treason, with one of the charges against him being that he wanted to unseat the king by marrying John to Margaret Beaufort, whom he unrightfully considered as in line to the throne. It was a defence that was easily checkable, and there would have been no point in him saying he had told many he wished to marry his son

What is Better than a Good Woman?

to Anne Beauchamp if he had not actually done so. Therefore, he and Alice presumably truly did hope to make Anne their daughter-in-law one day.

All they actually did in 1446 was take custody of the child. She was moved to Ewelme, there to live with Alice's son in the nursery.[31]. We can assume that Alice saw to it that Anne, much like John, was given only the best, and took special care of her establishment in their household. Whether she left court to do so we do not know, but she is not mentioned in any of the material we have reporting what went on at court in 1446, so it seems likely. Alice was surely pleased, not only in securing a good future marriage for her son, but also by her son getting a playmate who was of his own standing that meant he did not grow up alone.

Though Alice and William were most likely planning to marry the children, they never seemed to try and actually make them go through a marriage ceremony. In 1446, of course, they would have been too young but technically, both John and Anne would have been old enough by fifteenth-century standards, to go through such a ceremony in 1448, age six and four respectively, this did not happen.

This fact has sometimes been taking to mean that William was in fact lying, that he and Alice never actually meant to marry their son to Anne Beauchamp, but always wanted him to marry Margaret Beaufort, but that does not explain why they did not instead arrange for a marriage ceremony to be enacted between them at the first possible moment. Presumably, they simply wanted what they considered best for their son and thought he should be old enough to understand what was happening when he actually married, not do it as a child. In 1446, they could afford to wait. Anne Beauchamp would not officially come of age, and therefore be able to have control over her own lands, until she was fourteen, so that there were still twelve years during which to arrange the ceremony. There was no sign they would be losing power and

Alice's Relationship with Margaret of Anjou

influence with the king and queen and therefore be stripped of Anne's wardship. They had all the time they needed.

The year 1446 would, however, prove to be their last comparatively peaceful year together. By the beginning of 1447, trouble was brewing,[32] trouble in which William and Alice both were at least claimed to be involved, though the evidence they were is very sketchy. It started when Henry VI's uncle Humphrey, Duke of Gloucester, was accused of treason in February.

Despite his wife's disgrace and imprisonment in 1441[33] and Humphrey's withdrawal from court following it, he had remained an important figure. He remained popular with the commoners and was ready to give his opinion on matters of state if he thought it was warranted. In 1444, he had not hesitated to make his opinion about his nephew's marriage to Margaret of Anjou known.[34] He was not the only one who did that, but he was doubtlessly the most influential. When he also spoke against the terms of the marriage treaty, making clear that he thought it was shameful England had given up Anjou and Maine, he was in open conflict with his nephew's government, without having done anything that could in any way be construed as treasonous. It did put him in open conflict with many others at court, such as William himself, which was why many considered the treason charge that came against him in February 1447 to be fabricated. Many suspected that William, as the one who had actually negotiated the marriage treaty which had so upset Humphrey, had been behind this charge, convincing the king to accuse his uncle of treason. Other voices blamed the young queen, saying she wished no one who had been so against her becoming Henry's wife to be left alive.[35]

It is quite likely that both William and Margaret were happy that someone so obviously opposed to them and their political efforts no longer had any influence, but the evidence for them actually convincing Henry VI to accuse him of treason is scant. Henry was now an adult and had shown before he was able to act independently.

What is Better than a Good Woman?

The fact he often appeared somewhat childlike in his trust of his advisors, not only William, and seemed not to understand, or did not want to understand, that they might be advising him in their own best interests, has led to some to conclude he was utterly incapable of making his own decisions. The fact that several years later he struggled with serious mental health issues and at times could not even take care of himself seems to corroborate this.

In this case, however, it seems that it was actually Henry who made the decision to accuse his uncle of treason,[36] though how much support he found for this from William, Margaret, and in fact Alice, we do not know. They were not the only ones who would eventually profit if Humphrey was executed for treason,[37] so that, if influences on Henry to make this decision are explored, other nobles should be named as well, most notably Alice's cousin Cardinal Henry Beaufort.[38]

Most contemporaries did not blame Henry or the cardinal, but Margaret and William, and in some cases Alice as well. The accusations against her were much more low-key than those against her husband, but they were made.[39] There is no evidence she left court or in any other way abandoned her position at her husband's and her queen's side in the face of them. Instead, she stayed at court as the treason trial of Humphrey, Duke of Gloucester was prepared. Tempers were running high, but as it turned out there would be no trial. Humphrey was arrested on 20 February, but he did not live to stand trial. On his way to do so, he died on 23 February 1447.

It is generally accepted today that he died of natural causes, as was claimed then, but the most widespread belief at the time, as reported by the *Croyland Chronicle*, was that Humphrey had been poisoned.[40] No individuals were named, though in the following years William's name would be bandied about as his murderer[41] and, by 1450, Alice presented as his willing accomplice.[42]

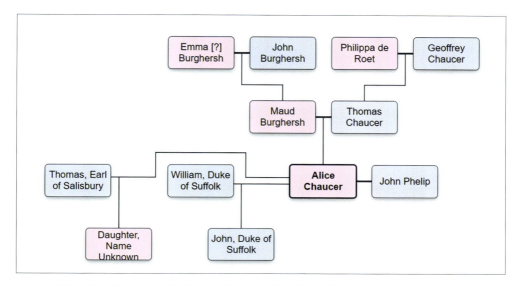

Alice's family tree, including her three husbands and her children.

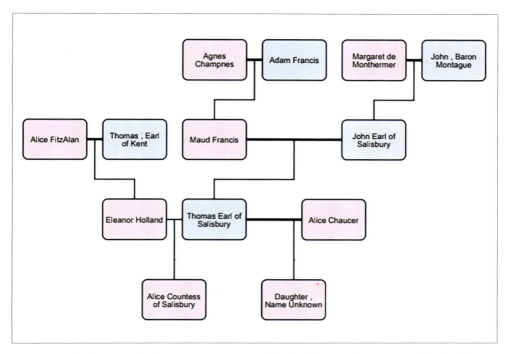

The family tree of Thomas Montacute, Earl of Salisbury, Alice's second husband.

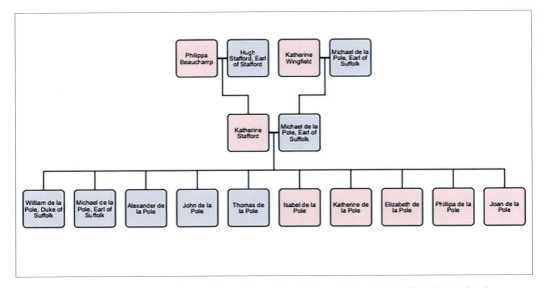

The family tree of William de la Pole, Earl and later Duke of Suffolk, Alice's third husband.

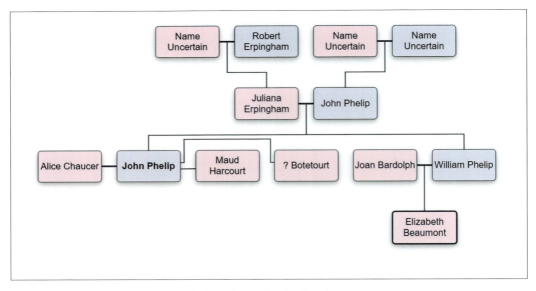

The family tree of John Phelip, Alice's first husband.

The effigies of Michael de la Pole, 2nd Earl of Suffolk **(1367-1415)** and his wife Katherine Stafford. They were the parents of Alice's third husband William de la Pole. There is no evidence Alice ever met them and they were both dead when Alice married William.

Coat of arms of Michael de la Pole, 2nd Earl of Suffolk of Wingfield Castle in Suffolk (or of his son William de la Pole, 1st Duke of Suffolk (1396-1450)), detail from a misericord, circa 1480, on the south side of the chancel of East Harling Church, Norfolk. (**Colin / Wikimedia Commons / CC BY-SA 4.0**)

Above: A mural depicting the procession of pilgrims of *The Canterbury Tales*, the most famous work of Alice's grandfather, the poet Geoffrey Chaucer. D*etail from mural by Ezra Winter, 1939. (Library of Congress)*

Opposite, left: Michael de la Pole sr, the grandfather of Alice's third husband. A controversial figure, he eventually died abroad, having been exiled as a traitor. (Library of Congress)

Opposite, right: King Henry V, the king who led the campaign into France in which Alice's first husband died. (Library of Congress)

Opposite, below: The siege of Mortagne near Bordeaux, 1377, one of the many sieges of the Hundred Years War. From Jean de Wavrin's *Recueil des Chroniques d'Angleterre*.

Below: The Battle of Agincourt, a famous English victory of the Hundred Years War. The French fighter Charles d'Orléans was captured and imprisoned after it; he would spend some time in Alice's household in later years. Also significantly for Alice, during the battle Michael de la Pole, 3rd Earl of Suffolk, died, leaving his title to his younger brother William, Alice's eventual third husband.

Left: The siege of Orléans, which saw the birth of the legend and eventual sainthood of Jeanne d'Arc. Alice's second husband Thomas Montacute, Earl of Salisbury, died at the beginning of the siege. A highly romanticised work by Frech painter Jules-Eugène Lenepveu (1819-1898). *La Pucelle* did not wear plate mail.

Below: The Battle of Jargeau. Led by Alice's eventual third husband William de la Pole, Earl of Suffolk, the English forces suffered a defeat. William was imprisoned; his brother John died during the battle.

Above left: Henry VI of England, to whom Alice and her third husband William became parental figures. The picture states that Henry was king not only of England but of France, a claim which led to escalating warfare during his childhood.

Above right: Henry VI and his guardian Richard Beauchamp, from the Rous Roll.

Henry VI's coronation as a young child. Henry VI was crowned both King of England and King of France before he was ten years old, but the pressure of trying to fulfil both roles against all odds played a part in causing the mental illness he suffered from as an adult.

Above: The wedding of Henry VI and Margaret of Anjou, a union that Alice's third husband William de la Pole had a big part in arranging.

Left: Philip the Good, Duke of Burgundy. The duke was well known for his expensive festivities and colourful court life. He tried to seduce Alice at a wedding they both attended in 1424, while she was married to Thomas Montacute, Earl of Salisbury. Alice did not think much of his attempts to do so and told him.

Right: Picture from a manuscript held in the British Library, in which over one hundred of Charles d'Orléans' poems are kept, as well as some by 'an English friend'. These were almost certainly penned by William de la Pole and dedicated to Alice.

Below: The Jack Cade rebellion, which erupted after the murder of Alice's third husband William de la Pole. Alice herself was seen as a high-ranking enemy by the rebels, who called for her to be charged with treason. 'Jack Cade Rabblement' by Keeley Halswelle, 1867. (Acquired as part of the Whitehead Gift by Bury Art Museum)

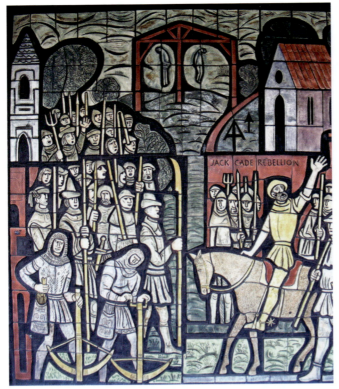

Left: A representation of the Jack Cade rebellion, showing nicely that the rebels were all meant to be of low-standing, as seen by their choice of weapons. Completed in 1965 by Adam Kossowski, 'The History of the Old Kent Road' is a mammoth 1,000-square-foot mural.

Below: Pembroke Castle, associated with the title of Earl of Pembroke. Alice's husband William held it from 1447 onwards, making Alice Countess of Pembroke, but her son John did not inherit the Pembroke title, as it was taken from him after his father's murder.

Queen Elizabeth, the controversial wife of Edward IV of England. Alice was one of the very few people of standing in England who did not take a side, either for or against her, after Edward had secretly married her.

Richard, Duke of York, a possible suspect behind the orchestration of the murder of Alice's third husband. Alice eventually made peace with him and married her son John to Richard's daughter Elizabeth. Her personal feelings about him are not known, though there are suggestions her son John did not like him.

Above: The Battle of Tewkesbury, fought when Alice was almost 67 years of age.

Below: The Battle of Towton, which is considered the bloodiest battle on English soil. Alice's son John fought in this battle, but survived without any injury.

Above right: Margaret Beaufort, Alice's daughter-in-law, wife of her son John for a time while both were still children. The marriage was dissolved before either John or Margaret were 11 years of age. Little is known of the relationship, if ever there was any, between Alice and Margaret after that. Even while the marriage still existed, there does not seem to have been much contact between the youthful couple or their mothers.

Right: Coat of arms of John, Earl of Lincoln, Alice's oldest son. He was created Earl of Lincoln in 1467, when he was only four years old.

Below: Wallingford Castle, an important keep in the 15th century, of which Alice was constable for a while after being widowed for the third time.

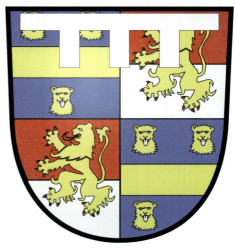

A window depicting medieval coats of arms at Montacute House, which was built on lands once belonging to the family of Alice's second husband, Thomas Montacute. The house itself was built around a century after Alice's death. (Courtesy of IDS.photos under Creative Commons 2.0)

Alice's effigy in the church at Ewelme, where her parents and possibly her daughter, were also buried.

Alice's tomb, including an effigy that was almost certainly worked from life, was planned by her before her death, and at the very least begun, if not finished, in her lifetime. It is a rare surviving example of a transit tomb, which shows the deceased as she was in life on top and as a corpse in a separate chamber beneath.

Modern view of the almshouse at Ewelme. It was founded by Alice and her husband William in the late 1430s, and Alice supported it for the rest of her life. (Courtesy Joanna Arman, from *Margaret of Anjou: She-Wolf of France*)

The village of Ewelme, where Alice was born and where she spent a large part of her life, as a child, a wife, and eventually a widow and grandmother. She was also buried in the church of the village.

Interior of Ewelme Church. (Courtesy of Joanna Arman)

Alice's Relationship with Margaret of Anjou

There is no evidence to support such a view, and no evidence that Humphrey died of anything but a heart attack. Even so, it was a conspiracy theory that gained traction, and though still not placing William at the centre of it, it definitely marked the beginning of him, and, by extension, Alice, becoming widely despised figures. Neither of them seemed to realise the extent of this, or how dangerous it could get. That this did not occur to either of them is rather baffling, since Duke Humphrey's example showed how quickly even someone of higher standing than them, who was widely popular to boot, could fall from grace. It also shows the extent of their trust in King Henry and Queen Margaret; they seemed to believe that something like it could never happen to them.

It is impossible to decide whether William or Alice was the more involved in politics and for whom it meant more, but Alice's actions after William's death make the question inevitable. Alice's withdrawal from politics after William's death, which will be discussed in Chapter 15, could very well have been simple prudence and born of a wish to be always close to her son. It is notable that she never again ignored budding dangers in a way she and William did in 1447, perhaps she learned a lesson William didn't. He ignored their unpopularity and insisted on rising further at court, ignoring all warning signs.

Lessons learned or ignored, in 1447 their rise became ever steeper. Their enemies, such as Richard, Duke of York, lost power,[43] with the leader of their faction, Duke Humphrey, dead. In William's defence, if it was really him who ignored the growing dangers to him and his family, it would have been very easy to do so. Favoured by the king, his wife a favourite of the queen, constantly given royal presents, they were on top of the world, untouchable, the second couple in the realm. But if they saw themselves like that, so did others.

On 11 April 1447, Alice's first cousin once removed, Cardinal Henry Beaufort, died. Since he was in his seventies, it would

What is Better than a Good Woman?

have been a loss for Alice though hardly an unexpected one, not one that could be taken as an omen of anything worse; but the following years would bring strife, difficulties and heartache. There were not only political setbacks. At some point in late 1447 or early 1448, Alice became ill.

We do not know what she was suffering from, but it must have been something serious; two grants from the pope survive, dated 8 June 1448.[44] The first of these was an indult to 'Alice, marchioness and countess of Suffolk ... who is of weak health, that her confessor may dispense her to eat flesh and milk meats, by advice of her physician, during Lent and on other fast days'. The next one, issued on the same day, was an indult to her to 'to choose her confessor, who may absolve her, even in cases generally reserved to the apostolic see, once only, and grant her plenary indulgence, once only, in the hour of death'.

It was quite common for high-born nobles to get a papal indult to eat meat in Lent, usually on the pretext of weak health, as it was for them to get an indult to choose a confessor for the time of their death. The latter was, however, only issued when the person in question was old and could therefore expect to die at any time, or else sick. It was not one that was valid for the rest of her life, but only for the immediate future. The indults being issued together also point towards her being genuinely ill, with the first grant intended to help her recover and the second one being for the safety of her immortal soul if she did not.

For these indults to be issued by June 1448, the application for them would have to have been sent off several months before, which is confirmed by one of them being for her eating meat in Lent, two months before. Though technically, the indult also mentioned 'other feast days', there were not very many of those between Easter and Advent, and certainly not enough to be worth applying for such an indult. Therefore, either Alice must have been so sick it was expected she would be still ailing by advent and, or else she or William sent to Rome for the indult before Lent, and it was a retroactive dispensation when it arrived. This seems rather more likely, as we know that Alice suddenly drops from all records pertaining to court life in early 1448.

It was thought at the time that meat was particularly helpful for patients who had lost a lot of blood, so that this might narrow down the possible case of her illness. Alice might have simply had an accident of some sort, resulting blood loss, but this would have been recorded somewhere. Similarly, given that she lived for nearly thirty years after receiving these indults, it seems unlikely she had some disease that, by itself, caused an extreme loss of blood, as this would have been all but untreatable at the time.

The most likely reason for loss of blood was that Alice had a miscarriage in late 1447 or early 1448, one so damaging she was considered on the brink of death. By then Alice was forty-three years old. Though old to be pregnant, it would not be impossible. Since there was no reliable contraception, and using contraception was considered a sin in any case, it is perfectly possible that Alice conceived a child in late 1447. A catastrophic outcome did not even need to be connected to her age. Pregnancies and births were highly dangerous in the fifteenth century, and a near-fatal blood loss could have happened to a woman at any age. It would make perfect sense if this was what happened to Alice in 1448.

If Alice truly lost a pregnancy in 1448, this would not only have been physically extremely dangerous but also an emotional blow. If she and William had hoped for a younger sibling for John, they would have known after this loss that it was never to be. It seems unlikely they would have wanted to risk it, too, if Alice nearly died when miscarrying.

Even if this was not the cause of Alice's illness, this must have been a trying time for her, William and even John, at nearly six old enough to understand what was happening. Presumably, given what we know of them, Henry VI and Queen Margaret

What is Better than a Good Woman?

would have made sure masses were read for Alice's recovery, and William, too, would have made such arrangements.

Presumably due to Alice's illness, William spent the first part of the year away from court,[45] but in spring he was once more at Henry's side. When Alice was recovering, it would have been William's duty to return to court. Both he and Alice would have wanted this; Henry VI would have understood his wish to be at his critically ill wife's side, but if William wanted to remain his primary advisor he could not afford to be gone from court too long. Henry needed close advisors, and if William did not fill the position of his closest man for long, someone else would fill the vacancy. Given the mood in those years, this would not only be a blow for William's ambition, and possibly Alice's ambition for him, but could actually have been dangerous for them both.

William had to leave Alice's side once she was on the mend. William's situation might have been made slightly more bearable by the fact that both king and queen must have been worried about Alice as well, so that they would have made allowance for any absent-mindedness on his part.

8

ALICE AS A DUCHESS

Whatever Alice was ailing from, she must have received comfort from an honour Henry VI chose to bestow on William that summer: an elevation to a dukedom,[1] the greatest honour he possibly could give him. To then dukedoms had been reserved only for royalty, by birth or marriage, which meant that for many, Henry making William a duke was taken as him signalling he saw him as quasi-royal. This would have caused jealousy and ill-will towards anyone without royal blood who received the honour, but it was seen as particularly undeserved in William's case. His comparatively unimpressive ancestry had been used as a jibe against him before 1448, but from then on, it was a massive part of the campaign to destroy him. Alice's ancestry, too, came under fire, as while it was generally recognised that the dukedom was a grant to William, from which she simply happened to profit, it was noted that her ancestry did not entitle her to hold such a distinguished title any more than William's did.

Even though the grant immediately came with trouble, William and Alice must have been pleased. They could not rise any higher, having a quasi-royal title from then on. It was a dazzling rise even for William; for Alice, it must have seemed all but unbelievable.

What is Better than a Good Woman?

Perhaps it was this rise in their fortunes, perhaps it was the fear of how deeply they could fall, with many people being clearly against them, or perhaps it was simply Alice's close brush with death in the beginning of the year, but shortly after becoming duke and duchess, William and Alice chose to make extensions to their almshouse at Ewelme. Their order for this still survives. Its beginning is particularly interesting:

> In the name of God. Let it known to all true Christian people, the content of this present foundation seeing, hearing and understanding. We, William de la Pole, Duke of Suffolk, and Alice my wife, Duchess of Suffolk, desire health in body, grace in soul, and everylasting joy to obtain. Because all Christian people meekly and devotely confiding by the upholding and maintaining of done service. And by the exercise of works of mercy in the state of this deadly life in the last dreadful day of doom they shall with the mercy of our Lord take their part and portion of joy and bliss. With them that shall be found aught of venom have a great and a fervent desire and a busy charge in mind to uphold and maintain done service and to exercise fulfil and to do works of mercy before the end of this deadly life.[2]

Sadly, this order does not actually reveal what changes he and Alice actually chose to make to the almshouse, only a suggestion that it was being expanded. The wish for 'health in body' suggests Alice's illness had been a factor in their turning towards religion again. It was a reminder, at the very height of their power, of death and the transience of life. It was something that was on William's mind in these first months after he received his dukedom, when he decided to write a will in January 1449. It would be a mistake, however, to connect such thoughts too closely with Alice's illness. While they had been reminded of the importance of having their

Alice as a Duchess

affairs in order in case something unforeseen happened, it is also possible that William simply thought his elevation to a dukedom required him to touch up an earlier will to make sure that there could be no doubt thrown on it and his wife and son possibly disadvantaged in the event of his death. The medieval concept of the wheel of fortune, a reminder that a big rise could come before a big fall, would hardly have been unknown to William, and it might have been that, more than Alice's illness, which prompted him to write this will:

In the name of the Father, Son, and Holy Ghost, one God in three Persons, Be it known to all Christian men, that these presents shall hereafter have, or see, that I, William de la Pole, Dile, Marquis and Earl of Suffolk, in good health of body, and in my good mind, the seventeenth day of January, the twenty-seventh year of King Henry the Sixth, and of our Lord 1448, make my testament in the wise that followeth.

First, I bequeath my soul to the highness and mercy of Him that made it, and that so marvellously bought it with His precious blood; and my wretched body to be buried in my Charter-house at Hull, where I will my image, and stone be made, and the image of my best-beloved wife by me, she to be there with me if she lust; my said sepulture to be made by her discretion in the said Charter-house, where she shall think best, in case be that in my days it not be made, nor begun, desiring, if it may, to lie so, as the masses that I have perpetually founded there for my said best-beloved wife and me, may be daily sung over me. And also the day of my funeral, and the day of my burying, that the charge thereof be byset upon poor creatures to pray for me, and in no pomps, nor pride of the world. Also I will, that my lands and goods be disposed after that that I have disposed them in my last will of the date of these presents. And only ordain my best-beloved

What is Better than a Good Woman?

wife my sole executrix, beseeching her, at the reverence of God, to take the charge upon her for the weal of my soul, for above all the earth my singular trust is most in her; and I will for her ease if she will, and else not, that she may take unto her such one person as she lust to name to help her in the execution thereof, for her ease, to labour under her, as she would command him.

And last of all, with the blessing of God, and of me as heartily as I can give it, to my dear and true son, I bequeath between him and his mother, love and all good accord, and give him her wholly. And for remembrance, my great balays to my said son.[3]

The earlier will William mentions in this one has not survived, so that we have no knowledge of how he wished his 'lands and goods be disposed'. We can only make guesses from the way they were distributed after his death. It is possible that given the circumstances of his death, changes were made then to what William had actually said in his will.

Even so, though not very illuminating about the legal aspect of William's bequests, it is an interesting document, particularly for a work about Alice, as Alice seems to be central to it. Naturally, as William's wife, it was only to be expected that he would mention her prominently in his will, but there was no need for him to make her the focus of the entire document, nor was that the normal custom. The will gives the impression of William only thinking of her, with their son being an afterthought.

This could be explained, of course, by the fact he was still only a small boy of six years old when William wrote this will, and had William lived to see him come of age, he would have changed his last wishes to include John more prominently. Though the single bequest to John, William's 'great balays [ruby ring]', seems fairly small, it was actually significant. Being his father's second son and

Alice as a Duchess

therefore not his heir, William had received the exact same bequest from his father Michael as he left to his own son.[4] It must have been the same ring, and therefore what looks at first glance like a slight was in fact a rather touching reminder of his own father and doubtless meant a lot to William. Nevertheless, John came second after Alice. The very fact that he felt the need to state he 'bequeath[ed] between him and his mother' his 'love and good accord', rather than just stating his love for his son without any qualification, suggests that his love for Alice was his predominant emotion when writing this will, and quite possibly in life as well.

The will was not only a testimony to William's affection for Alice. It is also testimony to the trust he put in her and her skills. He charged her with making all the arrangements for his funeral by herself, leaving her to work out the details, and he made her sole executrix of the will. It was fairly rare to only have a single executor, especially for wills that by necessity would require a lot of attention to detail concerning a great many possessions, the situation for any titled nobleman. William clearly thought Alice would be capable of performing the job, and as later events would show, his trust in her was not displaced. William had made the will simply as a precaution, not because he was worried or frightened for his life. It would not take long for him to be so.

Fall from grace

1449 was to prove a very difficult year for Alice, William and their small family. At first, it must have seemed as if everything was going their way. Richard, Duke of York, William's greatest opponent in political matters since the death of Humphrey duke of Gloucester, had been sent to Ireland, ostensibly to be regent there,[5] a promotion with a sting. It was a sign of trust, but it also took him away from court and the centre of power, leaving William without any obvious rival for the king's ear. However, even if that might have seemed like a fortunate decision for William and Alice, taking

What is Better than a Good Woman?

some pressure away from them and giving them the chance to win back the trust of the people in addition to keeping the trust of the king, it was to prove anything but. Shortly after the departure of Richard, Duke of York to Ireland, what could be called a smear campaign against William started.[6] It did not include Alice, though she was implicated by association, but it was quite vicious towards William himself.

In recent years, there has been a push to clear Richard, Duke of York of the charge of being the mastermind, or one of the masterminds, behind this campaign, but the evidence for him being at least involved is fairly compelling.[7] The few men who were charged eventually with passing on songs and poems disparaging William were all connected to Richard.

It was only with the start of this distribution of slurs and even songs against William that he really became unpopular.[8] Much has been made of William's unpopularity, particularly in modern scholarship, with the implication always being that while he did not deserve his fate, his own actions *and character* made him unpopular, and eventually caused his death. This theory does not hold up to much scrutiny, nor does the idea that Alice herself was extremely unpopular through her own actions and disposition. In fact, the opposite holds true. Neither she nor William were ever attacked on their personal merits[9] and none of the charges came from anyone who had ever met them who did not have a political axe to grind. As personalities, both of them seem to have been very attractive and well-liked.

This did not help them in 1449, as the smear campaign was designed to make William's supposed political flaws larger than life and obscure the real man behind them, to turn him into a villain. This was extremely successful, and after a few months the hatred against William, and hence Alice, became obvious in the population.[10] This must have been frightening for them both, but neither of them were cowards and they faced the hostility in the

Alice as a Duchess

only way they could: continuing to do what they could for king and country, no matter how much it was disparaged, and hoping it would all blow over.

It would not; and it was not just politically that it was to be a sad year for Alice. In June 1449, Anne Beauchamp died at Ewelme at the age of five.[11] What she died of is no longer known, but child mortality was extremely high at the time and for very long afterwards, so that while doubtlessly tragic, there is nothing sinister about it. Despite all the charges thrown against William in the year to come, nobody ever suggested little Anne's death was anything but natural, perhaps of a childhood illness that is easily curable today but was fatal at the time.

Her death would have been harder to endure for Alice than William. She had been more involved as her guardian for the last three years. It was also sad and shocking to John, who had presumably been raised with the expectation of marrying her one day. While John must have sad at losing his little playmate, his parents would have known that it meant his future was once more rather uncertain. As long as Anne was considered his future bride, he had a bright and secure future in front of him, not just as the future Duke of Suffolk as his father's heir but as Earl of Warwick in his wife's name, and owner of large swathes of land and a fortune in her name as well. Given the ever-increasing hatred of his parents in the population and the nobility, it would not have seemed very likely that a similarly great match for him could be secured anytime soon. Perhaps due to this, and due to them wanting to keep their son away from the hatred directed at them, William and Alice did not immediately seek a new match for their son. Perhaps they hoped the hostility would blow over and considered it prudent to keep their heads down.

After Anne's death, Alice stayed in Ewelme with her son for the rest of the year. It has sometimes been suggested that Alice's failure to be at William's side in court as often from 1448 onward meant

What is Better than a Good Woman?

that she could not cope with the pressure.[12] This is possible but is not the most straightforward explanation. Alice was ill in 1448 and probably was not yet strong enough to face court life for the first months after becoming a duchess. That she joined William again in late 1448 and early 1449 suggests it was not that she disliked the pressure, simply that she had needed a long while to recover. Perhaps she did not want to face the hostilities. It could, however, have been fear, not for herself but for John. By summer 1449, the English population was becoming not only hostile but increasingly violent against William,[13] and was starting to lambast the king for his trust in and reliance on him.[14] This was more dangerous than anything; as long as it was only against William himself, the king could reasonably be expected to protect him. The moment such protection became a danger to the king himself, William would be considered expendable.

It is strange that William himself does not seem to have realised this, or perhaps he did not want to realise it. His actions show complete trust in the king, a touching if less than worldly-wise conviction that nothing would happen to him due to the king's protection. It seems, however, that Alice did not share that confidence, or if she did, she still did not want to stake her son's life on it. She might have thought that if William was actually protected by the king, the enraged population might want to find another way to hurt him, and hurting his only son and heir would be the obvious way to do it. Perhaps she made that decision together with William, and his faith in the king did not extend to a trust that his protection would stop the population from harming his family, and it would be better for Alice to be out of the limelight and for her to make all the arrangements in person to see that whatever happened, nothing would harm John.

Interestingly, whatever William thought, neither then nor in the years to come did Alice ever show any apprehension about her own personal safety. Maybe she, too, trusted in the king to

Alice as a Duchess

protect her and simply did not want to leave even a slight chance of something happening to her son, or she was very brave and did not let any fears she might have had for herself affect her actions.

The decision to stay with John was an intelligent one. Things were turning very nasty very quickly against William, with rumours of an uprising in London and William being one of the main targets. He was being used as a scapegoat for everything that happened:

The Rote is ded,
the Swanne is goone,
The firy Cressett hath lost his lyght;
Therfore Inglond may make gret mone,
Were not the helpe of Godde almyght
The castelle is wonne where care begowne.
The Portecolys is leyde adowne
Iclosid we have oure welevette hatte,
That keveryd us from mony stormys browne
The White Lioun is leyde to slepe,
Thorouz the envy of the Ape clogge;
And he is bownden that oure dore shuld kepe,
That is Talbott oure goode dogge.
The Fisshere hathe lost his hangulhooke;
Gete theym agayne when it wolle be.
Oure Mylle - saylle wille not abowte,
Hit hath so longe goone emptye.
The Bere is bound that was so wild,
For he hath lost his ragged staffe.
The Carte nathe is spokeles,
For the counseille that he gaffe.
The Lily is both faire and grene;
The Coundite rennyth not, as I wene.
The Cornysshe Chowgh offt with his trayne Rex.
Hath made oure Egulle blynde.

What is Better than a Good Woman?

The White Harde is put out of mynde,
Because he wolle not to bem consent;
Therfore the commyns saith is both trew and kynde
Bothe in Southesex and in Kent
The Water - Bowge and the Wyne - Botelle,
With the Vetturlockes cheyne bene fast.
The Whete - yere wolle theym susteyne
As longe as he may endure and last
The Boore is farre into the west,
That shold us helpe with shilde and spere
The Fawkoun fleyth, and hath no rest,
Tille he witte where to bigge his nest.[15]

This was one of the more harmless examples of poems circulating at the time. William is blamed for the death of a man dying of natural causes in 1432, solely because this man died impoverished due to the French wars. The very fact that William had fought by his side for all but one year should have been enough to show the utter absurdity of this charge, but clearly, facts no longer mattered.

If William or King Henry VI had reacted the moment the campaign against him started, what happened next might have been prevented, but it is doubtful. William's fate was sealed from the moment he became a duke and, as has been pointed out by Henry's biographer Lauren Johnson,[16] Henry's very personality made something of the sort all but inevitable. In any case, by late 1449 it was too late for anything to be done about it, and this must have been fairly obvious to William. By the time Parliament opened in November 1449,[17] the hostility towards William had begun to spread to all those associated with him as well, and it was in that month that his treasurer, Adam Moleyns, was forced to resign, unable to stand the extreme animus against himself and his employer.

It was then that William surely realised just how bad everything had become, and that he could do nothing to make things better.

Alice as a Duchess

In fact, this is true in two ways: nothing he did would diffuse the situation, and doing nothing was his best bet to weather the storm. Men were starting to disobey him, and this disobedience was blamed on him. When Parliament adjourned over Christmas, William left court and went home to Alice and his son.

Though they would have celebrated Christmas with at least some pomp and circumstance to please their son and to also please themselves, it could hardly have been a season of good tidings of great joy for Alice and William. Following the violence that was by that time habitually visited upon those associated with William, they must have known there was a very real chance of it being their last Christmas together, of something happening to either or both of them.

It was probably with that in mind that they decided to make the best arrangements they could for their son, so that whatever happened, he would have as secure a future as they could offer him at the time: nearly six years after being granted the wardship of Margaret Beaufort, they decided to marry her to John.[18] This decision is one that has been much discussed, with a question mark hanging over who decided, Alice or William or both, when exactly it happened, and, in recent years, if it even happened at all. The last question can be answered definitively: there is proof that John and Margaret married,[19] though due to their extreme youth all the time this marriage existed, it was never more than a marriage in words, but it is recorded in the Papal Calendar that this marriage took place.[20]

The other questions about it are not so easily answered. As mentioned above, it has long been considered a fact that William was eager to marry Margaret to his son,[21] but this is not borne out by evidence. Conversely, there has also been a suggestion he did not want it at all, and it was Alice, after his imprisonment, who quickly saw to it that her son was married to the little girl still in her wardship. Given the complete trust William had shown in Henry VI, it could be that he did not actually see the need to salvage for John what he could in the face of an uncertain future,

What is Better than a Good Woman?

and it was Alice who insisted on it. We do know that the marriage was made before William was arrested on 28 January.[22] We also know it happened after Christmas 1449, so probably after it became apparent to Alice and William just how rapidly everything was falling apart. On 9 January 1450, William's treasurer was murdered,[23] a killing celebrated by a mob that was also baying for William's blood. It was becoming clear that William, and even Alice herself, might not survive the public's wrath, and that the best they could do for their son at that moment was make sure he was husband to a rich wife and by marriage more connected to the powerful Beaufort family than he had previously been by relation. Making this connection was the main reason for their hasty arrangement of this marriage, more so than Margaret's wealth: the hope of giving their son a powerful protector.

For the marriage to be legal, a dispensation from the pope allowing the children to marry despite being related in the prohibited degree was required. Usually, a wedding would have had to wait until such a dispensation arrived, but there was no time for that in January 1450. Since John and Margaret would not be old enough to consummate their marriage for several years in any case, William and Alice probably thought that it was a detail that they could pay attention to later, and in fact, it later fell to Alice to do this.[24]

Presumably, their wedding ceremony was the first time John and Margaret met. It also seems to have been the last time they met for several years. It would have been dangerous for Margaret to be too closely associated with William and Alice, as in fact it was already dangerous for John. Nobody would have had an interest in unnecessarily putting her in danger as well.

Since Parliament reassembled on 22 January,[25] shortly after the wedding must have taken place, this ceremony was probably the last time William ever saw his son. It might also have been the last time Alice saw William. With what had happened in the last few

Alice as a Duchess

months, especially after Christmas, they must have known there was a good chance that they would never see each other again. There were cries, becoming ever louder, to have William tried and executed for high treason,[26] and even if he still clung to the belief that the king would do all he could to protect him, he must both have known that there was a chance he would not be able to, even if he was willing, without risk to himself.

With Alice's name appearing more and more in the condemnations of William, they would have also known that it was quite possible something could happen to her as well, though even if their enemies succeeded in having her tried and condemned for treason, they would have known that as a woman, she would not be executed. Perhaps William considered it his duty to face his enemies himself and by offering himself up to whatever it was his enemies wanted done, taking the pressure away from his wife and son; that he knew what he had to do, or thought he had to do, and probably told Alice so before he left. They knew that this farewell could be the last. Perhaps Alice promised to be present should he be executed, to take care of their son, assured him of their love.

9

SUFFOLK'S MURDER

William stopped trying to weather the storm and instead threw himself on the mercy of king and Parliament. On 22 January, the first day Parliament reassembled, he made a speech to Henry VI, a speech that designed to pre-empt the treason charges he must have known were impending. This speech is recorded in the Parliament Rolls in its entirety.

It was clearly a passionate and well-thought-out speech, not one he made on the spur of the moment. Quite possibly, he discussed it with Alice. Even if he did not, she must have known what he was going to do upon returning to Parliament and must have waited with bated breath for news of how this speech went, what was happening in the capital.

It was not good news that she received, probably with a delay of some days. William's speech, as impassioned and doubtlessly heart-felt it had been, had not prevented treason charges being brought against him. On 28 January,[1] six days after he had attempted to clear himself of all charges before they were even brought, William was impeached by Parliament and shortly afterwards arrested and imprisoned in the Tower of London.

Though it cannot have been completely unexpected, it must still have seemed like a realisation of her greatest fears to Alice. William being executed as a traitor was no longer a remote possibility, a curse against him by his enemies, but something likely to happen. The list of highborn men, even of king's favourites, accused and tried for treason was a long one, even then; the list of such men being accused but acquitted was short. Alice must have known the most likely outcome was William being executed, leaving Alice a traitor's widow, their son disgraced and disinherited, and Alice in danger of being attainted as well.

Her fear must have been mixed with fury, as even if she tried, she could have hardly remained ignorant of the fact that William's arrest was celebrated by many, even with poems.[2]

Suffolk's trial for treason and Alice's reaction

Alice simply had to wait for what happened next, and perhaps, as the first week of February passed and she got no word of the charges against William being prepared or a trial proceeding, she hoped that arresting William and taking him out of the spotlight, giving the mob at least partially what they demanded, was all that would happen, that he would be quietly acquitted after a while. In fact, perhaps this is what Henry VI originally had in mind. Though the Tower of London is nowadays associated only with prison, it was not only that but also a royal residence in the fifteenth century. While William was there as a prisoner, it might have been as much to keep others out, to stop them from trying to form a lynch mob and kill him, as it was to keep him inside. He would have been kept in comfortable quarters, not in a dungeon, and perhaps Alice took some comfort from that.

William could send messengers and letters from the Tower even though imprisoned with a treason charge. In fact, men in his position were sometimes even allowed to have their wives visit them, but in William's case this would have been impossible. It would have been extremely dangerous for her to travel to London, as well as dangerous for their son to leave him behind. Alice and

What is Better than a Good Woman?

her son could not have left their manor at Ewelme at all during this time; they, too, were imprisoned in a golden cage, knowing that if they left, they were likely to face an angry mob.

Despite the fact William remained imprisoned for over six weeks,[3] the wrath against him did not dissipate. On the contrary, it seemed to get worse, with more and more people calling for the treason trial to go ahead. Henry VI caved under the pressure; on 13 March 1450, William was summoned to him to answer to the charges of having 'falsely and traitorously plotted, contrived, proposed, envisaged, performed and committed various high, great, heinous and horrible treasons'.

The charges against him had been put before the king on 12 February and again on 9 March[4] by nobles clearly impatient to cut their ties with him and Alice, lest they be dragged into the infamy surrounding them and by a House of Commons by then in a veritable frenzy trying to convict him.

Both sets of charges are recorded in the Parliament Rolls. The first set, presented to the king on 12 February, were very much based on pre-existing claims against William, which makes it hard to argue they were anything but a pretext used in 1450 to facilitate his fall from power. It basically listed all his actions in the previous years, most notably his negotiations to return his freedom to Charles, Duke of Orléans, and the ones for Henry VI and Margaret of Anjou's wedding, and attached the most negative interpretation to them.[5] That William's peers accused him of several actions they themselves had been involved in, such as the release of Maine and Anjou, and actions they had sworn only six years earlier not to blame on William,[6] must have infuriated Alice.

The charges by the House of Commons issued on 9 March[7] were less personally hurtful to Alice, as they did not come from men she and William had closely worked with, had even considered friends, such as Viscount Beaumont. This would not have made the charges any less alarming. William's earnest attempts to

Suffolk's Murder

make peace were described as treasonous. These charges, too, are completely recorded in the Parliament Rolls, and pretty much echo the ones made by the peers. Some of the charges were downright absurd, such as the last one, which claimed that William intended to turn the princes of Germany against Henry VI. Others took perfectly well-known facts and turned them against William, and by extension Alice.

No one really believed all of the charges against William, the nobles who would judge him once it came to trial would have known most if not all of the charges were fabricated. However, there were so many charges that even those most inclined to sympathy for William might have started to be doubt.

More material, not put before the king as a charge but simply as evidence of his supposedly bad character, was also circulated and recorded in the Parliament Rolls:

People fell from him, and worse [people] were encouraged to stay in the king's service and wars [?] worshipful taking without reproof or cowardice. The night before he was captured, he lay in bed with a nun whom he took out of her holy orders and defiled. Her name was Malyne de Cay, by whom he had a daughter who is now married to Stonor of Oxfordshire. He was coming from his position down to the place over the bridge past Jamet de Tille, which sinful abandonment [of his post] was not only the cause of his shameful capture but also of the death of his brothers and of many a notable person there [?] same time behaving badly [?] which is shameful to hear of in the case of a man who bears a noble title. And where he claims that he paid for his finance and ransom the sum of £20,000 and more, know in truth that he was [put to ransom for] 12,000 marks at the most, to which he sealed an agreement with the Frenchmen and his brother which we [?] at Oxford he stood as pledge for him etc.

What is Better than a Good Woman?

To whom falsely sworn, he let him die in prison. And because the sealed agreement lay in the hands of the French [?] and he could not by any scheming be quit of it without criticism (reproof) he therefore conspired with the duke of Orléans who was in his keeping and with the [?] Conace and Jamet de Tylly and others of the French camp to work for the release of the said duke of Orléans, so that he might have the sealed agreement back, accomplishing this without making other payments of finance, ransom or expenditure and taking in addition great sums in gifts and reward, and never redeemed the king or the lands, which matter shall be more fully declared hereafter in the future with the mercy of God.[8]

The list of charges was much longer, but these accusations, attacking William's relationship with his dead brother, were the most painful. This list also included Alice, which might have scared both her and William more than anything else. This mention is brief, but very clearly shows that she was considered complicit in most charges: 'Also where the said duke excuses himself and my lady his wife from the charge that they have always lived off the king and queen, it is not necessary to recall that article as the truth is so obvious.'[9]

Since this was not actually part of the official charges, it is not certain Alice knew of this, but it seems likely. She must have tried to be informed about everything that went on, and perhaps these accusations shocked her more than the official ones. They not only attacked her husband's character in ways it had not been attacked before, levelling charges of lewdness, cowardice and similar against him, they also included her own person.

William's speech before Henry VI in which he swore to being innocent is recorded, and presumably Alice would have had a report of it.[10] It was a brave speech, and probably it was an honest one. When addressing the treason charges, William said nothing

Suffolk's Murder

that is contradicted by any evidence, and many of his rebuttals are very much supported by it, such as the matter of John's marriage.

Interestingly, though some of the charges implicate Alice, William did not mention her at all. It was a common tactic for men on trial to protest their innocence by speaking about their flawless personal life, often mentioning wife and children. William did not; the only time he mentioned his family at all was to protest he had not originally meant to marry his son to Margaret Beaufort. William and Alice had often been involved together in politics, mentioned together in sources and had generally spent a lot more time together than many others in their position. Though, as discussed above, it has been suggested that Alice could not cope under the pressure and the couple had drifted apart somewhat since they had become duke and duchess,[11] this does not seem the most likely explanation for William's not mentioning her. Even if William and Alice had parted in conflict, William could still have introduced his son as testimony to his upright private life. His reticence might be because of the claim that his illegitimate daughter was conceived when he slept with a nun.[12] The accusation did not seem to hold much weight in the proceedings and was not addressed elsewhere, but it might also not actually count as slander against William, since it is perfectly possible that Jane actually was a nun's daughter.[13]

The charges against him, much like the explicit charges against Alice would be later, had been more or less free of any personal slurs until the supplementary accusations were read out in Parliament. Perhaps William figured addressing the political charges was more important, but there is another possibility: that he did not want to draw any attention to Alice, instead focusing all the public's wrath on him.

Usually, the wives of accused or convicted traitors were not in danger, though they did suffer from their husband's notoriety, particularly if they were executed.[14] In Alice's case, the fact she

What is Better than a Good Woman?

was actually closely connected with her husband's political life and had played a prominent role in it meant that William's disgrace imperilled her. Though she was not in danger of being executed, she and William would both remember what had happened to Eleanor Cobham nine years earlier. Perhaps, William refused to mention Alice mainly for that reason: to keep the focus on himself. Whether either had any hope that William could escape execution at that time is doubtful. Such hopes they had were vested in the king. But they knew there was only so much he could do without putting himself in danger.

The worst did not happen, not then. Four days after William had given his answers to the king and council, Henry summoned him as well as all the noblemen present to Parliament.[15] The matter of William was discussed, but no actual trial took place, a point that was stressed,[16] emphasising that William had not actually asked for a trial. Perhaps he realised that the moment a trial was held, nothing but a guilty verdict would be accepted by the population.

For all intents and purposes, the gathering on 17 March served as a trial,[17] with Henry presiding over it. Henry VI asked for the advice of his lords, but that was almost certainly only a formality, unlikely to influence the decision Henry was going to make regarding William: William was 'acquitted' of treason. He was not adjudged guiltless of the other charges and sentenced to five years in exile.[18]

Though doubtless a painful punishment for William, taking him away from his family, his home and, not least, his position of influence, this decision was made by the king to protect him.[19] It removed William from King Henry's court, so that his enemies had reached their goal of removing him from power. For the population, wanting to see him punished, it was clear that his way of life had been taken from him, if temporarily. It left the possibility open after his return of once more assuming a position of importance at King Henry's court. For this reason, the punishment was not received as intended by the population. The very fact William was

Suffolk's Murder

not executed angered many people and the mob screaming for his blood was not satisfied with his exile as a punishment. In fact, if anything, it only fed the anger against him, and once more, as before his imprisonment, there was violence against his servants.

Alice must have been happy that William would not be executed, but at the same time, afraid what the angry mob might do to her and their son, but what precautions she took, if any, are not known. Perhaps she simply hoped to be able to keep her head down, as, rather unusually for her, her movements and actions are not recorded during this crucial time. William did not leave prison immediately, though he was free to go. Not leaving prison after the punishment became known was a security measure; it is doubtful he would have survived doing so. A mob assembled in front of the Tower of London when the verdict was announced, waiting for him to emerge.[20]

Under normal circumstances, it would be virtually certain that William sent word to Alice to inform her when he would be leaving the Tower and where he intended to go to prepare for his exile, but given how tense the mood in the capital was, this might have been considered too dangerous, in case somebody intercepted his messenger, or the messenger was bribed to disclose the information. It cannot be said for certain Alice did not know, but it is a possibility.

William left the Tower during the cover of night in mid-April[21] to go to one of his manors, there to lie low until it was time to leave England, which, according to Henry VI's command, was on 1 May. It is not known where he went, but since he was so connected in the public mind to Ewelme, it is extremely unlikely he went there. It seems he went somewhere without his family.[22] Presumably, this was to protect Alice and little John, in case the outraged mob caught up with him.

That this was no idle fear was apparent by the fact that despite the precautions he took when leaving prison, William very

What is Better than a Good Woman?

narrowly escaped a mob of London inhabitants trying to catch and almost certainly murder him. He was not caught; but one of his servants and one of his horses were, and they were tortured – both of them.[23] If the mob was intent on learning where William intended to go by doing this, they were to be disappointed, but it shows just how badly the mood had turned against him, and that rather than calming everyone, William's sentence had only aroused the fury of many people even more.

As for Alice, neither her whereabouts nor her actions are known during this time. A letter William wrote to his son before leaving England suggests that he did not see him for some time before he left,[24] but that is all that can be said. There is no indication to show if John was with his mother at the time or not. Maybe Alice wanted to be with him to personally make sure nothing would happen to him, and there was less danger of him being sold out by servants. On the other hand, it is also possible that Alice wanted to remove their young son from both her and William's presence, thinking he would be less likely to be caught in the crossfire. Whatever Alice decided on, she must have done it well. Absolutely nothing about her whereabouts at the time is known, or her son's; frustrating to historians, but it shows that she knew what she was doing.

It seems as if William was preparing never to see his son again. Perhaps, he hoped or even planned with Alice that she might visit him while he was in exile, with his son staying in England so as not to be brought back into danger. Making preparations for John's life to go on without him was among the plans he made during the month between leaving prison and then England, alongside arranging to go to France, where he would be welcomed. There was no way to be low-key about issuing a safe conduct and the very fact that the French king was so prompt in issuing it to William was taken by his enemies as a sign that the treason charges against William had been correct, that he had been working together with the French king the whole time. William could not have known

Suffolk's Murder

that this would be the outcome of his applying for a safe conduct and even had he known, he had no choice.

The very last of these preparations, one day before he left England, was to write to his son to give him some advice. The letter shows William's concern and love for his son, but also his love and respect for Alice:

> My dear and only well-beloved son, I beseech our Lord in Heaven, the Maker of all the World, to bless you, and to send you ever grace to love him, and to dread him, to the which, as far as a father may charge his child, I both charge you, and pray you to set all your spirits and wits to do, and to know his holy laws and commandments, by the which you shall, with his great mercy, pass all the great tempests and troubles of this wretched world. And that also, knowingly, you do nothing for love nor dread of any earthly creature that should displease him. And there as any frailty maketh you to fall, beseech his mercy soon to call you to him again with repentance, satisfaction, and contrition of your heart, never more in will to offend him.
>
> Secondly, next him above all earthly things, to be true liegeman in heart, in will, in thought, in deed, unto the king our aldermost high and dread sovereign lord, to whom both you and I be so much bound to; charging you as father can and may, rather to die than to be the contrary, or to know anything that were against the welfare or prosperity of his most royal person, but that as far as your body and life may stretch you live and die to defend it, and to let his highness have knowledge thereof in all the haste you can.
>
> Thirdly, in the same way, I charge you, my dear son, always as you be bounden by the commandment of God to do, to love, to worship, your lady and mother; and also that you obey always her commandments, and to believe her counsels and advices in all your works, the which dread not but shall

What is Better than a Good Woman?

be best and truest to you. And if any other body would steer you to the contrary, to flee the counsel in any wise, for you shall find it naught and evil.

Furthermore, as far as father may and can, I charge you in any wise to flee the company and counsel of proud men, of covetous men, and of flattering men, the more especially and mightily to withstand them, and not to draw nor to meddle with them, with all your might and power; and to draw to you and to your company good and virtuous men, and such as be of good conversation, and of truth, and by them shall you never be deceived nor repent you of. Moreover, never follow your own wit in nowise, but in all your works, of such folks as I write of above, ask your advice and counsel, and doing thus, with the mercy of God, you shall do right well, and live in right much worship, and great heart's rest and ease. And I will be to you as good lord and father as my heart can think.

And last of all, as heartily and as lovingly as ever father blessed his child in earth, I give you the blessing of Our Lord and of me, which of his infinite mercy increase you in all virtue and good living; and that your blood may by his grace from kindred to kindred multiply in this earth to his service, in such wise as after the departing from this wretched world here, you and they may glorify him eternally amongst his angels in heaven.

Written of mine hand,
The day of my departing from this land.
Your true and loving father[25]

As he did in his will, written seventeen months before this letter, William shows his complete trust in Alice to raise their son correctly. There are no stipulations, simply a straightforward charge to his son to listen to Alice 'in all your works'. Clearly, his complete trust in his wife had not changed throughout their marriage. If he wrote a similar letter to Alice it has been lost, and

Suffolk's Murder

it would not be the only letter William wrote before his death that has been lost,[26] so it is possible. William may have had the chance during April 1450 to speak to her in person.

Even if he did, even if Alice stayed with William for as long as possible, on 30 April, on the day William wrote the letter to his son, they must have parted. There is a piece of circumstantial evidence to suggest that Alice did not in fact stay with William for so long: that letter to John. If Alice had been with him when he wrote it, he would not have sent it via a messenger, which seems to have been what happened, but given it to Alice herself to pass on to their son.

John's copy was not the only one. In fact, the letter was circulated in the time after William's death. Usually, it is assumed logically enough that William himself arranged this. If so, it was a risky move, and it would be interesting to know what Alice thought of it. It would draw everyone's attention directly to John. It could have drawn the attention of the mob, soon to be deprived of a chance to hurt William when he left England, to his young and defenceless son. While making sure he would be in everyone's mind and therefore making an attack upon him harder to get away with, it also made him a target. There can be no doubt that Alice was aware of all this, and it would be interesting to know if she agreed with William's reasoning, if indeed he was the one to make the decision to have the letter to John circulated, or if she was angry with him for putting their son in danger, no matter how good his intentions were.

It is also possible that the letter was circulated not by William but because the messenger William had sent was intercepted, or he decided for himself to copy and circulate it when hearing the news of William's death. He could have been paid.

Suffolk's murder and Alice's reaction

The letter is unlikely to have reached John before 2 May, and even if Alice was with him then, as is usually assumed, she could not

What is Better than a Good Woman?

have known about it before that, and by the evening that day or at the very latest the next morning she must have learned of what happened when William left England.

On 1 May, as he had been commanded, William boarded a ship for France.[27] With him he had some of his servants as well as his safe conduct to France and the one in England Henry VI had given him,[28] saying he was not to be harmed while still in the country. What happened next has been recorded in several chronicles, such as the *Croyland Chronicle* and the *Great Chronicle of London*, but the best description and the most contemporary version, penned only three days later, is to be found in the Paston Letters:

… And with him met a ship, called Nicholas of the Tower, with other ships waiting on him, and by them that were in the spinner, the master of the Nicholas had knowledge of the Duke's coming When he espied the Duke's ships, he sent forth his boat to weet what they were; and the Duke himself spoke to them, and said, he was by the King's commandment sent to Calais-ward; and they said, he must speak with their master. And so he with two or three of his men, went forth with them in their boat to the Nicholas; and when he came, the master bade him. 'Welcome traitor', as men say. And further, the master desired to wete if the shipmen would hold with the Duke; and they sent word they would not in no wise: and so he was in the Nicholas till Saturday next following. Some say, he wrote much thing to be delivered to the King, but that is not verily known. He had his confessor with him, and some say he was arraigned in the ship on their manner, upon the impeachments, and found guilty. Also he asked the name of the ship, and when he knew it, he remembered Stacy that said if he might escape the danger of the Tower, he should be safe and then his heart failed him, for he thought he was deceived. And in the sight of all his men, he was drawn out of the great ship into the boat, and there was an axe, and a stock; and one of the lewdest of the ship bade him lay down his head, and he should be fairly ferd with, and die on a sword. And took a rusty sword, and smote off his head within half a dozen strokes, and took away his gown of russet, and his doublet of velvet mailed, and laid his body on the sands of Dover; and some say his head was set on a pole by it, and his men sit on the land by great circumstance, and pray. And the sheriff of Kent doth watch the body, and sent his under-sheriff to the judges to weet what to do, and also to the King, to know what shall be done.[29]

Alice was a widow once again.

Widowhood once more

William's death is sometimes seen as the end of the frenzy around him,[30] with the rebellion brewing in the capital at the time considered either as a completely disconnected event, or as something that was squarely William's fault and which his death before the rebellion truly started defused it before it could become truly dangerous.[31] Neither is correct. Though the smear campaign against him and Alice had started as an attack solely on them, the king being considered simply a weak puppet doing their bidding,[32] the mood had turned, and there was genuine rage against the king, with William being a very convenient scapegoat for the many things that had gone wrong since Henry had come of age. The Paston letter shows William's murderers not only as murderers and as such naturally outside the law, but also as explicitly flaunting the king's authority, dismissing or even ripping up his safe conduct.

It is usually claimed that it was an angry mob who killed William, an understandable assumption given that he had been all but followed by angry mobs for nearly half a year, mobs that had already come very close to him, mistreating his servants. His treasurer had been murdered by just such an angry mob in January,

What is Better than a Good Woman?

and since Adam Moleyns had been a bishop, this shows just how volatile the mood had been for several months before William's death. There is no doubt that many cheered William's death and considered it a good thing, and that there were many who had actively called for it and had in fact tried to make it happen.[33]

A rumour circulated, which was used in the rebellion in the summer of 1450, that some Kentish sailors had taken the decision to kill William into their own hands[34] and that Alice, his outraged widow, had convinced the king to raze the entire county of Kent in revenge. This was actually in the manifesto of the rebels, stating this would be unfair to the many people of Kent who had not supported the deed.[35]

This claim is interesting not just for the light it throws on Alice, which will be analysed below. It seems to indicate that some Kentishmen had taken William's fate into their own hands, supposedly outraged by some unspecified deeds by William against the whole of Kent, and that they had been a small select group, not normal Kentish commoners. Both cannot be true at once, and other details show that it is less likely William was killed by commoners who were either fed up with something he had actually done against them or simply so riled up by the smear campaign that had been run against William and angry that he had not been sentenced to death that they decided to kill him.

For one, there is the fact that his murderers intercepted William on a ship that either had once belonged, or still did belong, to the royal fleet.[36] This makes it almost impossible that his murderers were common sailors. Even if the ship was no longer a part of the royal fleet, there is no way that common soldiers would have had the money to acquire the ship, run it and find men to command it, all without being noticed by any of the king's men. At the very least, this implies some help from someone of higher standing.

William's death does not sound as if it was at the hands of an angry mob, even one as inexplicably organised as this one is supposed to

Suffolk's Murder

have been. William's death was a show, a message. This has worked exceedingly well; even today, William's murder is often referred to as an execution, and the absolute horror of it glossed over. It was intended not only to make William's death as terrible as possible and also to send that message. If everything Paston said in his letter was true, then William was intentionally humiliated: explicitly dragged into a by-boat 'in the sight of all his men', threatened with torture if he did not comply, and even when he did, murdered with a rusty sword that took half a dozen strokes to kill him.

All of this is horrifying and unlikely to have been planned by any mob. For several centuries, it has been the accepted truth that in fact, there was a nobleman behind it, Richard, Duke of York.[37] However, in recent years, when the Duke of York's own name has started to be cleared of several unjust accusations and an unjustly bad reputation,[38] this has begun to be doubted.

While Richard, Duke of York's guilt can hardly be certain, and there are several candidates who are equally likely to have been involved in some way, the attempts to clear his name have sometimes taken on absurd dimensions, for example assigning explicitly republican motives to William's murderers that were not voiced at any other point during the fifteenth century to explain the obviously political staging of William's death.

A better defence for Richard is that he was in Ireland at that time, and he would not have been able to foresee William's movements well enough to be able to arrange his murder. However, that overlooks the fact that no matter if he was in England or Ireland at the time, he is unlikely to have been anywhere close to the location of William's murder, and would have had enough men to make arrangements with, or more likely, they could make the arrangement themselves, with only general instructions from Richard himself.

Once the whole furore around William's death and the following rebellion had calmed down, several men were arrested and executed for the distribution of the poems that started the smear

What is Better than a Good Woman?

attack against William in 1449[39] and also for his actual murder, and all those men had connections with Richard, Duke of York. It could be argued that the men were actually picked for that reason, to harm Richard by being associated with William's murder, but given the contempt in which William's name was still held even then it does not seem particularly likely. The most likely explanation is that Richard was indeed behind William's murder.

Alice must have asked herself such questions at the time, and perhaps she came to the same conclusion, that Richard was responsible. Certainly, her son seemed to think so when he grew up.[40] Who was responsible for her husband's death would not have been a question Alice wanted answered to take revenge. At the time, it could very much have been a matter of life and death, knowing who she could, or could not, trust. This included knowing whose lands it was safe to cross.

Alice apparently thought she had to travel. As John Paston said, the sheriff of Dover, probably eager to be rid of William's body, which many were trying to despoil,[41] had sent to the king to ask what to do with it. Henry VI, who was reportedly shocked and distressed at the news of William's death, gave the order that Alice was to decide what was to be done with his body.[42]

She, more than anyone else, would have known if several of the details relayed by Paston were correct, such as that he had consulted an astrologer named Stacy who had told him 'if he might escape the danger of the Tower, he should be safe'.[43] Since Paston gives this astrologer a name, thus clearly not repeating a vague story, it seems accurate. However, others have pointed out that Paston also includes details he could not possibly have known, such as William's emotions upon being told the name of the ship he was being held on. Moreover, the story sounds very like other, similar, stories of men being led astray by unspecific predictions,[44] and could very well have been simply a rumour picked up before the story was told by Paston. If he ever was told that he would survive if he escaped the Tower,

Suffolk's Murder

Alice would have known. If it was not true, the story might have added to her anguish, but upon learning that once more violence had left her a widow, she had bigger problems. Simply staying alive and salvaging what she could from William's possessions for her son would have taken all of her time.

Her first action we know of after William's death is giving orders for his funeral. We have no exact date for this, but writing on 5 May, John Paston reported that the sheriff had sent someone to the king, without any information as to what the king had decided. If the sheriff's messenger was known to have arrived to pose the question, it is most likely rumours would have circulated about his decision, even if those rumours were not accurate. That Paston did not mention anything of the sort suggests that the messenger did not see the king before 5 May. After giving the doleful news to Henry, the king would still have needed to make a decision, then sent a messenger to Alice. The first task of such a messenger would have been to inform Alice of her husband's fate, and then that the king had authorised her to make decisions as to how, where and when her husband was to be buried. Even if Alice started making arrangements the moment she had finished speaking to the royal messenger, it is unlikely the first preparations for William's interment were made before 7 May.

The fact King Henry could send a messenger to Alice at tells us he knew where she was staying. This information was not picked up by anyone else. Alice was of high interest at that moment, yet nobody recorded even a guess at her whereabouts. This means that either William had known of Alice's plans and passed them on to the king in case something happened to him, or else that Alice had informed the king of her whereabouts herself, throwing herself on his mercy and trusting he looked out for her and for her son, making sure they would not be attacked and that the information would go no further.

As Alice prepared for the burial, Henry VII issued a grant that confirmed the one he had made in 1444, stating that Alice was to remain her son's guardian. Issued on 8 May, it was made within days of learning of William's death.[45] Quite possibly, Henry VI informed Alice of this at the same time as he informed her of her husband's death. From what we know, she followed the wishes William had expressed in the will he had written in 1448 as far as was possible. If there was any procession to give money to the poor is unknown but given how much focus was on Alice during these days, the fact we know nothing of such a procession indicates that there wasn't one. This must have been out of a desire not to draw any attention, and perhaps Alice instead gave the money as William had requested privately.

The very first order she would have given was to have William's body brought from Dover to Hull, where he was to be buried. It has been claimed that Alice did not heed William's wishes in this instance and that in fact he was laid to rest in Wingfield,[46] a town where his family held an important manor.[47] But it is known that Alice saw to it William's body was brought to Hull, to fulfil his last wishes. This was not an easy task; the men in charge of bringing William's body to Hull had to travel at night and lie as low as possible during the day. There were many who wished to deny William a proper burial.

Such preparations were a completely new experience for Alice. Though she had twice been a widow before, she had been a highly esteemed lady both times, and her late husbands regarded as heroes. Being the widow of a widely hated man would have been entirely different. This seems obvious, but still, some have dismissed Alice's ordeal at that point, saying as it was her third widowhood she must have been inured to the politics of mourning.[48]

Alice appears to have been present at William's funeral, so she travelled to Hull. Though the sources also indicate that there was no more immediate physical danger for Alice, nor in fact for John at that time,[49] it seems unlikely Alice would have wanted to run any risk and they must have travelled in secret. The whole ordeal must

Suffolk's Murder

have been made worse by the fact that wherever they travelled the news of William's murder would have been known and, in many cases, celebrated. Poems once more circulated, openly mocking William, implying or trumpeting outright that his death was good for England.[50]

From the highest position possible, as a duchess, wife of the king's most favoured advisor, favourite lady of the queen, with immense power at her fingertips, Alice had fallen far: though still technically a duchess, she was in danger of losing that title if the king gave in to the many voices demanding William be posthumously attainted. Her name was spoken with hatred,[51] she was considered a malign influence, and some people even demanded she herself should be tried for treason.[52] She doubtless had to witness people celebrating the death of her beloved husband as she tried to keep herself and her son safe. John, who was only seven years of age, had to be kept as calm as possible, presumably the level of danger they were in kept from him.

It was an enormous task that would have taken immense mental and physical strength from Alice, but one she was to prove equal to. All the religious and secular tasks that arose from William's death were taken care of.

She did not order William's and her effigy to be made at that time. Who would have done it? This is another reason why it is sometimes assumed that Alice did not follow William's wishes but made her own arrangements for him at Wingfield, but this overlooks the fact that she did eventually ask for 'statues' of her own person as well as William to be made in Hull, some thirteen years after his death.[53]

Was Alice angry at her late husband for the danger and the mess he had left her and their son in, so did not wish to go above and beyond necessities at that point, and only gave the order when she had grown more mellow towards his memory in 1463? It is possible Alice was angry at William in 1450, that she cursed

What is Better than a Good Woman?

him for leaving her in such a difficult situation. But she was best placed to understand the difficulties he had faced and just how little responsibility he himself bore for what had happened. She was in a similar situation, her disgrace and conviction for treason demanded by many. In part, this was because she was William's wife, but to ignore the part her own actions played in this is wrong, as will be discussed below. The most likely explanation for Alice delaying the creation of the effigies William had asked for in his last will and testament is that she wished for it to be done to her satisfaction and in the hectic atmosphere of spring and summer 1450, she could not have found a stonemason to do it.

What little evidence there is suggests that after the funeral was over, Alice took herself and her son to see the king, a calculated risk. The king would have been able to offer her and John greater safety than could find anywhere else in England. While the danger of someone finding out they were living in any one of Alice's manors, and bribing their servants or simply storming their home, was high, no such danger would have existed while they were at court, in close proximity to the king. Of course, it had happened before that an angry mob wanted to storm the king's palaces,[54] and some of the political poems and ditties circulating in 1450 were a warning to Henry VI that he could not go against his subjects' wishes too far, but the feeling against him was not presently strong enough that they wanted to challenge him in such a drastic fashion.[55] Doing so meant that for any rebel, they had crossed the point of no return. With William dead, it might have seemed extremely unlikely to Alice that anyone would actually try committing such blatant treason simply to reach William's wife and son. Even if some had been so inclined, Alice may have hoped that not enough would be happy with attacking the king's person to harm a woman and a child, a calculation that was correct. Once she reached court, she did not seem to have been in physical danger anymore, and neither was John. Being at court also meant

Suffolk's Murder

she could hope to influence what happened after William's death. He had not died attainted, which meant that John was to inherit all his father's possessions and titles.

The fact that the population would not like it was, of course, the greatest disadvantage to Alice and John coming to court in late spring 1450. Though physically safe, it meant that the anger against Alice would not die down, would be stoked even more by her ostensibly proving what she and William had been accused of – that they were too close to the king and queen, that they influenced them unduly. It was the lesser of two evils for Alice, but Henry VI and Alice herself seemed like to pay the price shortly afterwards.

However, perhaps Alice did not really have a choice. There is a theory that Alice was actually with Queen Margaret when she received the news of her husband's death. This seems unlikely as surely this would have been recorded, but it is possible that Alice had been aware from the first that the court was the safest place to be and she and William had arranged to send John to be with the king or the queen when William left prison. John was still so young he was very unlikely to be recognised, so that it would not have been overly dangerous for him to be sent to court with several servants. At least he would have been out of physical danger.

If so, it would explain why King Henry knew where Alice was, as surely, she would have told the servants with John how to reach her in case she was needed in some way, her son suddenly became sick, or something similarly unforeseen. It might also explain why the letter William sent to his son circulated – it would have been hard to keep any secret at court.

In fact, such a course of action by Alice could make sense of an otherwise rather inexplicable hiccup in several chronicles: the claim that King Henry took 'the Duke of Suffolk' with him to Leicester when Parliament was reconvened.[56] Usually, it is claimed that this was William, and that Henry wished to protect him from the very exile he himself had sentenced him to a month earlier,

What is Better than a Good Woman?

but this is not possible. Not only do we know when William left prison, that he left it at night and that a servant and one horse of his were attacked when he escaped the angry mob awaiting his release in front of the Tower of London, it is a fact that Leicester is too far away from Dover for William to have been able to make the journey between 29 April, when he was supposedly with Henry, and 1 May, when his ship was intercepted shortly after he boarded it in Dover.

However, no chronicle would have been written immediately after it happened, and the one saying that Henry was with 'the Duke of Suffolk' is from several years later[57] – at a time when the Duke of Suffolk was Alice and William's son John. Since absolutely nothing is known about his whereabouts at pretty much any point in 1450, there is nothing contradicting the idea that Alice sent John either to Queen Margaret or King Henry, who may, in fact, have been his godfather.

If John had been with King Henry from late March, then it is very understandable that Alice's first instinct after William's funeral was to go to court: this would not have been motivated by any thoughts for her own safety, or even any political wish to keep her son's inheritance as safe as possible, but simply a mother's instinct, wishing to be reunited with her son after such a trying time.

In a way, John's absence would have made her task easier; she only had to keep herself safe and did not have to worry about sheltering John not only from dangers, but also from the emotional effect it would have had on a seven-year-old boy to witness people celebrating his father's death.

10

THE JACK CADE REBELLION

We can imagine that, whether John arrived with her or had been with the king and queen the whole time, Alice was relieved when arriving at court, but that relief cannot have been very long-lived. There is almost no possibility that Alice arrived before mid- to end of May. Shortly afterwards, the discontent that had been brewing for a while erupted into a full-blown rebellion,[1] an uprising that went down in history as the Jack Cade rebellion, so-called after the supposed name of its leader.

In some ways, this rebellion heralded the upcoming civil war, the decades-long series of conflicts known as the Wars of the Roses. Some historians consider the Jack Cade rebellion the starting point of those Wars, though traditionally, the First Battle of St Alban's of May 1455 has been selected. The rebellion has been seen as the uprising of rightfully disgruntled men rising up against the high and mighty abusing their power. Primary sources do not support this idea. Though most of these sources were written after its failure and the chroniclers writing them had a vested interest in damning the rebels, some facts are verifiable. For one, the rebels who marched on London were extremely violent. Led by a man who has become known to history as Jack Cade[2] but called himself Edmund Mortimer, it was an uprising

What is Better than a Good Woman?

of commoners,[3] some with legitimate grievances against the nobility, others who just seemed to enjoy making trouble. Even those with grievances did not seem to be particularly interested in addressing them, though. The rebellion started with violence. Only a month after William's death, they formed a mob and dragged Bishop Ayscough, Lord Say and his son-in-law out of their palaces to hang them.

With that, they were unforgivable; killing not only a nobleman but a bishop as well. This seems to have been a warning shot towards the king, but they must have known it was a gamble, one that relied on Henry's perceived chronic vacillation, intended to pressure him into listening to their demands, which they presented after the murder of the two men.

These demands included that Alice be tried for treason,[4] along with a number of men who had been close to her husband and the king, and had been connected with Henry's unpopular policies over the last few years. The charges against Alice were rather vague, that she was too close to the king and queen, rose far above her station as someone who was born a commoner and a woman.[5] Unlike William, there were no specific charges levelled against her, no actual actions she was supposed to be tried for, only rumours of actions she was supposed to want to take – and generally behaving in a way unnatural to her sex.

Alice must have begun to fear not only for her livelihood but also for her life. As a woman, she would not be executed for treason, even if King Henry agreed to have her put on trial. However, the mob was obviously calling for her blood and while there was no precedent for execution, she must have feared that she would simply be murdered by them, as Adam Moleyns had been. Being the king's favourite had not saved her husband, and if the rebels were to prove more and more successful, there would be no way he could continue protecting her, just as he had not been able to protect her husband.

The Jack Cade Rebellion

Charges against Alice

For once, King Henry held out. He refused to listen to the rebels, or even see them, as King Richard II had done during the Peasants' Revolt. Instead, he withdrew – possibly with Alice and her son. His wife stayed near London and saw her husband's forces arrive. It is unlikely Alice was with her at that point. Alice was a courageous woman, but she was not a stupid one.

When the king did not listen to their demands, the rebels decided to take the law into their own hands. Some sources suggest they set up a court and started holding treason trials for the absent Alice and the noblemen they wanted to see condemned.[6] Unsurprisingly, this mock trial for Alice returned a guilty verdict, though there is some doubt that the 'trial' ever took place.

We can once more only imagine Alice's reactions as she waited for news from the capital, news that could not only endanger her life but also her son's, and her relief when she heard that the king's forces had been successful. They had beaten down the rebellion and the leading rebels had been hanged. The immediate danger to her life was over.

The fallout of the rebellion still had to be dealt with, and in any case, unless she was extremely naive, she must have known that even once the storm had died down and law and order had returned it would take months, possibly years, for the hatred the common people of England felt for her and William to dissipate.

Who was the instigator of the rebellion? Though it was officially pretended that the commoner 'Jack Cade' was simply a malcontent who had been able to stir the masses, the name he chose for himself hinted at the upheaval of the following decades: by calling himself Edmund Mortimer, 'Jack' claimed to be related to Richard, Duke of York and focused people's attention on the duke's royal descent from the Mortimer family, considered by many to be more important than Henry VI's own descent from John of Gaunt, Duke of Lancaster.

What is Better than a Good Woman?

This and the fact that not long afterwards Richard began protesting against the government, a protest that would escalate into a full-blown civil war and that eventually led to him claiming the throne, has led many to believe, both then and in the centuries afterwards, that the duke himself was behind the rebellion. Unsurprisingly, he strenuously denied culpability, pointing out that he himself had been a victim of the rebels, as they had stolen valuable jewels from him and his wife.

While it is possible Richard was speaking the truth, that 'Jack' had chosen his name by himself, it is equally possible that the duke, understandably angry at the bad treatment from the king he had received in the last years despite serving him well and faithfully, had tested the water with this rebellion, while staying far enough away from it to retain plausible deniability.

This question was one that Alice herself had to deal with in the summer of 1450. She had to decide who was trustworthy and who was not, if any of the high and mighty at court were involved in not only her husband's murder but the calls for her own execution for treason, calls that were at the same time calls for her son to be disinherited.

It is known that in August 1450[7] a dispensation was issued for her son John and Margaret Beaufort, a dispensation ostensibly addressed to the two children themselves, saying that their marriage was valid despite their being 'in the fourth and fourth degrees of kindred', and referring to a letter the two children had supposedly written, stating that if they were to divorce 'grave dissensions and scandals would probably be stirred up between their parents and friends.'[8]

At the ages of six and seven, of course Margaret and John had not written this letter themselves. William was not involved, as the letter quoted by the dispensation was obviously written after the wedding, at a time when William was already in prison. Given that it was issued in August, the request must have been sent to Rome

The Jack Cade Rebellion

before his death, but even so, the authors of this letter asking for a dispensation were Alice and Margaret's mother, Margaret Beauchamp.

The dispensation must have given Alice a greater sense of security, as it tied her son closely to Henry Beaufort, Duke of Somerset, one of the king's closest men at court, and therefore someone who could protect John if she found herself not able to do so. It was one of the very few things she could be happy about that year. Even by November 1450, she was not yet safe. When parliament met that month, the House of Commons demanded that Henry VI have several men and one woman banished from his presence for being a bad influence on him.[9]

The treason charges that had hung over her head only months earlier were gone, but it still hurt to hear herself accused of 'improper behaviour'. The king was informed: 'Your possessions have been greatly diminished, your laws not executed, and the peace of this your realm not observed nor kept, to your great harm and the distress of the liege people of this your realm and the likely subversion of the same without your good and gracious attention to this matter in all appropriate haste.'[10]

This was mostly a demand made for appearance's sake, not with any expectation of it actually being acted upon, and it was not. Henry VI attempted to compromise:

His highness is not sufficiently appraised of any reason why they should be removed from the presence of his highness; nevertheless, his highness has agreed by his own volition and by no other authority that save for the person of any lord named in the said petition, and also save for certain persons, who are few in number, who have been accustomed to wait continually upon his person, and who know how and in what way they may best serve him to his pleasure, his highness has agreed that the rest shall remove themselves

What is Better than a Good Woman?

from his high presence and from his court for the period of a whole year; within which time any man who can and will make any objection against any of them by which it might be considered reasonable that he should be removed from his high presence and service and from his court, he who so objects will be patiently heard and listened to, saving always that if it happens the king takes to the field against his enemies or rebels, that then it shall be lawful for him to use the service of any of his liege people, this notwithstanding.[11]

Nobody would have been fooled by the pretence of a compromise. Henry VI's decision completely rejected the bill from the House of Commons, the only people being affected by the accusations being commoners, the nobility were exempt.

In this case, King Henry made the right decision. He has often been castigated for not listening to the House of Commons, much more than any other king, but at the time the decision was considered a good one. It appeared to take heed of the House of Commons views without caving in to their demands or rewarding the rebels who had murdered several of his closest advisors by giving in to their demands once they were formally made in Parliament.

As far as Alice was concerned, this meant that she could have continued being at court, being close to king and queen, without having to fear anything. The decision in Parliament effectively spelled the end of all the troubles of 1450, at least for a good while.

11

A WOMAN ALONE

Even so, it seems that Alice had no interest in staying at court for long after 1450. In a significant change to her and William's actions in the previous years, when Alice became a widow for the third time she seems to have become disillusioned with politics and abruptly withdrew from court life, never fully to return to it.

Her decision, if considered at all, is usually seen as that of a widow who felt it was her place to stay at home and raise her son.[1] This is historically nonsensical and smacks more of Victorian values than of any exhibited by those close to power in the fifteenth century. It is not what Alice did when Thomas Montacute died, leaving her a pregnant widow.

Of course, the simplest explanation is that she had no interest in exposing her son to the vicissitudes of politics. It is notable, however, that from 1450 on, Alice received no more presents from Queen Margaret, or only very insignificant ones. At least no more are recorded, only formal ones as given to all ladies of standing. This has usually been interpreted in a way that leaves Alice almost completely out of the equation, a reaction to the fate of Alice's husband William. The argument is that Margaret had given presents to Alice to please William, not because she actually liked Alice or wanted to please her. That these presents stopped

What is Better than a Good Woman?

after William's death is taken as evidence that he was the reason these presents, though it is not explained why Margaret, assumed to want to make William notice her as a woman and not just wanting to please him as a friend, figured the best way to do it was by giving presents to his wife.

Much more logical explanations are available: like Alice, Margaret may have seen the risk of too much closeness with any one courtier, and Alice in particular, and wanted to distance herself from her, to make sure that there would be no risk of them both being in danger of being accused of any abuse of power.

This political explanation is perhaps the most obvious, but another possibility is some personal disagreement. This is unknowable, but that does not mean it is impossible. Alice and Margaret may have disagreed over something, or Alice and Henry did and Margaret sided with her husband, from conviction or duty. It is simply a possibility that should not be discarded, as doing so discards the humanity of Alice and Margaret – something that still, based on the Victorian reading of the situation, often happens.

Whatever the reason Alice chose to withdraw from political and court life, it is hard to blame her. In the years 1449 and 1450, being a courtier had brought her nothing but bad luck and heartache. She must have been longing for some peace and quiet. While Alice was still a presence at court, or even while her husband was when she was not at court because she wanted to be with her son or was ill, her movements were recorded. Such records become far rarer for the years following William's murder. The scarcity of records has led historians to make guesses as to what she did when, and why. One of these speculations, based on some scant evidence, is that shortly after William's death she took a vow of chastity.

The case for this is given by Karen K. Jambeck[2] who suggests that Alice's clothing on the effigy of her tomb indicates she was a vowess, something she could have been without giving up her

A Woman Alone

possessions but not without taking a vow of chastity. It was a decision some women made after the death of husbands, but it was uncommon. Though she chose to distance herself from king and queen after William's death and the events of 1450, there is no sign of an open rift, and therefore Alice could have relied on them not to demand she marry someone else for political reasons. Therefore, if she did indeed take a vow of chastity, it must have been a sign of her love for William.

What she actually did in the years following William's death is hard to reconstruct. Her first and foremost task was surely taking care of her son and his education. Alice would be extremely close to John even when he was an adult, as she had been when he was a baby as discussed in Chapter 10. When he was an adult, it was an unusually close relationship even by modern standards, though not unnaturally so. This closeness may have come from the time after William's death, when it seems the two of them stayed together for long periods of time, with Alice's focus mostly if not exclusively on her son.

We do know some of the arrangements Alice made for John's education, which give us an insight into her own priorities. Alice took care that her son was as well-educated as any prince. John was scholarly, could read English, Latin and French and had a number of books on history, religion and science in those languages.[3] One book Alice used for his education was Vincent of Beauvais' *De morali principis institutione*,[4] 'Moral Instructions for a Prince', or 'Moral Education for a Prince', a tract often used for the education of actual princes thorough Europe. We do not know when she considered John old enough to be introduced to this work, only that she ordered an Oxford clergyman called John Courteys[5] to copy and translate it for her use at some point in the 1450s, and that the same book was used again for the education of her grandchildren when they were still fairly young.

What is Better than a Good Woman?

This care taken with this book suggests that Alice put similar care into all other aspects of John's education. Since she was responsible for it herself, with no power of decision going to anyone else, it is logical to think that she chose similar focuses for her son's education as her own parents had for hers. Though as we have seen, William had prepared for the event of his death before his imprisonment, so that it is not far-fetched to think he had made preparations not only for his son's financial and marital future, but also his education. In the aspects that a father was usually expected to make arrangements for his son, such as martial arts, this would make a lot of sense. However, since no evidence survives for any arrangement, and only very scant evidence of the decisions Alice actually made for her son, there is no way of making sensible deductions. Nothing at all survives about what sort of education Alice enjoyed, only that she, like her son was highly intelligent and able to at least speak and understand two languages.

It does not seem that anyone considered John's education particularly remarkable, though, or that anyone thought there was anything at all wrong with it, which indicates that Alice managed to prepare him well for what martial and intellectual challenges were in his future. That this would have included employing men not only to teach him how to fight, but also how to make conversation, how to dance and other fine arts in addition to knowledge of mathematics, history and logic is something we can assume based on custom.[6] Similarly we can also only assume that Alice employed tutors for these tasks and did not undertake them herself. While she would have been unable to teach John how to fight, it is not impossible she could have taught him the more intellectual subjects and the social graces herself, though going by the customs of the day it is unlikely.

Having John's wardship, Alice held all his lands and possessions until he came of age,[7] which meant most of the

A Woman Alone

lands and possessions she and William had possessed, and she had to manage them alone. This was a new situation for her; though of course she did not have to do all the actual work. Her task would have mostly consisted of choosing the right people to do it for her and John, and checking what they were doing. Sometimes it meant arguing with nobles when they made a claim on the lands.

Naturally, it was not all new to Alice, who had been a wealthy landowner since she had been eleven years of age, but after William's death it was the first time she had to do it without anyone close to her to advise or help. For the first decade or so of her owning vast lands, we have seen that her father Thomas had been responsible for most of the management,[8] and Alice did not have to do anything. When she then assumed responsibility, he had been there to help her during her second widowhood and into her marriage with William, until his death. The situation would have been much different and much more fraught after her third husband's death.

Alice was aware that the worst she could do was hesitate or show any weakness to those lurking, waiting to pounce and lay claim to lands belonging to her and her son. That speaks against Alice devoting all her time to teaching John. While Alice devoted her time to her son after William's death until John married Elizabeth Plantagenet, this would have consisted of more than looking after his physical well-being and his education and development. It also meant securing his inheritance and money.

In 1450, this may have seemed all but impossible. King Henry VI had been as kind to John as he could, but he did not inherit everything his father had owned. The title of Earl of Pembroke, given to William in 1447,[9] fell to the crown and was passed by the king to his oldest half-brother Edmund Tudor. So did several of the possessions and lands Henry had granted to William in the years of his prominence at court.[10]

What is Better than a Good Woman?

For all his high standing, and his ducal title, William had not been a notably rich man. By comparison to almost everyone in the country, he had riches beyond their wildest dreams, but William was one of the poorest courtiers. John was therefore heir to a dukedom his income from his lands could hardly support, a situation worsened by the fact several of his father's lands did not go to him. John would suffer a chronic shortness of money for the rest of his life.

Probably, given the mood in 1450, there was really nothing Henry VI could do to allow John to keep all possessions and titles. It would have been dangerous not only to him but to John himself. Alice must have been maddened by the partial disinheritance of her son nevertheless. In fact, it could be this was what caused a rift between her and the king and queen.

During this time, Alice gained a reputation as a tough businesswoman, mostly because of her quarrels with the Paston family,[11] an important family living in Oxfordshire who are remembered by history for their vast collection of letters. While William had been alive, he and Alice had quarrelled with them about the ownership of lands[12] and Alice continued doing so as a widow. Similarly, in the early 1450s[13] she challenged John Tiptoft, Earl of Worcester, when he acted in such a way that it put her stewardship of the castle at Wallingford in question. Worcester accepted her rebuke, and Alice had her way.

Though most people at the time seemed to consider such quarrels as something to be expected of a woman in Alice's situation and of her standing, they have affected Alice's reputation. There are often accusations of her being too tough, too unkind,[14] even accusations of not always 'being charming' or not having inherited her father's likeability, as discussed above.

At the time, at least during the first years of Alice's third widowhood, there was no criticism of her actions. In fact, there is very little comment on her at all, as she tried to stay in the

A Woman Alone

shadows. She was too successful in this in the long run. It seems that Alice's plan was to wait for the hatred still aimed at her, William, and by extension their son after Parliament in 1450 to blow over. It did, as new favourites took William's place at Henry's court, but it meant that Alice was more removed from Henry VI's own heart. Her importance had waned. She was no longer a political force.

In the years 1451 and 1452, Alice and John were safe in the knowledge that if nothing unforeseen, such as an illness killing Alice, Margaret Beaufort or John himself, their future was secure. Rich little Margaret was the best match Alice could have hoped for for her son. But in 1453, something did indeed intervene, not an illness or death. It was politics: William was dead, Alice had withdrawn from court and political life, was of no more political importance. Others had come to the fore, and one of them was a close relative of little Margaret: her cousin Henry Beaufort, Duke of Somerset.

He was, of course, also related to Alice, if rather more distantly. This branch of the Beaufort family was not as close to her as Cardinal Henry Beaufort had been. This Henry had no interest in the success or well-being of Alice and her son, but he was interested in little Margaret's future, and he did not consider that John, a duke but shaping up at the age of ten not to be politically particularly significant nor very wealthy, would be a suitable husband for her. There was someone else at court who was slowly emerging as a player: Henry VI's oldest half-brother, Edmund Tudor.[15]

There is some doubt if it was in fact Margaret's uncle influencing Henry to strip her wardship from Alice and see to it her marriage to little John was annulled, though it is often assumed, or whether Henry himself wanted to reward his half-brother and decided this was the best way to do it. Henry had a track record for this, taking a reward away from someone he had given it to

What is Better than a Good Woman?

previously and giving it to someone else he wished to favour.[16] While it is still a widespread assumption that Henry Beaufort influenced the king, Henry's illegitimate half-brothers hardly had any money and Edmund had a title he needed to fund, and the support Henry wanted from them would not be possible without their owning some lands. Their parents had not left them anything to inherit. Henry had a way to offer them an incentive to stay loyal to him.

That this was necessary is often overlooked when discussing the short-lived, never consummated marriage between John and Margaret. In the years of Alice mostly taking care of her son's needs, the political situation in the kingdom had not become any more stable. In 1452, Richard, Duke of York, had first spoken against the king by criticising his advisors,[17] of whom Henry Beaufort, Duke of Somerset, was one of the most important by then. This criticism and the following actions against king and government had been a disaster for Richard, but it had proved, if any proof was needed after 1450, how deeply divided the country was – Edmund and Jasper Tudor had sided with Richard against Henry Beaufort.

The decision took from her son the future Alice had planned for him with William, in the last months of William's life. She must have known Henry VI was involved in the decision making, though until recently this was not the historical consensus, the decision assigned to Henry Beaufort, Duke of Somerset, or even to little Margaret herself.[18] This was claimed from as early as 1509,[19] being first mentioned at her funeral, and quite possibly it was a legend she herself encouraged. It is also a legend that has absolutely no supporting evidence.

There was nothing Alice could do about the decision, and so she accepted it when the wardship was taken from her, her son's marriage was annulled and Margaret's future separated from her son's as Jasper and Edmund Tudor took her wardship. At the

A Woman Alone

time, there was no open rift between Alice and king and queen. Alice continued her quiet, low-key life after her son's 'divorce', continuing to take care of him, his education and his lands. In 1453, there were two events that happened which we know she must have had an interest in.

The first one was in March 1453. Three men were arrested who admitted to having been the driving forces behind William's murder.[20] They were executed for it. If Alice believed that these men were guilty, it must have been satisfying for her to see the men responsible for her husband's death killed, but it is possible that she, like many of her contemporaries, was sceptical. Many people in the fifteenth century, as well as many historians, considered these men to have been chosen for their connection with Richard, Duke of York. If Alice shared this opinion, she may have been rather angry at her husband's murder being used like this, for a political end.

The other event of interest to Alice that year is something about which there is less speculation: Queen Margaret's confinement.

Alice's changing relationship with Margaret of Anjou

In early 1453, after eight years of marriage, Margaret had finally fallen pregnant.[21] Some have linked Alice's difficulties in pregnancy with Margaret's long wait to conceive and suggest Alice would have sympathised with the queen. Alice's problem, however, was not conceiving, her problem was obviously keeping pregnancies, so while she may very well have sympathised with Margaret's difficulties they were not the same problems she suffered. Moreover, such a claim usually assumes that Margaret and Alice were still close, and the fact that Alice was present during Margaret's churching ceremony in November 1453 seen as evidence for this. Alice's mention in the source reporting this is the only mention of her in any source at all for that year.

While there is no evidence the two were estranged, and no reason to assume this, there is equally no evidence that they

What is Better than a Good Woman?

were still as close as they had been before William's murder. Since William's murder, there had been no more gifts from Margaret to Alice recorded, and while in 1450 this would have been sensible, there would have been no reason why Margaret could not have made Alice a present later if she had been so inclined. Since all evidence there is for these years suggests that Alice rarely spent time at court, and Queen Margaret's actions suggest the closeness they had once shared was no longer there, this is the most likely guess.

Even so, Alice chose to be present at the churching ceremony[22] after Margaret had given birth to a healthy boy in October 1453, who was called Edward. This must have been as good news for Alice as it was for everyone else. After all, the last time a king had not had an heir of his body despite being married for a fairly long time, it had resulted in the usurpation of Henry's grandfather and a lot of unrest in the realm. And with Richard, Duke of York, a controversial figure, considered Henry VI's heir unless he had an heir of the body,[23] it was considered more important than ever that Henry have a child. Even a daughter could have caused trouble, because while Salic law did not apply in England, the only time a daughter had been a king's sole heir it had led to an extended civil war. Queen Margaret giving birth to a healthy son was considered good news throughout England, even by those who did not like the queen and were politically opposed to her. Even Richard, Duke of York, who was relegated in the line of succession with the birth of Henry's son, showed every sign of pleasure at hearing of Edward's birth.[24]

It is often claimed that Alice was present with Margaret while she gave birth. A queen giving birth was a public affair, and it was quite common for high-born ladies to be present. In fact, the evidence is quite clear that she was not, only arriving several weeks later for the churching ceremony, which took place forty days after the birth.

The source gives a very clear picture of what Alice's position in this ceremony was: simply as one of the most high-ranking ladies.[25] This is interesting in that it shows Alice was perfectly happy to perform a part in an important ceremony like this one, but also that she and Margaret were not particularly close any longer. Alice is not singled out in the way she often was during the 1440s.

This seems to have been Alice's last appearance at court for quite a while. No other visits are recorded, which certainly means that even if she did occasionally come to court in the time between 1453 and 1460, her presence at court was not considered to make much of a difference in the grand scheme of things, as reported by chroniclers.

The beginning of the Wars of the Roses

We have no recorded reaction of Alice's to the news two months before the birth of Edward that King Henry VI had, in the words of a contemporary chronicler, gone mad. It was reported that he was utterly unresponsive, reacting to nobody and nothing, showing no sign of recognition when his wife, his courtiers, his cousin, tried to speak to him.

It was clear to everyone that even if Henry recovered quickly, which everyone hoped and apparently expected at the time, he needed a regent as quickly as possible to run the kingdom while he was unable to do so.[26] That this was urgent was not in question, but who this regent was to be was a question that was fought over in the months leading up to Edward's birth, and in the months after it. Queen Margaret wanted to be her husband's regent, an office she had grown up knowing her own mother performed for her father. However, Richard, Duke of York considered that as he was an Englishman and closely related to the king, it should be his task. He won this power struggle, but not easily. Though Queen Margaret was not popular, either to

What is Better than a Good Woman?

the nobility or the population, Richard himself was not the most popular of men either, and his uprising of only a year before was still in many people's minds. Henry Beaufort, Duke of Somerset was imprisoned for speaking against Richard as Lord Protector. While she performed her allotted role at Queen Margaret's churching ceremony, Alice was not keen to be mixed up in the quarrel. Even if she and Queen Margaret had had a falling out, of which there is no evidence, the queen could not have afforded to shun Alice and the support she and, in due time, her son could have brought when the situation started escalating. It must have been Alice's decision to keep herself and her son out of it for as long as she could.

She managed it for a long period because she was no longer considered to be politically influential, and her son was too young to play any part in events for most of the 1450s. Alice was probably glad of this when it became apparent the power struggle that started when Henry VI became catatonic would not be solved without violence.

Henry VI came to his senses on Christmas Day 1454.[27] Alice, who had once been close to him, might have been happy about this, but several others were not, chief among them Richard, Duke of York. Upon Henry VI reassuming his position, Richard was banished from court and his enemy Henry Beaufort, Duke of Somerset was released from prison and once more became the the king and queen's closest man. Richard was unlikely to accept this, and he did not. After several months of attempting to solve the situation and constantly being rebuffed for it, he and his supporters finally gathered an army to meet the king's forces. It was claimed by Richard at the time,[28] quite possibly truthfully, that he did not actually intend to use force against the king and his men but was prepared to do so in his own defence.

On 22 May, the first battle of the series of conflicts now known as the Wars of the Roses took place in the town of St Alban's.

A Woman Alone

Richard's forces won the day, after his assurances that he only wanted to rid the king of his bad advisors.[29] Such promises would only have made Alice more determined to keep her nearly teenaged son away from court. After all, William had died under just that pretext.

It must have become clear to her as the conflict continued that she would not be able to keep John away from it forever. He was growing up and would be expected eventually to take sides. Moreover, those closely related to Alice started to do so, most notably her stepdaughter, Thomas Montacute's daughter Alice, and her husband Richard Neville, as well as their oldest son, Richard, Earl of Warwick.

As the situation worsened, Alice decided that the best course of action was to strengthen her and her son's ties to the Yorkist side of the conflict. It would be fascinating to know why – if it was a purely political decision, if disillusionment with king and queen fed into it or if it was a mixture of these motives – but sadly, there is absolutely nothing to shine any light on this. We are left only with the bare facts, which is that by late 1457, two-and-a-half years after the Battle of St Alban's, Alice decided to ally herself and her son to Richard, Duke of York, by arranging a marriage for John to one of Richard's daughters.[30]

Arranging a marriage for her son

It is not known if this was her idea, or if Richard approached her with the idea. Generally, it is believed to have been at Alice's instigation.[31] Marrying her son to a girl who was nowhere near as rich as either Anne Beauchamp or Margaret Beaufort but of higher birth than both, would by her connection make sure that he would not be persecuted as a member of the Lancastrian party, purely for who his father was. John was also a good match for Richard's daughter, and Richard may very well have been aware of the chances such an alliance offered. John was a duke, and Richard

What is Better than a Good Woman?

could hope that John would support him if the conflict escalated any further.

Whoever proposed the marriage, the other party quickly agreed. Richard had two unmarried daughters at that time. The older of the two, Elizabeth, was chosen as John's bride. The arrangements made between her and Richard, Duke of York are still on record and give a picture of the money that was brought to the marriage by Richard's daughter, and the way it was to be paid.[32]

The names mentioned in these bonds, such as Bishop Wayneflete, are impressive, a list of the connections Alice either made or strengthened by marrying her son to Elizabeth Plantagenet, and even if the money she and John would receive from the match was not so impressive, this must have pleased her. What John thought of it all is unknown, but it would have been considered irrelevant, and he would have known this. Most likely, Alice simply informed her son, who was then fifteen years old, of her decision, and it is doubtful he was anything but accepting of this, having always known that a marriage would be arranged for him.

Neither Alice nor Richard wanted to lose any time. On or by 2 February[33] the wedding of their children went ahead, the details of which are sadly lost to history. We can imagine it was a grand affair, the marriage of a duke of the realm to the daughter of one of the most foremost men in England, but perhaps neither Alice nor Richard saw any need for any great celebration. Nobles did sometimes marry quietly.

John's bride Elizabeth, then aged thirteen years, moved into their household[34] to get to know John and learn all the tasks required from her as his wife before they were old enough to run their own household. Alice's relationship with her daughter-in-law is rarely alluded to in all records. In fact, there is much more interest in her relationship with Margaret Beaufort, a woman she probably met once, than with the woman who had been married to her son for

A Woman Alone

seventeen years when Alice died and had given John nine children by then.

There are indications that the two women had a very good relationship.[35] Alice and Elizabeth seemed to choose to spend a lot of time together, and to have a similar taste in art and literature.[36] While this evidence of them enjoying the same things and often enjoying them together only exists from much later in their lives,[37] there is every reason to assume Alice got on well with the teenage girl from the first.

Even if she did not, it would not have mattered. When agreeing to marry her son to Elizabeth Plantagenet, Alice had agreed to take the girl into her household and to continue whatever education she had received so far. Elizabeth was to grow up a very intelligent and highly literate woman who, like Alice, could at the very least read French and Latin as well as English, and probably speak French in addition to English.[38]

John and Elizabeth seem to have taken to one another fairly quickly, so that even if Alice would have preferred for her and her son to continue their calm life until he was old enough to run his own household, she must have been pleased by that. It is just as possible that Alice was delighted that Elizabeth came to her household and welcomed the change, something new and interesting happening that did not present any danger to her or her son.

It is likely that Alice was also starting to think of grandchildren. At the time of their marriage both John and Elizabeth were considered young for consummation, which was usually delayed until both bride and groom were sixteen.[39] While there were exceptions, they were rare. However, when the wedding took place, it was only two-and-a-half more years until Elizabeth would turn sixteen.

It is possible that she and Richard had an agreement that John and Elizabeth would not in fact consummate the marriage before she turned sixteen. Such formal agreements were common in the

What is Better than a Good Woman?

case of a young bride being married, though usually only if the groom was much older than the bride. In the event of both bride and groom being very young, it seems to have usually been an informal arrangement, not to stop a much older man of taking advantage of a far too young wife, but to make sure that two teenagers did not listen to their hormones. The pattern of births of the many children John and Elizabeth would go on to have suggest that they kept to the normally accepted age of sixteen years for the consummation.

The 1450s are, apart from Alice's childhood, the part of her life we have the least evidence for. She became more active again, even in politics, in the 1460s, once Edward IV was on the throne, secure in the knowledge that unless he did something monumentally stupid or illegal himself, John was safe as the king's brother-in-law. Her 'disappearance' in the 1450s may have been prompted by wanting John to become a teenager, old enough to start forming connections of his own, to be seen as his own person, not just her and William's son. Perhaps the conflict made her think it too dangerous for them to return to court, risking John picking the losing side.

Of course, if so, her eventual decision to marry him to Elizabeth Plantagenet sounds rather contradictory, but it may not actually have been so, or at least not as much as it looks at first glance. It is often claimed by making this decision, Alice saw the writing on the wall, that Richard, Duke of York would eventually be on the winning side, and she decided to ally with him for that reason. This is a sensible explanation but not the only one.

In fact, there is evidence from late 1460 indicating that Alice intended to have a foot in both camps, and not only intended it but actually succeeded. This must have been quite a feat for her to accomplish, as her decision to connect her son to Richard, Duke of York by marriage not only seems to historians as if she was siding with him, it also seemed so to contemporaries. It was seen

A Woman Alone

as actively treasonous, and according to John Benet's chronicle, [40] there was talk of stripping John of his dukedom as a punishment for his marriage. The chronicle stated he actually was stripped of it, but if so, this was never legally enacted as no such demotion is recorded in any legal documents. [41] Alice must have expected such a reaction from king and queen, but it seems that somehow she managed win them round.

The argument that she was simply protecting her son might have worked with Queen Margaret, who was the one, rather than her husband Henry VI, who seems to have become close to Alice again by 1460. After all, Margaret was famously extremely protective of her own son Edward, by then almost seven years old, and she might have been prepared to accept that Alice would do whatever it took, whatever was necessary, to make sure John was safe and well.

By the end of the decade, it was at the very least rumoured that she was once more close to the queen. A churchman called Friar Brackley, himself a firm Yorkist, [42] wrote a letter to John Paston stating that Alice, with 'other aforementioned persons' was one of the 'leader[s] of those most inclined towards [the queen] with all their strength' [43], which the friar condemned.

It is easy to argue that Friar Brackley was mistaken about the information he relayed to Paston, but there are two counter arguments. One is that the rest of the information given by the friar in the letter is accurate, including his complaint that Alice's son had not yet picked a side in the steadily worsening quarrel. The second is that if ever there was an intention to punish John for his marriage, it had not happened, and despite being York's son-in-law he was appointed on Commissions for the Peace for Norfolk and Suffolk. [44]

Since he had never shown any inclination to side with the king and queen, despite being nearly eighteen at the time, it is not unreasonable to assume that such trust in him was because

What is Better than a Good Woman?

of his mother. Or it was less Alice's own charm and ability to convince, more the fact that they could not be choosy about their supporters.

At the end of 1459, it had seemed as if the Yorkist forces would lose. After October,[45] the Duke of York had to flee abroad with some of his closest supporters, including his two sons, Edward, Earl of March and Edmund, Earl of Rutland, his brother-in-law Richard Neville, Earl of Salisbury and his wife Alice Montacute, as well as their oldest son, Richard, Earl of Warwick. This fact might have drawn Alice more closely toward the Yorkist forces than she might have wanted to be or wanted to show, as the Earl and Alice Montacute, the 5th Countess of Salisbury were her stepdaughter and stepson-in-law. However, we do not know how close, if at all close, they were to Alice at this point, and it seems as if Alice did all she could to become indispensable to the king and queen.

If she, or they, were hoping that the civil war was over, they were to be disappointed. Edward, Earl of March and Richard, Earl of Warwick returned from exile in Calais in summer 1460,[46] and several battles were fought that turned the tide. Several of the royal couple's closest advisors died that summer, which made Richard, Duke of York feel safe enough to return to England from Ireland, were he had been with his second oldest son Edmund.

At that point, Alice was quite obviously trying to play both sides, something to which Friar Brackley's letters bear evidence. It was in October 1460 that he reported that Alice was one of the queen's chief supporters, with 'all her force'.[47]. However, in another letter, also written in October that year, he reported that 'the Lady of Suffolk hath sent up hyr sone and hise wyf to my Lord of York to aske grace for a schireve the next yer'.[48]

As the Duke of York was Elizabeth's father, there was nothing untoward in Alice making use of this connection to ask for a favour from the duke. Though asking shows that she was eager to

A Woman Alone

keep up a cordial relationship with him, in spite of similar efforts with king and queen.

It was in both their interests to try and make the best of it, but it is interesting to note that there is some evidence Alice's son was not ready to fight for his father-in-law, though he did not hesitate to fight for the Yorkist cause once Richard was no longer involved.

John has been accused of being a coward, unwilling to fight, by historians,[49] and Alice has been disparaged for encouraging this supposed cowardice.[50] No contemporary ever claimed this, and evidence speaks against it. There is no way to know how John would have reacted had the Duke of York lived longer.

After returning from exile in October 1460, Richard, seeing that all his earnest attempts to be treated what he considered fairly by the king, queen and their advisors were doomed to failure, decided to claim the throne for himself. It was not a popular move[51] and Alice was probably as shocked by it as everyone else; even Richard's supporters were. The king and queen eventually reached a compromise whereby Richard was formally to be Henry VI's heir, with his and Queen Margaret's son being disinherited, but Henry was to remain king until he died.[52]

It must have been apparent to most that this was not a compromise that would hold very long. By December 1460, the country was at war again, and on 30 December[53] the Lancastrian troops, ignoring a Christmas truce, assembled at Wakefield.[54] The Duke of York gathered his own men and met them, together with his son Edmund, his brother-in-law the Earl of Salisbury and one of Salisbury's sons, Thomas.

It was to be a catastrophe. The Duke of York either died in this battle or was beheaded on the battlefield. Salisbury's son Thomas died in the battle, and Salisbury himself was beheaded by the Lancastrians a day later. What was considered the worst of all by contemporaries was the fact that York's son Edmund was taken prisoner after the battle and, instead of being held hostage

What is Better than a Good Woman?

for money as was customary, he was killed by Lord Clifford, who supposedly took out his anger with the Duke of York on his seventeen-year-old son.

Even men who supported the Lancastrian side in these conflicts were appalled. It might have been this that finally convinced John and Alice to side with the Yorkists. We know from Friar Brackley's letter that she was considered to have enough money and power to provide fighting men,[55] but if she ever did, we have no evidence of it.

John finally made a decision and sided with York's oldest son, Edward, Earl of March, who upon his father's death stepped into his shoes and took up his claim to kingship. It is tempting to assume that John's decision to do so after Richard, Duke of York was dead meant that he was prepared and even happy to support the Yorkist claim but would not fight for the man many considered to have given the order for his father's murder. What we do know is that John fought not in the next battle, which took place at on 2 February 1461 and became known as the Battle of Mortimer's Cross, but that he was present at the battle two weeks later, the Second Battle of St Alban's, which the Yorkist forces lost.[56] It was an inauspicious beginning, and doubtless Alice was worried for her son, then and during the next several weeks when John accompanied his brother-in-law on his military campaign.

The training Alice had chosen for him was obviously enough to prepare him for the realities of battle. Though his presence in battle was occasionally noted, nobody ever made any more than a passing comment about him during these conflicts, suggesting that he comported himself well without drawing attention, positive or negative. Nothing about his fighting was very notable, which was exactly what Alice surely hoped for.

The battles in those months were brutal, and they culminated in the biggest ever fought on English soil, the Battle of Towton, which took place on Palm Sunday, 29 March. With supposedly up

A Woman Alone

to 80,000 men involved in it and up to 20,000 dead, it was a huge bloodbath. It was also the battle that at least temporarily decided the conflict. When Edward, Earl of March and his forces emerged victorious, Edward became King Edward IV. Alice's son was brother-in-law to a king from then on, and her daughter-in-law was a princess of the blood.

Victorian historians such as Henry Alfred Napier[57] tried to analyse Alice's feelings about this outcome, claiming she must have either been crowing with victory or feeling regret.[58] There is no way to decide, but we do know that her life changed a lot in that year, not only because of Edward IV's ascension. The most dramatic of these changes happened between the end of March, when the Battle of Towton made Edward IV king, and June, when his coronation took place: John and his wife Elizabeth left Alice's household to go live at Wingfield Castle, one of his father William's ancestral manors and now his.

This was done because they were both old enough to run their own household, not because of any sort of quarrel with Alice, who remained on the best of terms with both of them, Even with Alice knowing she would always be a welcome guest in their household, it would have meant that her life was to be very different from then on, different from anything she had ever known. Never before had she lived on her own, with nobody to take care of, or to take care of her. At the age of nearly sixty, Alice had a new start. This might have been rather sad for her, but if so, one piece of news sweetened the blow: Elizabeth was pregnant and was expected to give birth to Alice's first grandchild in the autumn of 1461. Alice was to prove a very involved grandmother by the standards of the fifteenth century.

The first court event she took part in since 1453 was Edward IV's coronation. Sadly, this coronation is nowhere near as well recorded as that of Richard III over twenty years later, or Henry VII even later. The only reason we know that Alice was

What is Better than a Good Woman?

present is because of a record of her being granted clothing for it. Clearly, she was considered a supporter, or at least not a danger, to Edward IV by that time, and it is even possible she performed a small part in the service.[59]

Possibly, it was helping her son and his wife prepare for the arrival of this child that occupied Alice for most of the rest of the year. Alice was not present when her first grandchild was born, nor does her son appear to have been. Since Alice appears to have been present for the births of several later grandchildren, it is possible that her presence at Elizabeth's confinement had been planned. What seems to have happened was that the then 17-year-old Elizabeth had miscalculated, been mistaken about the conception date, and went into labour unexpectedly while travelling to London in late October 1461. A rather frantic letter from her survives, which can be dated with some certainty to that year, in which she begs John Paston to allow her to take quarters in his home, since she urgently needed a place to stay.[60]

This suggests that it was urgent enough for her not to travel on for several more miles to take lodgings in her brother's palace at Westminster, and that Alice was not in London then, though she would spend a lot of time there in the following years. Though no answer to Elizabeth's letter survives to this day, and perhaps none was ever written, it seems John Paston did as asked, letting Elizabeth lodge with him and she gave birth in his lodgings.

Since women usually went into confinement around a month to six weeks before the birth of a baby was expected,[61] and since Elizabeth's baby survived, it is almost certain that the child was not too early but the parents had simply miscalculated. Elizabeth gave birth to a healthy daughter, Alice's first grandchild, who was christened Elizabeth after her mother. It is usually assumed that Alice's first grandchild was her famous grandson, John, Earl of Lincoln, but the scant evidence that survives for his age[62] and the

A Woman Alone

even more scant evidence for his sister Elizabeth's age, such as her marriage date, suggest that she was older.

Alice was close to her grandchildren once they were a little older, this is all we can say with certainty. Perhaps she stood as godmother to her own granddaughter, which was quite a common decision. Technically, since John himself was barely nineteen when his first daughter was born, still a ward of his mother's, little Elizabeth also became her grandmother's ward, but in practice this did not influence her life in any way, nor Alice's.

The child's parents returned with her to their main home at Wingfield once the mother had recovered. Alice made the decision to move to London for the time being. Though we have little by way of evidence what she did there, the Paston letters make it pretty clear she was not in Ewelme in Oxfordshire in the years 1462 and 1463. Moreover, we have three letters signed by her asking a servant to bring her several items to 'my inne in London'.[63] The first reads: 'To William Bylton... I grete you wele. and pray you my good William yef my books be in myther closette by grounde, yt ye woll put them in some other place for takyng of harme. And God kepe you. Writen in myn Inne the xxiiij day of Janyver. Alice.'

The second one is concerned with similar issues, written around two months later:

> To William Bylton. My good Cok of Bylton. I grete you wele, and wol and pray you that ye take my litill Cofre of Gould, and wrappe it sure, and fast in some cloth, and seele it wele, and send it heder to me by some sure felyship that cometh betwix, and in any wise yt it be surely sent. And God have you in his merciful keeping. Writen at London in myne Inne ye xiiij day of Marche.[64]

The third one is not dated, though its contents suggest that it was written after the second, not very long afterwards as it, too, was

What is Better than a Good Woman?

concerned with money being sent to her, and with payments being made to absent servants:

> To William Bylton. Cok of Bylton. I grete you well, and woll yt ye send me by Robard Ffrere berer hereof xxli 33 in grotis oute of a bagge leeing upon the coffre in my closet, oute of the whiche Bagges I suppose Sr Symond hath hadde oute gere (&c.) and I woll also yt ye take oute of the said bagge for John Edmonds 1 noble. the Marchal 1 noble, yrself 1 noble. Shauples 1 noble. The grome porter iijs iiijd, Thom. Baker iijs iiija, William of the stable iijs iiija, and for Richard Bauge xx, and write these names in a bille that I may se redely what have be taken oute of the said Bagge. to Adam Browdrer 1 noble. Take good hyde aboute you ffor sherewes ben nyghe.[65]

On the face of it, these were fairly mundane letters, dealing with everyday life. Even so, they reveal quite a lot about Alice's circumstances at the time, and about her personally. The fact she asked for a 'coffer with gold' to be sent to her, and the servant William Bylton to put her books out of harm's way are the best indications of when these letters were written, though they are not dated, and could in fact have been written at any point in her life. Nothing in the letters itself even dates hem to her third widowhood, even less to the 1462/3. However, since we know a lot about her whereabouts during her marriage to William, we can say for certain that they cannot date from those years. Moreover, the early years after William's death are also unlikely since it would have been noted, and for the first two or three years, might have even caused outrage that she lived in London – in easy reach of the palaces the king and queen stayed in most often. There is no mention of John and no tutor, nurse or anyone else charged with the care-taking, upbringing and education of her son mentioned among the servants

A Woman Alone

Alice wanted William Bylton to pay, servants she considered important enough to mention by name. This narrows the time frame down massively, since while Alice lived for another 14 years after 1461, when John and Elizabeth first moved away to establish their own household, she spent only five of those years alone. By 1466, she once more shared a household with her son, his wife and their children.

Since by this time, when once more establishing herself and her family in Ewelme at her palace there, Alice asked for several of the items mentioned to William Bylton to be send to her there, from London, the obvious conclusion is that they were sent to her in the years between 1462 and 1466. As will be seen below, the years 1464 to 1466 are unlikely due to other evidence we have as to her whereabouts, and even 1463 is unlikely to have been when she wrote the first letter. This puts dates them to early 1462 and gives us the valuable insight that Alice had chosen, for the time being, to relocate to London. Why she made this decision, we have no idea.

The well-being of her books was the first thing Alice wrote a letter about, before even she demanded that her money be sent to her. This supports the picture often painted of her as a literate person who had many books and very much prized them. The letters reveal another, rather unconventional, side to her as well.

While the first letter is a fairly conventional one in terms of language, it already shows a very familiar tone with her servant, 'good William'. There was nothing very wrong about that; it was not frowned upon for nobles to use such language with their servants. However, by the second letter, Alice's familiarity with William Bylton had deepened, as rather than 'good William', she addressed him as 'Cock of Bylton'. This is not actually sexually suggestive, though the modern associations with the word suggests so to modern readers. At the time, 'cock' meant something like 'hothead'. Alice's greeting meant 'Dear hothead of Bylton' – an

What is Better than a Good Woman?

informal form of greeting that suggests she either knew the man well or had come to know him well between her first letter written in January and her second in March. The tone is teasing. If anything, it suggests an insider joke between Alice and her servant William Bylton.

This shows two things: that Alice had a somewhat mischievous sense of humour, and the frequent accusation levelled against her by historians, especially since the nineteenth century, of her being aloof and full of herself does not tell the full story. As previously discussed, such accusations are mostly sexist, as it is highly unlikely that noblemen would be accused of such a lack of proper behaviour, as Alice frequently has been. The letters to William Bylton show that, if anything, the opposite was true for Alice. There are few examples of nobles of her standing, men and women, young and old, choosing such a familiar tone with their servants. Was Alice widely despised after her husband's death? Clearly, she was on the best terms with her servants at least, could rely on them and was a kind employer to them, and they were loyal to her.

In the early part of 1462, Alice must have learnt she was to be a grandmother again by autumn; her daughter-in-law having fallen pregnant again so quickly after the birth of her namesake daughter makes it doubtful she and John waited even the customary six weeks after birth until Elizabeth was churched, before trying for their next baby. Around October, she received news that Elizabeth had given birth again and that she and her new child were healthy. This time, she had given birth to a little boy, named John after his father. Before he was even of age, Alice's son therefore had an heir.

There was less pleasing news in autumn that year, too; a birth juxtaposed with a death: that of Alice's stepdaughter, Alice Montacute, Countess of Salisbury.[66] Her exact date of death is not known, since her Inquisitions Post Mortem were lost, but she was still alive in 1461, after her husband's death, when her son helped Edward IV win the throne[67] Her funeral, jointly with her husband

A Woman Alone

and son Thomas's, took place in late January 1463.[68] Since it was a grand affair that would have taken a while to arrange, she cannot have died much later than September or October 1462, while a date much before that also seems very unlikely, as no temporary burial is recorded for her, unlike for her husband and son.

It is therefore possible that Alice learned her son had an heir at nearly the same time as she learned of her stepdaughter dying. Though nothing is really known of their relationship in the last ten to fifteen years of Alice Montacute's life, it must still have been a sad reminder of the past to Alice. Since her stepdaughter had been almost exactly her age, it is also possible that her death was a reminder of Alice's own mortality, something that is suggested by an action she took in 1463.

Curiously, though the funeral of the Earl and Countess of Salisbury and their son Thomas is well recorded, there is no mention made of Alice's presence in the source detailing the guests and the whole ceremony. Her son and his wife were there, and perhaps Alice thought that their presence was enough, that they would represent her. Perhaps she was unable to attend the funeral herself, or she did not want to. Her absence is notable and somewhat strange.

It is possible to attach too much meaning to this, as very few of her actions of that sort are known. There are, for example, also absolutely no indications that have survived that Alice was interested in her own daughter's death, the death of Alice Montacute's much younger half-sister, and it stands to reason she was. While this could be taken as evidence that this daughter was in fact non-existent, all the evidence that supports her existence is indicative of something else unexplained. There is also no evidence of her having much interest in William's death. Nothing about his funeral arrangements survives, nothing about any prayers read for him, or any of the other customs usually followed after a death. Even for her own parents, no such grants for prayers survive, and

What is Better than a Good Woman?

we only know how they were buried and that Alice had buried them according to their standing because their graves happened to survive the centuries, unlike the graves of William, Thomas Montacute, his daughter and son-in-law, and that of Alice's daughter. It is likely that Alice did, in fact, have prayers read for her stepdaughter, as well as for William, Thomas Montacute, John Phelip, her daughter, her father and mother, and that no such orders have survived.

An order that has survived, though,[69] is one for the Hull Charterhouse, where William was buried, of statues of herself and him to be made. Whether they were intended to be on top of his grave, or if they were meant to be put elsewhere in the church as a reminder of their status as patrons, is unknown. Though the charterhouse is still in existence, having survived the Reformation and the civil wars in the seventeenth century, neither William's grave nor the effigies ordered by Alice are, so that this is another mystery that is no longer solvable.

Possibly, with her stepdaughter's death in mind, Alice also started giving orders for her own tomb to be erected, which can still be seen in the church at Ewelme that she and William supported so much, where her parents are buried. It is known that Alice made the arrangements for her tomb several years, perhaps even more than a decade, before her death, but the exact orders are not known any more than their timing.

It does not seem as if Alice went to Hull in 1463 to check on the progress of these statues, or even to give the order, but at some point towards the end of 1463 or the beginning of 1464, she seems to have gone back to Ewelme again, only for a short visit. Her orders for several items to be brought back to Oxfordshire are not dated before late 1466, but we can vouch for her presence in Ewelme in spring 1464.

Perhaps she went back there after visiting her son and daughter-in-law in late 1463, when they gave her a third

A Woman Alone

grandchild in as many years, another girl whose name we sadly no longer know. After visiting her perhaps she chose not to go from Wingfield Castle directly back to London, but visit Ewelme along the way, there to take a look at how her tomb was coming along, or to make up her mind about what she wanted and give orders later.

Possibly, though, she stayed in Wingfield a bit longer, not only to spend time with her son and his family but also for business reasons. In March 1463,[70] Edward IV had given his then twenty-year-old brother-in-law leave to enter into his inheritance, some months before he formally came of age. As Alice had held her son's wardship since William's death, there were probably no problems with this, but it is still likely that they had to discuss some details of land possessions and management that year, to make the transition as smooth as possible. It could even be that it was on this business that, after visiting her son, Alice went to Ewelme afterwards, to organise some of what was needed for this transition.

We know that she was staying Oxfordshire in early 1464 when the news broke that King Edward IV had been betrayed, that Edmund Beaufort,[71] a man closely related to Alice of course, had turned against him. Having been forgiven his loyalty to the Lancastrian cause in 1455-1461[72] and given a place of honour at Edward IV's court, Beaufort turned against the king using information he had gained at court to gather men, to engage Edward in battle and, if possible, unseat him.

Alice's son John was in the forces raised to fight for Edward under the leadership of John Neville, Earl of Northumberland, younger brother of Richard Neville, Earl of Warwick, another step-grandson of Alice's. John Neville was an accomplished soldier, and he defused the brewing rebellion, winning a decisive victory at the Battle of Hexham on 15 May 1464 and seeing to it the rebels were executed. There were few losses among the king's forces, but Alice's son John appears to have been catastrophically injured.

What is Better than a Good Woman?

We know this from a letter from Margaret Paston to her husband John, the same Paston family Alice had been quarrelling with repeatedly over the years. Margaret mentioned various men and their actions in connection to this military campaign and battle and stated that 'the Duke of Suffolk is come home again, and he either is dead or else right sick, and not like to escape.'[73]

This could have referred to any illness, nothing to do with the battle, given that it was written three weeks after Hexham. Coming as it does, however, in connection with other information concerned with this military campaign in this letter, and taking into account that after 1464, John never fought again and never was expected by any of his contemporaries to do so, it seems most likely he received a serious injury while fighting. He was rumoured to be dead already or about to die, with his chances of recovery not worth mentioning, Alice would have had the chance to look after her son herself; though John's wife and his three young children were still in Wingfield Castle, Margaret Paston obviously meant by John having 'come home', that he had been brought to Ewelme, to his mother.

This was most likely not a snub to Elizabeth, who appears to have left Wingfield Castle to come to Ewelme when hearing of her husband's plight. Most likely, it was simply easier, Ewelme being much closer to Hexham than Wingfield. Since Alice seems to have been there at the time, able to have everything prepared for her son's arrival, it must have been considered the best choice.

What she did to help him recover is sadly not known; no physicians' bills survive for that time, but whatever was done it was successful. Despite the dire prognosis given by Margaret Paston, John recovered from whatever was afflicting him. There is a suggestion, with him never fighting again and not expected to, that he retained some minor handicap. Alice had proved, when having her father buried, that she appreciated militarism,

A Woman Alone

considered being a soldier an important and honourable following. Once John recovered, she might have been proud of him risking everything for king and country.

Possibly because John was still somewhat weak, or because he and Elizabeth simply enjoyed staying with Alice, they remained at Ewelme with her for the rest of the year, and John even did so until Parliament was done in early 1465.[74] Perhaps Alice, after John left for Wingfield Castle, where Elizabeth soon became pregnant again, once more went to live in London.

If so, she was once again staying close to the king's court, usually if not always staying in Westminster. Though this was not yet a part of London, as it would become in later years, it was close, and Edward IV was close to London and its citizens, often coming to visit the town.

Being close to the king must have been fascinating in early 1465. In 1464, Edward's actions had caused a scandal. Being a young unmarried man of not quite nineteen years when he came to the throne, it had naturally been assumed that he would soon marry a foreign princess to make an alliance with another European nation. In fact, he had shown an interest in doing so as late as summer 1464, sending his cousin and chief advisor, Richard Neville, Earl of Warwick, to France to negotiate a marriage between himself and the French king's sister-in-law, Bona of Savoy.[75] Upon Warwick's return having successfully negotiated the marriage,[76] Edward announced to him and other nobles in September that in May 1464 he had married an English woman called Elizabeth, Lady Grey, who is remembered by history by her maiden name, Elizabeth Woodville. Daughter of a highborn Luxembourger noblewoman named Jacquette and a squire called Richard Woodville, Elizabeth was said to be a beauty, but did not have much to offer in a king's marriage. She brought no dowry, no alliance to another country, and since Edward sprung the marriage on everyone, it also insulted Spain, France and Milan.[77]

What is Better than a Good Woman?

Naturally, the marriage was unpopular among the nobility because of this. Alice never spoke against the new queen, or showed through any actions she did not approve of her, but nor was she ever numbered among her supporters. Like her son and daughter-in-law, she was one of the very few nobles who were neutral, or at least displayed neutrality, in the matter. Perhaps Alice recognised the potential troubles brought about by the marriage but was still sympathetic to the comparatively low-born queen, knowing first-hand how difficult it was to be taken seriously without a stellar noble ancestry. Conversely, she might have been very against the marriage and the person of the new queen, but known better than to say it loudly, remembering what had happened the last time she had openly taken sides in arguments about an unpopular queen.

Another possibility is that Alice slowly but surely was starting to feel her age. At the age of sixty, she was quite old for the time, and the fact nothing is known about her in those years, despite her new interest in politics after 1461, might indicate so. She didn't have the energy to engage. This might also explain her son and daughter-in-law's decision in late 1466 to once more move into her household.

12

AS *MATER FAMILIAS*

We know more about her son and daughter-in-law after 1464 than we do about Alice, that they made efforts to fight for possessions in Suffolk while staying at Wingfield Castle. In early 1466, Elizabeth gave birth there again, to a little boy whose name is also sadly lost to history, but who, though predeceasing his parents, would survive his grandmother. During that time, they showed no inclination to live with Alice, but by the end of 1466 they had made the decision.

At some point in autumn that year, John and Elizabeth and their entire household moved into the palace at Ewelme, to be with Alice. Various explanations have been suggested for that, such as their wishing to leave Suffolk after a particularly nasty quarrel about possessions with the Pastons the year before.[1] This was a quarrel in which Alice was involved,[2] so that it would make little sense for them to withdraw from the fallout it caused by going to live with her. None of the other possible explanations for them coming to live with her sound particularly likely either, except one: they wished to be with Alice, potentially because they were worried about her health.

Though there is no evidence for Alice actually being sick at this point, and her absence from sources in those years might simply be

What is Better than a Good Woman?

because she had not done anything anyone considered interesting or important enough to write down. Perhaps John simply thought that she was too old to live alone, or he wished to be close to her in case something happened.

So 1466 once more signalled a change in Alice's life. At the age of sixty-two, she lived in a household with several children for the first time. Though it is not known if John and Elizabeth's second-born daughter, who died at some point in babyhood or childhood, was still alive in 1466, they brought at least three children with them when they came to Ewelme: five-year-old Elizabeth jr, four-year-old John jr, and the infant boy who had been born at the beginning of the year. Elizabeth was already heavily pregnant again, and would give birth within some months of arriving back in Oxfordshire.

We know from the Ewelme Muniments for 1466[3] that Alice was the head of the household, and that Elizabeth and John were considered only members of it, a rather interesting decision for all three of them to make, but one they all seemed to agree with. Over the next few years, several mentions of them all together survive, indicating only goodwill among them. Alice was head of a household that was soon to house four or five children.

There is a great indicator of the trust her son and daughter-in-law placed in Alice: whenever they left Ewelme, which they were sometimes compelled to do, they left Alice in charge of their children. They might have modelled their children's upbringing on John's, although the evidence for that is only circumstantial. In 1466, one of the books Alice ordered to be brought to her from London to Ewelme was Vincent of Beauvais's 'De morali principis institutione',[4] which she had had translated for John's use in the 1450s. Since Alice's oldest grandchild was only five years old in 1466, the suggestion is that Alice, as well as John and Elizabeth, were making plans for a long-term stay at Ewelme.

240

As Mater Familias

The Ewelme muniments are a fascinating source and include many articles that have been used as evidence for Alice's possessions and even her personality.[5] There is a danger of overstating Alice's importance when working with this source, however, forgetting that the muniments record not only items owned by and delivered to Alice, but also to her son and daughter-in-law. While a lot of items which belonged to John and which he had delivered to Ewelme are either clearly marked as belonging to 'the duke' or are items which must have belonged to him as they would be of no used to a woman,[6] there is a lot of confusion as to what belonged to Alice and what belonged to Elizabeth. Both are referred to as 'duchess'. While it is clear from the nature of some items, for many, there can be no certainty.

This has caused many authors to assume that until otherwise marked, every item associated with 'the duchess' was Alice's,[7] an understandable assumption, given that Alice figured very largely in the life of her son and daughter-in-law, but nonetheless not always correct. Most of all, this faulty allocation is made in connection to the many books mentioned. While we know some of them belonged to Alice, such as the above-mentioned work by Vincent of Beauvais, others are more likely to have been Elizabeth's.

The most notable example of such a book, one that Alice's supposed possession of has often been used to make deductions about her character, is 'La Cité de Femmes' by Christine de Pizan.[8] Often cited as the first feminist book, it is comprised of the stories of both historical and fictional ladies.[9] This has sometimes been used as evidence for Alice's proto-feminist attitude, but the scant evidence for the ownership of the book suggests it was Elizabeth's, or possibly even John's, rather than Alice's, given that it was brought to Ewelme from Wingfield.[10] rather than London.

Even so, there is a connection between Alice and the book, given that it was brought to Ewelme for Elizabeth's confinement with her fifth baby. As has been pointed out by Rachel Delman,[11]

What is Better than a Good Woman?

Elizabeth appeared to allow Alice a free hand when preparing this confinement. Possibly Elizabeth simply agreed to or vetoed the plans Alice made. Alice allowed her daughter-in-law free use of all she owned when arranging the chambers for her confinement. Several tapestries which belonged to Alice were chosen, in addition to other decorations[12]. Confinement was intended to be a female only space[13] – though this was not a rule that Elizabeth seemed particularly interested in maintaining, as by late 1466, she was pregnant for the second time with a baby conceived while she was still in confinement after the birth of its closest sibling. Alice would have been the obvious person, alongside Elizabeth's ladies and servants, to visit and entertain her. So even if Elizabeth was the person to choose the books brought for that time, it would have been books she was interested in discussing with her mother-in-law.

These accounts also throw an interesting light on Alice's own living quarters, a point also made in Dr Delman's article. The subject of the article is female leadership, and Alice's example in this, but it also contains some interesting details beyond the topic. Over 15 years after his death, Alice still had her and William's coat of arms hanging in her chambers, for everyone to see who entered. Since these were not just in reception chambers, where her marriage, and thus her claim to the dukedom, would naturally be stressed, but also in her living quarters, she must still have had fond memories of him. There were no reminders of Thomas Montacute or John Phelip.

Alice was very much in control of the household, but John and Elizabeth had no problem fitting into it. It would have been expected, of course, for children and children's spouses to be respectful of their parents, but it is certainly telling that they chose to be a part of Alice's household and had no problems with being technically beneath her in the hierarchy several years after they had already run their own household. If Alice actually was sick, or they were afraid of what might happen to her on her own, they could

As Mater Familias

have invited her to live in their household rather than choosing to go to live in hers.

Alice was doubtless happy to have them around, and happy, too, when Elizabeth, probably in December 1466 or January 1467, gave birth to a healthy little girl, who was named Anne. Despite her short detour back into politics in 1462/3, it seems that once she lived with her son and daughter-in-law again, she once more focused on her family, ignoring all national politics.

Interestingly, for all the valid points that can be made about John being influenced by his mother in many ways,[14] points that were made even by contemporaries, in this case it is possible that it was Alice who was influenced by her son. John never showed much of an interest in politics, not as a young man and not in his later years. This was, of course, so very different to Alice, who had not only shown an interest in them but actively been involved until William's death. Since she was to show that her sudden withdrawal from them again in 1465 was not due to illness and she was perfectly able to get involved in regional disputes, her being influenced by John is the obvious explanation. Alice's involvement in regional disputes is where we get most evidence about her movements from for the next few years. Since John famously took up his parents' disputes with the Paston family, and since many letters from and to the Paston family have survived, we actually have a wealth of evidence of these disputes and of Alice's movements.

In 1466, her son and her daughter-in-law were involved in negotiations for Elizabeth's sister Margaret to marry Charles, son of the Duke of Burgundy,[15] son of the man who had made passes at Alice when she was newly married to Thomas Montacute. Alice herself was not at all involved, though she had good reason to follow events. On 13 March 1467, something happened that probably interested Alice far more: her oldest grandson, John, who was then only four years old, was given an earldom by his uncle Edward IV, became the Earl of Lincoln.[16]

What is Better than a Good Woman?

The following year, she took very close care of the new young earl and his siblings, when his parents left for Burgundy to celebrate the wedding of Elizabeth's sister to Charles,[17] who had become Duke of Burgundy upon his father's death in 1467. It seems that Alice was left to care for them all, and if John and Elizabeth made any arrangements as to what was to happen in case they did not survive the journey, they would have appointed Alice as the guardian of their children. After some months, John and Elizabeth returned safe and sound in autumn 1468. Shortly afterwards, in the winter of that year, Elizabeth gave birth to another baby, another granddaughter for Alice.

Quite possibly, Alice was happy not only about this but also for her son and daughter-in-law turning to more domestic matters in the year that followed, even if these matters included yet another quarrel with the Paston family. In fact, this is something Alice almost certainly supported whole-heartedly. As mentioned, despite not then living with John and Elizabeth, Alice had already been involved in John's quarrel with them in Suffolk, Presumably, she was even more involved when the quarrel flared up in Oxfordshire in 1469. According to the Pastons, she was very much a key player in that particular dispute.[18]

Of course, the Pastons' dislike of Alice went back a long way. All during the 1460s, they had recorded unflattering rumours about her, at one point even stating with no supporting evidence that the people 'love not in no wise the Duke of Suffolk nor his mother'.[19] Margaret Paston had warned her son not to be fooled by her, and, when making deals with her to take someone else along, for she would be likely to dupe him otherwise.[20] The truth of this cannot be ascertained, but it is obvious that Margaret did believe it. Alice did not hesitate to use all weapons she could when she was arguing about possessions. This also means that the Pastons' insistence that Alice was actually behind most of the attacks against them that have usually been assigned to John is quite possible.

As Mater Familias

As John continued the dispute about the manors, most vigorously in 1478[21] after his mother's death, the quarrel has usually been assigned to him, and no attention has been paid to the many references to Alice, especially to the escalation of bitterness 1469.[22] That the Pastons and Alice had been enemies for a long time means that not all claims they made about her, or her son, can be taken at face value.

Despite the many letters shining a light on the struggle, it is extremely one-sided, and there is no record of Alice or John's feelings about the whole affair, their spin on it. Since we only have the Pastons' version of events and some facts by which to judge this version but no counter argument from Alice or John, this has caused some commentators to take the Pastons at face value when condemning John, and to unquestioningly accept their judgement of Alice.[23]

While John is often rather unfairly judged to be the sole aggressor in these quarrels, Alice's characterisation given by Margaret Paston might be more accurate. The picture given by Margaret is one-sided, but not entirely wrong. Alice had proven before that she could be greedy, and that she thought of nothing but her own right and her family's when she considered herself under attack. It is not particularly hard to imagine that Margaret was also right about Alice being the driving force behind the quarrels about possessions that started up between her son and the Pastons in 1467, though it would be a mistake to blame her entirely. John had shown in 1465 that he was willing to argue the case with the same vigour his parents had before him, and perhaps the most likely version is that Alice simply recommended what she considered the best course of action to him. Elizabeth was not involved in this and seems to have tried to play the role of peacemaker. Though obviously supportive of her husband, she considered it more her duty to be approachable and less belligerent, in contrast to Alice.

Just how the quarrel mounted in 1469, we do not know. During the years before that, John and Elizabeth were involved in matters

What is Better than a Good Woman?

of state, such as the planning of the marriage of Elizabeth's younger sister Margaret to the Duke of Burgundy and were not as often at Ewelme as they would be a year later. John was prominently involved in several of the proceedings,[24] so perhaps the Paston family thought that if they did not act soon, John's position of favour with the king would make it impossible for them to act at all. Conversely, John might have considered that 1469 was a perfect time to establish his rights for just that reason.

By 1469, the country was slowly but surely lurching towards civil war again, and Edward needed what support he could get; he could not afford to reject, still less punish, men such as his brother-in-law. In fact, his insensitive treatment of several of his supporters was what had escalated the tension in England once more. In a situation echoing the one that Henry VI and Alice's husband William had been in, Edward's marriage had made him turn to advisors who acted, or were said to act, against his former advisors, such as his cousin the Earl of Warwick. For all the bad press Henry VI has received for ill-judged favouritism in the centuries since, Edward's failing in this is more clear-cut. Favouring the queen's family over several others which had helped him win the throne in the first place – and in particular riding roughshod over Warwick and his family – would prove to be a bad decision. By 1469, after having accepted Edward's slights over several years (which included marrying his aged aunt to one of the king's brothers with the stated intention of waiting for her death so he could inherit),[25] Warwick had had enough and was starting to act against Edward.[26]

It was against this background that the quarrel between Alice's son and the Paston family flared up again. There had been some physical confrontations, but nothing really serious, and the solution that was offered in the end[27] was probably not expected to last for very long. What is interesting is how deeply involved Alice clearly was, in the planning – and in person, accompanying

As Mater Familias

John and Elizabeth. This clearly indicates that she was involved in their life, not just a fixture in their household but actually an active participant.

As Edward could not afford to reject any offer of support, if Alice had wanted to get involved she would have been able to do so. She did not, which must have been her choice. Shortly after the quarrel with the Pastons had come to an end in 1469, Edward IV was taken prisoner by the Earl of Warwick.[28] John became involved, not Alice.

If it had been only Richard Neville, Earl of Warwick, whom Edward IV had provoked, perhaps he could have managed to keep the peace, but he also treated others badly while favouring his wife's family, not least his brother George, Duke of Clarence. While seeing to it that the queen's sisters all had marriages considered by many to be way above their station[29] and searching for a marriage for his youngest brother Richard, Duke of Gloucester, Edward had neglected his brother the Duke of Clarence, and when George, at the age of twenty, came to an agreement with the Earl of Warwick about a marriage between himself and Warwick's oldest daughter Isabel, Edward forbade it.

The marriage went ahead despite Edward's disapproval, in July 1469. Apparently having decided they would never prosper under Edward IV, Warwick and George had then moved to capture Edward and had also unlawfully killed two members of the Woodville family, Edward's father-in-law Richard and his brother-in-law John.

Edward IV was lucky that he still had fairly widespread support, and that there were Lancastrian malcontents who seized upon the rift in the Yorkist ranks. When the Earl of Warwick took Edward prisoner, they reacted, forcing the earl to gather an army to repel them.[30] However, many men were not ready to assemble in Edward's name without seeing Edward as a free man, leaving Warwick with no choice. Edward summoned the peers of the

What is Better than a Good Woman?

realm, and they arrived to ride alongside him to London. John was among those peers.

He as well as others probably hoped this would be the end of it. John seems to have returned home shortly afterwards to be with his wife who expecting the birth of yet another baby. Having had a girl in 1468, Elizabeth gave birth to another boy in early 1470, who was named Edward after her royal brother, a subtle statement of support with little risk. John was unable to fight owing to his injury received at the Battle of Hexham, and his oldest son was not yet eight years old in 1470. The family must have known that unless they acted rashly, the odds were they would survive, whatever happened. John, as was expected of him, was present during several council meetings of the king's in early 1470, discussing how to deal with the situation, but the moment everything started building towards a military confrontation between Edward and the Earl of Warwick, between Edward and the Lancastrians, John was of no more use to the king and he went back to Ewelme.

Just what Alice hoped would happen is impossible to say, but we do have an indication that with her own grandchildren's future in mind, she sided with Edward. If so, she must have been worried when in October 1470[31] the Earl of Warwick and George Duke of Clarence managed to drive Edward IV from England, together with several of his key supporters: his youngest brother Richard, Duke of Gloucester, his lord chamberlain William, Baron Hastings and one of his brothers-in-law, Anthony Woodville, Earl Rivers.[32]

It is possible that it was because of his wrongful execution of John and Richard Woodville that Alice turned against her step-grandson the Earl of Warwick, as it was not dissimilar to what had happened to William. During the period in which Edward was gone from England, Henry VI was released from prison and her former close friend Margaret returned to England to be its queen once more, there is not a single surviving mention of Alice. The obvious conclusion is that she spent her time at Ewelme, maintaining

As Mater Familias

a studied neutrality; looking after the Almshouse that she had founded with her third husband, seeing to it her grandchildren were well taken care of.

She was not as innocent as she may have appeared. It is known that Elizabeth, together with her mother Cecily and her sisters Margaret, Duchess of Burgundy and Anne, Duchess of Exeter, was writing letters to her brother George in England, as well as Edward and Richard in exile in Burgundy,[33] trying to convince them to make up, trying to convince George to side with his brothers when they returned from exile with an army.

This was treason. The fact she did this while in the same manor as John and Alice would have implicated them as well. In fact, there is little chance that they would not have known of this. Cecily was closely watched,[34] and since it stands to reason that Anne, married to a Lancastrian duke,[35] was as well, we can assume that Elizabeth would have been instrumental in these attempts, the one to organise the letters to go to Burgundy. It would have been all but impossible to do this without John and Alice being aware of it. Had she been against it, even if she had wished to see Elizabeth punished for it, there would have been no way for Alice to betray her without her son being implicated and her grandchildren suffering for it. However, since we do know Alice and Elizabeth continued to be on good terms after Edward IV took back the throne, it does not seem likely Alice was strongly opposed to her actions.

Whatever Alice thought of it, they were to succeed. By April 1470, Edward IV and his supporters landed at Ravenspurn in England,[36] together with an army paid for by his brother-in-law, Charles, Duke of Burgundy,[37] son of the duke who had once attempted flirting with Alice.

They were met by George, Duke of Clarence, who had taken his sisters' and mother's words to heart and had decided to abandon his alliance with the Lancastrian king and the Earl of Warwick and support his brother. George had many men he could command. When

What is Better than a Good Woman?

Edward IV and his brothers marched on London with their men, they were able capture Henry VI, who had been staying there while the Earl of Warwick had gathered men to meet Edward's forces.

Edward marched on to meet Warwick's men, as well as Queen Margaret and her son, seventeen-year-old Edward. They met the former at Barnet, on 14 April 1471.[38] It was a success for the Yorkists: many of the Lancastrian troops fled, and the Earl of Warwick, like his father and grandfather before him, fell in battle.[39]

Hearing of this, Queen Margaret, her son, and her son's wife, Warwick's younger daughter, fled towards Wales, where they intended to meet up with King Henry VI's half-brother, Jasper Tudor. They never made it. Edward's troops met them at Tewkesbury, and on 4 May 1471, thoroughly defeated them. Margaret's son died in battle and with her troops fleeing, Margaret herself and her daughter-in-law were taken prisoner.[40]

Edward of Lancaster's widow was soon released into the custody of her older sister, George of Clarence's wife, but Margaret remained imprisoned. Since she was not only a woman and as such exempt from being executed for treason, but also a queen and executing an anointed queen would have set an uncomfortable precedent, another solution had to be found for her. Eventually, Edward decided on something that could almost be taken as a kindness: he decided to give her wardship to Alice, having her imprisoned in Wallingford Castle.[41]

How the two women felt about probably depends largely on how much the erstwhile queen blamed Alice for her loss. Many historians, especially Victorian ones, have blamed Alice for not sticking by Margaret, Napier going so far as to say that Alice should have shared her disgrace.[42] But there is no evidence for Alice siding with either Edward or Margaret, and there was no open rift between them in 1460, when Alice's son had been married to Elizabeth Plantagenet for some time.

As Mater Familias

Why a gesture of kindness? Alice knew Margaret well, had for a time even acted as a substitute mother for her. She was the only person in England who had been close to Margaret once and yet could be trusted not to side with her. Under the circumstances, Margaret could not have hoped for anything better, and, if we go by an astoundingly dry letter one of the Pastons wrote about it, nobody was surprised at Edward's choice or considered it a mistake.[43]

However, it is equally possible that the choice was not intended to be a kindness, but to placate Alice. Edward had reason; his father had never paid Elizabeth's dowry completely, nor had he himself in the last ten years. By 1471 he still owed Alice the massive sum of 1000 pounds for his sister Elizabeth's dowry.[44] Giving her Margaret's wardship might have been a gesture to show that he trusted her and held her in high regard, and that she would get the money eventually. Conversely, Alice might have asked for it, using the fact the king was so indebted to her as leverage. It seems that Alice saw to it Margaret was well taken care of, that her imprisonment was an honourable one, but if that meant much to a woman who had lost everything is doubtful. This was not Alice's fault, and possibly she felt sorry for the woman who had once been a friend.

Holding Margaret's wardship was not the only reward the Suffolk family received after Edward IV regained the throne. John and Elizabeth were granted the wardship of Francis, Lord Lovell,[45] an adolescent who had been Warwick's ward since his father's death in 1465[46] and who had lived with the Earl of Warwick's sister Alice FitzHugh for the last two years before his wardship was given to the Duke and Duchess of Suffolk.[47]

The young lord and his two sisters moved into the Suffolks' household in summer 1471, which means that Alice must have met them. Of course, it does not have to mean anything more than that; there is no evidence she ever so much as interacted

What is Better than a Good Woman?

with them. Lord Lovell and his sisters were the closest living relatives of Alice's first husband, John Phelip, being the only great-grandchildren of his brother William. Since Alice had been close to William, perhaps she was pleased to see his great-grandchildren well. When in 1473 John and Elizabeth arranged a marriage for Joan Lovell, Alice was present.

The last years of Alice's life are sadly obscure. What evidence there is only refers to private matters. There is a grant from 1471 to John and Elizabeth:

> To my dere and welbeloved sone John duke of Suffolk and to my Lady Elizabeth his wife suster to our soveraigne lord Kyng Edward the fourthe alle me stuffe of plate of sylver of gilte and of golde. And all my beddys of clothe of gold and of solke and of arras and of tapiserye werke. And all my tapices of arras and of tapiserye. Excepte the plate and the olde beddes and olde tapices of silke and of tapiserye that dayly serven me. Which also after my decesse I yeve to my seide sone and my seide lady his wife. To have and to holde to my seide dere and welbeloved sone and to my seide lady his wife and to their chyldyr of their bodyes comyng alle the seide plate beddys and tapices with goddess blessing and myn for ever.[48]

That Alice gave 'all [her] stuff of silver of gold and of gold' to them, as well as such valuable items as her beds, excluding the ones she needed, suggests a degree of withdrawal from secular life. Possibly, Alice started ailing then. She was sixty-seven years of age in 1471, and may have decided to turn away from the vanities of this world toward God.

13

ALICE'S DEATH

It is possible that at the same time that she made such arrangements, Alice also wrote her will, but sadly, we do not know when she did. It would make sense for her to have done it as at such a time, but it could just as well have been done ten years earlier, or only weeks before her death. Only parts of the will survive, though the parts that do suggest that Alice was still perfectly lucid when she wrote it:

> Item, I will that mine executors, immediately after my decease, take wholly the issues, revenues, and profits, coming and growing of my manor of Norton-under-Hampden, in the county of Somerset, with the appurtenances, which for the sum of 200 pounds sterling, I purchased of Dame Katherine, the wife late of Sir Miles Stapleton, Knight, now the wife of Sir Richard Harecourt, Knight; of my manor of Cotton Henmales, in the county of Suffolk; of my manors of Newenham Courtney, Swereford, in the county of Oxenford; of my manors of West Wythenham, Buryfeld, Langeley, Bradley, with all the lands and tenements in South Moreton, in the county of Berkshire; of my manors of Hatfield Peverell and

What is Better than a Good Woman?

Termyns, in the county of Essex, with all and every their appurtenances; and of all other lordships, manors, rents, lands, and tenements, with the appurtenances, which I have at any time purchased, seth the decease of my said worshipful Lord and husband, William, Duke of Suffolk, whom God assoil; paying therewith first my debts, and then all my bequests above specified, that is to say, such of the bequests as I perform not in my life; and thereupon I specially pray, require, and on God's behalf, charge my feoffees of the said manors, lands, and tenements, with the appurtenances, that they peaceably suffer my executors to take up, and receive all the profits, issues, and revenues, coming and growing, after my decease, of all the said manors, lands, and tenements, with all their appurtenances, in my will afore specified and recited, to the full accomplishment and performing of this my present will and testament, as they will answer afore God at the dreadful day of doom, for to the intent of fulfilling of this present testament and last will I have enfeoffed them, and none otherwise: nevertheless, I will, that all such of my servants as depart from me during my life, have no part of the bequests to them above made.[1]

The last sentence is particularly interesting, and suggests that it was written a while before her death, as it is unlikely she would have expected a departure of servants if she was certain to be dying soon. It also shows us that she was still a strong-willed woman, somewhat cynical about the world, and that she did not like anything to be out of her control. It is doubtful this would have changed much, even if she did lead a more God-oriented life, and she would still have taken a keen interest in what went on around her. The joy at the arrival of another grandchild in 1472, a boy called Edmund, would not have faded.

Alice's Death

However, by 1473, she was genuinely started to ail. Either she or her son sent for a dispensation from the Vatican, granted on 3 March 1474:

To Alice, duchess of Suffolk. Indult, she being broken with age, to choose a fit priest, secular or religious, as her confessor, who, after hearing her confession, may grant her absolution, and enjoin a salutary penance, once only in cases reserved to the apostolic see (with certain exceptions named, and in general the cases contained in the bull of Coena domini) [a papal Bull, so called from the feast on which it was annually published in Rome, the feast of the Lord's Supper, or Maundy Thursday, censures of excommunication] and in other cases as often as shall be opportune; and that the confessor of her choice may, once only, in the hour of death, grant her, being contrite and having confessed, plenary remission of all her sins, with the usual condition of making satisfaction to whom it is due, and the usual clauses against abuse of the present indult, and requiring fasting on Fridays for a year, or giving in alms six groats (sex grossos) of the money of that country, said to be worth half a gold ducat. If she do not so fast, the present grant shall be null and void, as far only as regards plenary remission in the hour of death. Sincere devotionis tue affectus.[2]

Though the language in such indults was often exaggerated, that she was said to be 'broken with age' suggests that Alice was no longer healthy by the time of the request to the papal court, and that she was starting to make arrangements for the hour of her death. That she was required to fast on Fridays implies that she was not suffering from any special illness, simply the effects of age. As we shall see below, she was still lucid shortly before her death, so even if she was physically ailing and unable to take part

What is Better than a Good Woman?

in the life John and Elizabeth led, or even if she was unwilling to do so, having decided to live a more religious life, she must have at least have been interested in the birth of yet another grandchild in 1474, another boy, Humphrey. In the same year, her oldest grandchild, Elizabeth, then thirteen years of age, was married to Henry Lovell, cousin of John and Elizabeth's ward Francis.[3] It can be assumed that Alice at the very least attended this wedding, if it was physically possible, but it must remain just that: an assumption. No evidence about this marriage survives, and all we know is that Elizabeth continued living in her parents' household for the time being.

For a woman whose life is so well-recorded in comparison to her contemporaries, we have no knowledge what her last months of life were like. Only one of her letters survives from 1475, to her step-grandson William Stonor, son of her third husband William's illegitimate daughter Jane:[4]

> Right trusty and entirely beloved friend, we greet you well, desiring and praying you, all excuses laid apart, that in the moment this letter seen you come to us to Ewelme, for certain great causes concerning our well [sic] and pleasure, which at your coming you shall understand more plainly, and thereupon you to depart even at your pleasure, so that you fail not herein at this time, as our perfect trust is in your [doing], and as in greater case we will be glad for you, that knows our lord, who have you ever in governance. Written at Ewelme, the 5 day of March.[5]

She clearly considered the matter urgent and she promised him something for the future. She was making preparations for her death, and perhaps would ask him to help his uncle John with the execution of her will. We do know that this was a matter Alice was concerned with before her death. We have it in John's own words

Alice's Death

that he 'promised her Ladyship to be well willing and helping with all my power, and never to let or suffer, nor make to be let any thing thereof, after my power, and to be of such demeaning, I ensured her upon my truth, and upon a book.'[6]

It seems that John kept that promise,[7] but it is revealing that Alice felt the need to have him swear it to her, swear it on the Bible ('upon a book') as well. This could be taken as an indication that she did not trust him, but nothing else suggests any such rift in their relationship. A more likely explanation is that by making him swear, she ensured his security – it would be hard to accuse him of not having done something he had sworn on the Bible to do.

If by 5 March she was expecting to die soon, she was to be proven correct. It does not seem, though, as if her death was considered imminent, even a week before it happened. On 14 May 1475,[8] Alice's oldest grandson, John, Earl of Lincoln, who was then twelve, was knighted by his uncle Edward IV. He and his father, and possibly his mother as well, were at court for this occasion, without there being any indication of worry about leaving Alice behind.

Her son and grandson rushed home suddenly, not long after the ceremony in which the twelve-year-old John jr was knighted, perhaps having received news that Alice had taken a turn for the worse. They arrived in time when on 20 May 1475 the dowager duchess of Suffolk, dowager countess of Salisbury, died, apparently peacefully, in her ancestral manor of Ewelme.

14

THE AFTERMATH

There is some doubt whether Alice's date of death was 20 May, as her Inquisitions Post Mortem give it as 9 June 1475. However, the inscription on her tomb, ordered by her son, records 20 May, and since he appears to have been present when Alice died this has to be considered the more trustworthy of the two dates. It is not uncommon for Inquisitions Post Mortem to be wrong on such details, so that it can be said with reasonable certainty that she did died at the age of exactly seventy years.

She was laid to rest in the same church as her parents,[1] in the splendid transit tomb she had made for herself. Her funeral must have been a big affair, one quite possibly attended by a disgraced former queen.[2] Her daughter-in-law, a princess of the blood, was present, laying to rest a woman who had been born a commoner, but who had risen to unlikely heights in her life and had died a highly respected matron.

Her family would continue rising after her death. Her oldest grandson John was even heir to the throne for a while, ten years after her death. But of course, she never saw it. She died in the circle of her family, presumably as she had wanted it. Her body still rests in the church in Ewelme, and though the manor she lived in for most of her life is long gone, her tomb still exists,

The Aftermath

proclaiming her connections, her steep rise, her fascinating life story to the world.

Though long gone, Alice did not suffer the fate of most of her contemporaries: in the centuries since her death, her life story has never been forgotten.

ENDNOTES

Chapter 1

1. Marion Turner, *Chaucer: A European Life* (Princeton and Oxford: Princeton University Press, 2019)
2. ibid, p.22
3. ibid, pp.43-70
4. ibid, p.103
5. Henry Morley, *English Writers: An Attempt Towards a History of English Literature, Volume 5* (London, Paris & Melbourne: Cassel and Company Limited, 1890), p.248
6. Marion Turner, *Chaucer: A European Life* (Princeton and Oxford: Princeton University Press, 2019), p.153
7. Thomas A. Prendergast, Stephanie Trigg: *30 Great Myths about Chaucer* (Hoboken, New Jersey: John Wiley&Sons, 2020) 'Myth 5: Thomas Chaucer was John of Gaunt's Bastard'
8. ibid
9. *Life Records of Chaucer* (London: Kegan Paul, Trench, Trübner &Co, 1900) pp.55/6
10. ibid
11. Marjorie Anderson, *Alice Chaucer and Her Husbands*, PMLA Vol. 60, No. 1 (Mar., 1945), p.46

Endnotes

12. http://www.inquisitionspostmortem.ac.uk/view/inquisition/
    21-648/651A

13. ibid

14. P.R.O. DL28/3/2http://www.inquisitionspostmortem.ac.uk/view/
    inquisition/25-527/

Chapter 2

1. Albert C. Baugh, *Kirk's Life Records of Thomas Chaucer*, PMLA
   Vol. 47, No. 2 (Jun., 1932), pp. 461-515. p.463

2. William Hunt, 'Chaucer, Thomas', from: *Oxford Dictionary of
   National Biography*, 1885-1900, Volume 10

3. ibid

4. Chris Given-Wilson, *Henry IV.* (New Haven and London: Yale
   University Press, 2016), p.11

5. His death is the subject of Terry Jones's *Who Murdered Chaucer?*
   (London, Methuen Publishing Limited, 2013)

6. *The Worthies of the United Kingdom; Or Biographical Accounts of
   the Lives of the Most Illustrious Men, in Arts, Arms, Literature
   and Science, Connected with Great Britain. With Numerous
   Portraits, Etc.* (London: Knight & Lacey, 1828) p.81

7. http://www.inquisitionspostmortem.ac.uk/view/inquisition/
   24-346/349

8. http://www.inquisitionspostmortem.ac.uk/view/inquisition/
   24-680/681

9. Nicholas Orme, *Medieval Children* (New Haven and London:
   Yale University Press, 2001). pp. 35-43

10. ibid

11. *The Worthies of the United Kingdom; Or Biographical Accounts
    of the Lives of the Most Illustrious Men, in Arts, Arms,
    Literature and Science, Connected with Great Britain. With
    Numerous Portraits, Etc* (London: Knight & Lacey, 1828) p.81

12. Albert C. Baugh, *Kirk's Life Records of Thomas Chaucer*,
    PMLA Vol. 47, No. 2 (Jun., 1932), pp. 461-515. p.466

What is Better than a Good Woman?

13. ibid, p.467
14. https://www.british-history.ac.uk/no-series/parliament-rolls-medieval/october-1407
15. Martin B. Ruud, *Thomas Chaucer*, University of Minnesota Studies of Language and Literature, No. 9 (Minneapolis, 1926)
16. Larry Scanlon and James Simpson, *John Lydgate: Poetry, Culture, and Lancastrian England* (Indiana: University of Notre Dame Press, 2006)
17. See below, her interaction with Margaret of Anjou and Philip Duke of Burgundy.
18. https://www.british-history.ac.uk/no-series/parliament-rolls-medieval/november-1411
19. ibid
20. Albert C. Baugh, *Kirk's Life Records of Thomas Chaucer*, PMLA Vol. 47, No. 2 (Jun., 1932), pp. 461-515. p.470
21. *The Worthies of the United Kingdom; Or Biographical Accounts of the Lives of the Most Illustrious Men, in Arts, Arms, Literature and Science, Connected with Great Britain. With Numerous Portraits, Etc* (London: Knight & Lacey, 1828) p.81
22. Marjorie Anderson, *Alice Chaucer and Her Husbands*, PMLA Vol. 60, No. 1 (Mar., 1945), pp. 24-47 p.25
23. For instance: https://www.british-history.ac.uk/inquis-post-mortem/vol20/pp109-123
24. C138/13/42
25. Henry Alfred Napier: *Historical Notices of the Parishes of Swyncombe and Ewelme in the County of Oxfordshire.* (Oxford: James Wright, Printer to the University, 1863) p.32

Chapter 3

1. ibid, pp.30/1
2. https://www.british-history.ac.uk/inquis-post-mortem/vol20/pp109-123
3. Rowena E. Archer, 'Alice Chaucer, Duchess of Suffolk (d.1475), And Her East Anglian Estates', in: Peter Bloore, Edward

Endnotes

A. Martin: *Wingfield College and Its Patrons: Piety and Patronage in Medieval Suffolk* (Woodbridge: The Boydell Press, 2015) p.188

4. Albert C. Baugh, *Kirk's Life Records of Thomas Chaucer*, PMLA Vol. 47, No. 2 (Jun., 1932), pp. 461-515. p.473

5. Henry Alfred Napier: *Historical Notices of the Parishes of Swyncombe and Ewelme in the County of Oxfordshire.* (Oxford: James Wright, Printer to the University, 1863) p.63

6. PCC 43 March. An edition of wills proved in the Prerogative Court of Canterbury

7. ibid

8. ibid

9. https://www.british-history.ac.uk/inquis-post-mortem/vol20/pp.109-123

10. Matthew Lewis, *Richard, Duke of York: King by Right* (Stroud: Amberley Publishing, 2016) p.35. See also: Ian Mortimer, *Henry V: The Warrior King of 1415* (New York City: RosettaBooks, 2009, 2013) 'August'

11. Matthew Lewis, *Richard, Duke of York: King by Right* (Stroud: Amberley Publishing, 2016) p.37

12. Ian Mortimer, *Henry V: The Warrior King of 1415* (New York City: RosettaBooks, 2009, 2013) 'September'

13. ibid

14. Matthew Lewis, *Richard, Duke of York: King by Right* (Stroud: Amberley Publishing, 2016), p.108

15. Ian Mortimer, *Henry V: The Warrior King of 1415* (New York City: RosettaBooks, 2009, 2013) 'September'

16. ibid

17. ibid, 'October'

Chapter 4

1. C138/13/42

2. Henry Alfred Napier, pp.98-9

What is Better than a Good Woman?

3. Paul Murray Kendall, *Richard the Third* (London: George Allen & Unwin, 1955-1956) p.51
4. Ian Mortimer, *1415: Henry V`s Year of Glory* (London: Random House, 2009) pp.388-464
5. Albert C. Baugh, *Kirk's Life Records of Thomas Chaucer*, PMLA Vol. 47, No. 2 (Jun., 1932) pp. 461-515. pp.475/6
6. https://www.poetrynook.com/poem/departing-thomas-chaucer

Chapter 5

1. Marjorie Anderson, *Alice Chaucer and Her Husbands*, PMLA Vol. 60, No. 1 (Mar., 1945) p.27
2. http://www.inquisitionspostmortem.ac.uk/view/inquisition/23-262/282
3. ibid
4. See below, Chapter 5
5. Marjorie Anderson, *Alice Chaucer and Her Husbands*, PMLA Vol. 60, No. 1 (Mar., 1945) p.28
6. See, for example: translated by Thomas Johnes, Esq: *The chronicles of Enguerrand de Monstrelet; containing an account of the cruel civil wars between the houses of Orleans and Burgundy; of the possession of Paris and Normandy by the English; their expulsion thence; and of other memorable events that happened in the kingdom of France, as well as in other countries. Beginning at the year MCCCC., where that of Sir John Froissart finishes, and ending at the year MCCCCLXXVII., and continued by others to the year MDXVI.* (London, William Smith, 1845); and Piers de Fenin, *Mémoires de Pierre de Fenin comprenant le récit des événements: qui se sont passés en France et en Bourgogne sous les règnes de Charles VI et Charles VII, 1407-1427* (Histoire) pp.224-239
7. Ian Mortimer, *1415: Henry V`s Year of Glory* (London: Random House, 2009) p.517

Endnotes

8. https://sourcebooks.fordham.edu/source/1420troyes.asp

9. ibid

10. Lauren Johnson, *Shadow King. The Life and Death of Henry VI* (London: Head of Zeus Ltd, 2019) 'That Divine King your Father'

11. ibid, pp.28-9

12. ibid, pp.17-19

13. Henry Alfred Napier, pp.35-6

14. https://www.british-history.ac.uk/no-series/parliament-rolls-medieval/january-1401

15. Chris Given-Wilson, *Henry IV* (New Haven and London: Yale University Press, 2016) p.445

16. William Hunt, 'Montacute, Thomas de', *Oxford Dictionary of National Biography*, 1885-1900, Volume 38

17. Marjorie Anderson, *Alice Chaucer and Her Husbands*, PMLA Vol. 60, No. 1 (Mar., 1945) pp. 24-47, p.30

18. See below, Chapter 12

19. Piers de Fenin, *Mémoires de Pierre de Fenin comprenant le récit des événements: qui se sont passés en France et en Bourgogne sous les règnes de Charles VI et Charles VII, 1407-1427* (Histoire) pp.224-239

20. ibid

21. ibid

22. 'Lateran Regesta 260: 1425-1426', in *Calendar of Papal Registers Relating to Great Britain and Ireland: Volume 7, 1417-1431*, ed. J A Twemlow (London, 1906), pp. 439-451. British History Online http://www.british-history.ac.uk/cal-papal-registers/brit-ie/vol7/pp439-451 [accessed 10 March 2021].

23. ibid

24. http://www.inquisitionspostmortem.ac.uk/view/inquisition/25-527/

25. ibid

26. ibid

What is Better than a Good Woman?

27. ibid

28. Albert C. Baugh, Kirk's Life Records of Thomas Chaucer, PMLA Vol. 47, No. 2 (Jun., 1932) pp. 461-515, p.491

29. ibid, p.492

30. Henry Alfred Napier, p.98

31. Piers de Fenin, *Mémoires de Pierre de Fenin comprenant le récit des événements: qui se sont passés en France et en Bourgogne sous les règnes de Charles VI et Charles VII, 1407-1427* (Histoire) pp.224-239

32. Helen Castor: *Joan of Arc. A History* (London: Faber and Faber Ltd, 2014) 'This War, Accursed of God'

33. See, for example: Piers de Fenin, *Mémoires de Pierre de Fenin comprenant le récit des événements: qui se sont passés en France...* and translated by Thomas Johnes, Esq: *The chronicles of Enguerrand de Monstrelet...*

34. Piers de Fenin, *Mémoires de Pierre de Fenin comprenant le récit des événements: qui se sont passés en France...* pp.224-239

35. Translated by Thomas Johnes, Esq: *The chronicles of Enguerrand de Monstrelet...* p.445

36. ibid

37. ibid

38. http://www.inquisitionspostmortem.ac.uk/view/inquisition/23-262/282

39. Nicholas Harris Nicolas, *Testamenta Vetusta: Being Illustrations From Wills Of Manners, Customs & c. As Well As The Descents And Possessions From Many Distinguished Families. From the Reign Of Henry The Second To The Accession Of Queen Elizabeth. Volume I* (London: Nicols And Son, 1826) p.215-7

40. Kathryn Warner, *Edward II's Nieces: The Clare Sisters. Powerful Pawns of the Crown* (Barnsley: Pen & Sword Books Limited, 2020) pp.47-8

41. Nicholas Harris Nicolas, *Testamenta Vetusta: Being Illustrations From Wills Of Manners...* p.215-7

Endnotes

42. http://www.inquisitionspostmortem.ac.uk/view/inquisition/23-262/282

43. National Archives UK: https://discovery.nationalarchives.gov.uk/details/r/C4944919?fbclid=IwAR10WgchjUqNEUlTCKxIuW6skCUE3cID6nawK-x6kpWLdX1_gTStHRISgoc

44. https://www.british-history.ac.uk/no-series/parliament-rolls-medieval/september-1429

45. National Archives UK: https://discovery.nationalarchives.gov.uk/details/r/C4513109?fbclid=IwAR2ROk3DwqXq-xLXTjcS2W9TVpjZfZYO3sMott3OfN1HtNJMJ9IciT1hyyA

46. https://www.british-history.ac.uk/no-series/parliament-rolls-medieval/september-1429

47. Albert C. Baugh, *Kirk's Life Records of Thomas Chaucer*, PMLA Vol. 47, No. 2 (Jun., 1932), pp. 461-515. pp.490-3

48. ibid, pp.428-30

49. Translated by Thomas Johnes, Esq: *The chronicles of Enguerrand de Monstrelet...* pp.446-450

50. For the whole story, see Helen Castor: *Joan of Arc. A History* (London: Faber and Faber Ltd, 2014) and Moya Longstaffe: *Joan of Arc and 'The Great Pity of the Land of France'* (Stroud: Amberley Publishing 2017)

51. https://www.british-history.ac.uk/no-series/parliament-rolls-medieval/september-1429

Chapter 6

1. Ian Mortimer, *1415: Henry V's Year of Glory* (London: Random House, 2009) p.517

2. ibid

3. ibid

4. Translated by Thomas Johnes, Esq: *The chronicles of Enguerrand de Monstrelet...* pp.557-8

5. Lauren Johnson, *Shadow King. The Life and Death of Henry VI* (London: Head of Zeus Ltd, 2019) pp.95-8

What is Better than a Good Woman?

6. 'Henry VI: November 1449', in *Parliament Rolls of Medieval England*, ed. Chris Given-Wilson, Paul Brand, Seymour Phillips, Mark Ormrod, Geoffrey Martin, Anne Curry and Rosemary Horrox (Woodbridge, 2005), British History Online http://www.british-history.ac.uk/no-series/parliament-rolls-medieval/november-1449 [accessed 11 March 2021]

7. Piers de Fenin, *Mémoires de Pierre de Fenin comprenant le récit des événements: qui se sont passés en France...* pp.224-239

8. Translated by Thomas Johnes, Esq: *The chronicles of Enguerrand de Monstrelet...*

9. Marjorie Anderson, *Alice Chaucer and Her Husbands*, PMLA Vol. 60, No. 1 (Mar., 1945) p.30

10. Susan Curran: *The English Friend* (Norwich: Lasse Press, 2011.) Position 243

11. Henry Noble MacCracken, *An English Friend of Charles of Orléans*, PMLA Vol. 26, No. 1 (1911), pp.142-180

12. Pierre Champion, *'La Dame Anglaise de Charles D`Orleans'*, Romania, XLIV, 1923.

13. ibid, p. 154. Translation author

14. ibid, p.152. Translation author

15. Ibid

16. Susan Curran: *The English Friend*. Positions 3385-3412

17. 'Henry VI: February 1449', in *Parliament Rolls of Medieval England*, British History Online http://www.british-history.ac.uk/no-series/parliament-rolls-medieval/february-1449 [accessed 11 March 2021]

18. Calenda of Patent Rolls, Henry VI, Volume II, p.86

19. ibid

20. See: H. T. Riley, *Ingulph's Chronicle of the Abbey of Croyland* (London: George Bell and Sons, 1908)

21. See: Albert C. Baugh, *Kirk's Life Records of Thomas Chaucer*, PMLA Vol. 47, No. 2 (Jun., 1932), pp.461-515

22. Susan Curran: *The English Friend*. Position 1120

Endnotes

23. National Archives UK: https://discovery.nationalarchives.gov.uk/details/r/C4944919?fbclid=IwAR10WgchjUqNEUlTCKxIuW6skCUE3cID6nawK-x6kpWLdX1_gTStHRISgoc

24. George Frederick Beltz, *Memorials of the Order of the Garter, from its foundation to the present time. Including the history of the order; biographical notices of the knights in the reigns of Edward III and Richard II, the chronological succession of the members* (London: W. Pickering, 1841)

25. Lauren Johnson, *Shadow King. The Life and Death of Henry VI* (London: Head of Zeus Ltd, 2019) pp.129-30

26. Susan Curran: *The English Friend.* Positions 3427-3440

27. The discussion about what caused her downfall is detailed in: Helen Castor: *Joan of Arc. A History* (London: Faber and Faber Ltd, 2014)

28. Lauren Johnson, *Shadow King. The Life and Death of Henry VI* (London: Head of Zeus Ltd, 2019) p.102

29. ibid, pp.103-4

30. ibid

31. ibid

32. Lauren Johnson, *Shadow King. The Life and Death of Henry VI* (London: Head of Zeus Ltd, 2019) pp.129-30

33. National Archives UK: https://discovery.nationalarchives.gov.uk/details/r/C4944919?fbclid=IwAR10WgchjUqNEUlTCKxIuW6skCUE3cID6nawK-x6kpWLdX1_gTStHRISgoc

34. George Frederick Beltz, *Memorials of the Order of the Garter...*

35. 'Henry VI: November 1449', in *Parliament Rolls of Medieval England*, British History Online http://www.british-history.ac.uk/no-series/parliament-rolls-medieval/november-1449 [accessed 11 March 2021].

36. Susan Curran: *The English Friend.* Position 3265

37. 'Henry VI: November 1449', in *Parliament Rolls of Medieval England*, British History Online http://www.british-history.

What is Better than a Good Woman?

ac.uk/no-series/parliament-rolls-medieval/november-1449 [accessed 23 March 2021].

38. ibid

39. 'Henry VI: November 1449', in *Parliament Rolls of Medieval England*, British History Online http://www.british-history. ac.uk/no-series/parliament-rolls-medieval/november-1449 [accessed 11 March 2021]

40. Henry Noble MacCracken, *An English Friend of Charles of Orléans*, PMLA Vol. 26, No. 1 (1911), pp.142-180

41. ibid

42. 'Henry VI: November 1449', in *Parliament Rolls of Medieval England*, British History Online http://www.british-history. ac.uk/no-series/parliament-rolls-medieval/november-1449 [accessed 11 March 2021]

43. Henry Noble MacCracken, *An English Friend of Charles of Orléans*, PMLA Vol. 26, No. 1 (1911), pp. 142-180

44. Pierre Champion, '*La Dame Anglaise de Charles D'Orleans*', Romania, XLIV, 1923.

45. Henry Noble MacCracken, *An English Friend of Charles of Orléans*, PMLA Vol. 26, No. 1 (1911), pp. 142-180

46. Pierre Champion, '*La Dame Anglaise de Charles D'Orleans*', Romania, XLIV, 1923.

47. Marjorie Anderson, *Alice Chaucer and Her Husbands*, PMLA Vol. 60, No. 1 (Mar., 1945), pp.33-4

48. Henry Noble MacCracken, *An English Friend of Charles of Orléans*, PMLA Vol. 26, No. 1 (1911), pp. 142-180

49. ibid, pp.151-179

50. Pierre Champion, '*La Dame Anglaise de Charles D'Orleans*', Romania, XLIV, 1923

51. Karen K. Jambeck, *The Library of Alice Chaucer, Duchess of Suffolk: A Fifteenth-Century Owner of a 'Boke of le Citee de Dames'* (Western Connecticut State University) p.122

Endnotes

52. Lauren Johnson, *Shadow King. The Life and Death of Henry VI* (London: Head of Zeus Ltd, 2019) pp.129-30

53. George Frederick Beltz, *Memorials of the Order of the Garter...*

54. http://www.inquisitionspostmortem.ac.uk/view/inquisition/24-346/349

55. Rowena E. Archer, 'Alice Chaucer, Duchess of Suffolk (d.1475), And Her East Anglian Estates', in: Peter Bloore, Edward A. Martin: *Wingfield College and Its Patrons: Piety and Patronage in Medieval Suffolk* (Woodbridge: The Boydell Press, 2015)

56. http://www.inquisitionspostmortem.ac.uk/view/inquisition/24-346/349

57. ibid

58. ibid

59. http://www.inquisitionspostmortem.ac.uk/view/inquisition/24-680/686

60. Albert C. Baugh, *Kirk's Life Records of Thomas Chaucer*, PMLA Vol. 47, No. 2 (Jun., 1932), pp. 461-515. p.502

61. ibid, 503-505

62. Henry Alfred Napier, p.44

63. He discusses Thomas's tomb but does not realise the oddity of the choice.

64. Martin B. Ruud, *Thomas Chaucer*, University of Minnesota Studies of Language and Literature, No. 9 (Minneapolis, 1926)

65. Henry Alfred Napier, p.44

66. For example: Edited by Lucy Toulmin Smith, John Leland, *The itinerary of John Leland in or about the years 1535-1543.*

67. ibid, p.112

68. Ed. Charles Lethbridge Kingsford, *The Stonor letters and papers, 1290–1483* (London: Offices of the Society, 1919)

69. James Gairdner, *The Paston Letters, AD 1422–1509. Volumes I-VI.* New Complete Library Edition (London: Chatto & Windus, Exeter: James G. Commin, 1904)

What is Better than a Good Woman?

70. Ed. Charles Lethbridge Kingsford, *The Stonor letters and papers, 1290–1483* (London: Offices of the Society, 1919) p.xx
71. ibid, pp.xxii
72. ibid, p.50
73. http://www.inquisitionspostmortem.ac.uk/view/inquisition/24-346/349
74. Rowena E. Archer, 'Alice Chaucer, Duchess of Suffolk (d.1475), And Her East Anglian Estates', in: Peter Bloore, Edward A. Martin: *Wingfield College and Its Patrons: Piety and Patronage in Medieval Suffolk* (Woodbridge: The Boydell Press, 2015) p.188
75. Susan Curran: *The English Friend*. Position 5708
76. The most famous example is of course found in the Parliament of 1450: https://www.british-history.ac.uk/no-series/parliament-rolls-medieval/november-1450
77. For example: James Gairdner, *The Paston Letters, AD 1422–1509. Volume IV.* pp.221-2
78. 'Henry VI: October 1435', in *Parliament Rolls of Medieval England*, British History Online http://www.british-history.ac.uk/no-series/parliament-rolls-medieval/october-1435 [accessed 12 March 2021].
79. Marjorie Anderson, *Alice Chaucer and Her Husbands*, PMLA Vol. 60, No. 1 (Mar., 1945), p.33
80. Susan Curran: *The English Friend*. Position 3859
81. 'Henry VI: October 1435', in *Parliament Rolls of Medieval England*, British History Online. Web. 12 March 2021. http://www.british-history.ac.uk/no-series/parliament-rolls-medieval/october-1435.
82. Henry Noble MacCracken, *An English Friend of Charles of Orléans*, PMLA
83. National Archives UK: https://discovery.nationalarchives.gov.uk/details/r/C4944919?fbclid=IwAR1oWgchjUqNEUlTCKxIuW6skCUE3cID6nawK-x6kpWLdX1_gTStHRISgoc

Endnotes

84. 'Chronological Arrangement of Vatican Regesta Documents', in *Calendar of Papal Registers Relating To Great Britain and Ireland: Volume 8, 1427-1447*, ed. J A Twemlow (London, 1909), pp. xv-xxxviii. British History Online http://www.british-history.ac.uk/cal-papal-registers/brit-ie/vol8/xv-xxxviii [accessed 12 March 2021].

85. ibid

86. National Archives UK: https://discovery.nationalarchives.gov.uk/details/r/C4944919?fbclid=IwAR10WgchjUqNEUlTCKxIuW6skCUE3cID6nawK-x6kpWLdX1_gTStHRISgoc

87. http://www.inquisitionspostmortem.ac.uk/view/inquisition/23-262/282

88. Henry Alfred Napier, p.35

89. ibid

90. http://www.inquisitionspostmortem.ac.uk/view/inquisition/24-680/686

91. Henry Alfred Napier, p.44

92. ibid

93. John Goodall: *God`s House at Ewelme: Life, Devotion and Architecture in a Fifteenth-Century Almshouse* (London: Taylor & Francis, 2017) p.23

94. ibid, p.23

95. ibid

96. Lauren Johnson, *Shadow King. The Life and Death of Henry VI* (London: Head of Zeus Ltd, 2019) p.164

97. ibid, p.124

98. ibid,

99. Stanley Bertram Chrimes, *Henry VII* (London: Yale University Press, 1999), pp. 8-11

100. Paul Murray Kendall, *Richard the Third* (London: George Allen & Unwin, 1955–1956) p.157

101. Lauren Johnson, *Shadow King. The Life and Death of Henry VI* (London: Head of Zeus Ltd, 2019), p.124

What is Better than a Good Woman?

102. ibid, p.122

103. Paul Murray Kendall, *Richard the Third* (London: George Allen & Unwin, 1955–1956) p.157

104. See below, Chapter 12

105. 'Houses of Benedictine nuns: Abbey of Barking', in *A History of the County of Essex: Volume 2*, ed. William Page and J Horace Round (London, 1907), pp. 115-122. British History Online http://www.british-history.ac.uk/vch/essex/vol2/pp115-122 [accessed 13 March 2021].

106. Lauren Johnson, *Shadow King. The Life and Death of Henry VI* (London: Head of Zeus Ltd, 2019) p.164

107. 'Houses of Benedictine nuns: Abbey of Barking', in *A History of the County of Essex: Volume 2*, ed. William Page and J Horace Round (London, 1907), pp. 115-122. British History Online http://www.british-history.ac.uk/vch/essex/vol2/pp.115-122 [accessed 13 March 2021]

108. ibid: there is no mention made of them

109. For example: Marjorie Anderson, *Alice Chaucer and Her Husbands*, PMLA Vol. 60, No. 1 (Mar., 1945)

110. 'Lateran Regesta, 359: 1437-1438', in *Calendar of Papal Registers Relating To Great Britain and Ireland: Volume 9, 1431-1447*, ed. J A Twemlow (London, 1912), pp. 1-13. British History Online http://www.british-history.ac.uk/cal-papal-registers/brit-ie/vol9/pp.1-13 [accessed 13 March 2021]

111. The act of Parliament against William in 1450 referred to him freeing Charles, Duke of Orleans against the best interests of England in that year, but this happened in 1440.

112. 'Henry VI: November 1449', in *Parliament Rolls of Medieval England*, British History Online http://www.british-history.ac.uk/no-series/parliament-rolls-medieval/november-1449 [accessed 13 March 2021]

113. Nancy Goldstone, *The Maid and the Queen: The Secret History of Joan of Arc* (London: Phoenix Paperbacks, 2013) pp. 225-6

Endnotes

114. 'Henry VI: November 1449', in *Parliament Rolls of Medieval England*, British History Online http://www.british-history. ac.uk/no-series/parliament-rolls-medieval/november-1449 [accessed 13 March 2021]

115. ibid

116. 'Henry VI: November 1449', in *Parliament Rolls of Medieval England*, British History Online http://www.british-history. ac.uk/no-series/parliament-rolls-medieval/november-1449 [accessed 15 March 2021].

117. Rachel M Delman: *Gendered viewing, childbirth and female authority in the residence of Alice Chaucer, duchess of Suffolk, at Ewelme, Oxfordshire* (2018) https://www.tandfonline.com/doi/full/10.1080/03044 181.2019.1593619?fbclid=IwAR3zANh8h84dUUpk qdX6R6_qz4DJ8v1TrljoQn22_vr_ffyFz43MqeGVdCw&

118. ibid

119. ibid

120. ibid

121. For example, King Edward IV`s wife Queen Elizabeth had her last child at the age of 43.

122. Susan Curran: *The English Friend*. Position 4701

123. 'Henry VI: January 1442', in *Parliament Rolls of Medieval England*, British History Online http://www.british-history. ac.uk/no-series/parliament-rolls-medieval/january-1442 [accessed 13 March 2021]

124. 'Henry VI: November 1449', in *Parliament Rolls of Medieval England*, British History Online http://www.british-history. ac.uk/no-series/parliament-rolls-medieval/november-1449 [accessed 13 March 2021]

125. Lauren Johnson, *Shadow King. The Life and Death of Henry VI* (London: Head of Zeus Ltd, 2019), pp.178-80

126. He was celebrated as a hero even in chronicles written during Tudor times.

What is Better than a Good Woman?

127. She even became the first woman to be officially attainted in later years.
128. See, for example: Roger Virgoe, B.A., Ph.D., *The Death of William De La Pole, Duke of Suffolk* https://www.jstor.org/stable/community.28211836
129. ibid
130. ibid
131. ibid
132. ibid
133. In fact, the incident had rather severe consequences. Since the Keeper of the woods was later imprisoned for acting against Alice and the city itself punished, complaints are on record against Alice and William.
134. Sheila Kant, *Alice, Duchess of Suffolk* (2000)
135. 'Henry VI: January 1442', in *Parliament Rolls of Medieval England*, British History Online http://www.british-history.ac.uk/no-series/parliament-rolls-medieval/january-1442 [accessed 14 March 2021].
136. No mention is made of him.
137. 'Henry VI: January 1442', in *Parliament Rolls of Medieval England*, British History Online http://www.british-history.ac.uk/no-series/parliament-rolls-medieval/january-1442 [accessed 14 March 2021]
138. Ed. Gwilym Dodd, Douglas Biggs: *Henry IV, The Establishment of the Regime, 1399-1406* (York: York Medieval Press, 2003) p.132
139. Calendar of Patent Rolls, Richard II, Volume VI, AD 1396-1399, p.464
140. Chris Given-Wilson, *Henry IV* (New Haven and London: Yale University Press, 2016) pp.138-157
141. See above, Chapter 3
142. http://www.inquisitionspostmortem.ac.uk/view/inquisition/25-527/

Endnotes

143. Ed Cecil Monro, *Letters of Queen Margaret of Anjou and Bishop Beckington and Others. Written in the Reigns of Henry V and Henry VI. From a manuscript found at Emral in Flintshire* (London: Camden Society. 1863) pp.96-7

144. ibid

145. ibid

146. ibid p.77

147. Calendar of Patent Rolls, Henry VI, Volume V, 1441-1446, p.596

148. Rachel M Delman: *Gendered viewing, childbirth and female authority in the residence of Alice Chaucer...*

149. See below, Chapters 11 and 12

150. Josephine Wilkinson, *Richard the Young King to Be* (Stroud: Amberley Publishing, 2014) p. 65

151. At least, there is no evidence of her being present at court, as there is for the previous years.

152. The lead-up to this is explained in: 'Henry VI: January 1442', in *Parliament Rolls of Medieval England*, British History Online http://www.british-history.ac.uk/no-series/parliament-rolls-medieval/january-1442 [accessed 15 March 2021].

153. Lauren Johnson, *Shadow King. The Life and Death of Henry VI* (London: Head of Zeus Ltd, 2019) pp.187-91

154. ibid, p.191

155. ibid, p.193

156. ibid, p.194

157. 'Henry VI: November 1449', in *Parliament Rolls of Medieval England*, British History Online http://www.british-history.ac.uk/no-series/parliament-rolls-medieval/november-1449 [accessed 15 March 2021]

158. It was part of William's protestation of innocence to point this out.

159. ibid

What is Better than a Good Woman?

160. Lauren Johnson, *Shadow King. The Life and Death of Henry VI* (London: Head of Zeus Ltd, 2019) pp.194

161. Ed. Thomas Basin and Charles Samaran, *Histoire de Charles VII: Tome Premier, 1407-1444* (Paris: Les Classiques de l'Histoire de France Au Moyen Age. Volume 15, 1933)

162. ibid

163. 'Henry VI: November 1449', in *Parliament Rolls of Medieval England*, British History Online http://www.british-history.ac.uk/no-series/parliament-rolls-medieval/november-1449 [accessed 15 March 2021].

164. ibid

165. ibid

166. Susan Curran: *The English Friend.* Positions 5283-5311

167. Lauren Johnson, *Shadow King. The Life and Death of Henry VI* (London: Head of Zeus Ltd, 2019) p.195

168. S. Bentley, *Excerpta Historica or Illustrations of English History* (London, 1831) p.4

169. Nicola Tallis, *Uncrowned Queen: The Fateful Life of Margaret Beaufort, Tudor Matriarch* (London: Michael O'Mara Books Limited, 2019)

170. H. T. Riley, *Ingulph's Chronicle of the Abbey of Croyland* (London: George Bell and Sons, 1908) p.399

171. S. Bentley, *Excerpta Historica or Illustrations of English history* (London, 1831) p.4

172. Nicola Tallis, *Uncrowned Queen: The Fateful Life of Margaret Beaufort, Tudor Matriarch* (London: Michael O'Mara Books Limited, 2019) Positions 773-801

173. ibid, position 185

174. See, for example: Nathen Amin, *The House of Beaufort. The Bastard Line that Captured the Crown* (Stroud: Amberley Publishing, 2017)

175. Henry VI: November 1449', in *Parliament Rolls of Medieval England*, British History Online http://www.british-history.

ac.uk/no-series/parliament-rolls-medieval/november-1449 [accessed 15 March 2021]

176. ibid

177. For example: Nicola Tallis, *Uncrowned Queen: The Fateful Life of Margaret Beaufort, Tudor Matriarch* (London: Michael O`Mara Books Limited, 2019) Position 785

178. See below, Chapter 8

179. He is referred to as marquis in the Calendar of Patent Rolls, Henry VI, Volume V, 1441-1446, p.409

180. Calendar of Patent Rolls, Henry VI, Volume IV, 1441-1446, p.319

Chapter 7

1. Ed. Thomas Basin and Charles Samaran, *Histoire de Charles VII: Tome Premier, 1407-1444.* (Paris: Les Classiques de l`Histoire de France Au Moyen Age. Volume 15, 1933

2. ibid

3. Lauren Johnson, *Shadow King. The Life and Death of Henry VI* (London: Head of Zeus Ltd, 2019), p.197

4. https://twitter.com/SylviaBSo/status/1301813823079436288?s= 20&fbclid=IwAR1-FtbKu63Cfp23ZLdJQNFxFceg4mPeGE Um9Y6UWx45EtGQjI-opPU2qUA

5. Ed. Thomas Basin and Charles Samaran, *Histoire de Charles VII: Tome Premier, 1407-1444.* (Paris: Les Classiques de l`Histoire de France Au Moyen Age. Volume 15, 1933)

6. ibid

7. Lauren Johnson, *Shadow King. The Life and Death of Henry VI* (London: Head of Zeus Ltd, 2019), p.197

8. For example: Henry Alfred Napier, p.61

9. Ibid, p.61

10. Jacob Abbot, *Margaret of Anjou. Makers of History* (Glasgow: Good Press, 2019) Original publication: 1861

11. For example: Lauren Johnson, *Shadow King. The Life and Death of Henry VI* (London: Head of Zeus Ltd, 2019), p.197

What is Better than a Good Woman?

12. Stanley Weintraub, *Uncrowned King. The Life of Prince Albert* (New York: Free Press, 1997). p.18

13. ibid

14. Nicola Tallis, *Uncrowned Queen: The Fateful Life of Margaret Beaufort, Tudor Matriarch* (London: Michael O'Mara Books Limited, 2019) Positions 991-1006

15. National Archives UK: https://discovery.nationalarchives.gov.uk/details/r/C4518120

16. This is detailed in: J.L.Laynesmith, *Cecily, Duchess of York* (London, New York: Bloomsbury Academic, 2017)

17. Lauren Johnson, *Shadow King. The Life and Death of Henry VI* (London: Head of Zeus Ltd, 2019), pp.198-200

18. 'Milan: 1458', in *Calendar of State Papers and Manuscripts in the Archives and Collections of Milan 1385-1618*, ed. Allen B Hinds (London, 1912), pp. 18-19. British History Online http://www.british-history.ac.uk/cal-state-papers/milan/1385-1618/pp18-19 [accessed 16 March 2021]

19. 'Henry VI: February 1449', in *Parliament Rolls of Medieval England*, British History Online http://www.british-history.ac.uk/no-series/parliament-rolls-medieval/february-1449 [accessed 16 March 2021]

20. As observed by: Lauren Johnson, *Shadow King. The Life and Death of Henry VI* (London: Head of Zeus Ltd, 2019) p.194

21. ibid

22. A typical example of this can be seen in the uprising of 1450: 'Henry VI: November 1449', in *Parliament Rolls of Medieval England*, British History Online http://www.british-history.ac.uk/no-series/parliament-rolls-medieval/november-1449 [accessed 16 March 2021]

23. As discussed in: Lauren Johnson, *Shadow King. The Life and Death of Henry VI* (London: Head of Zeus Ltd, 2019)

24. This is the angle chosen in: John Ashdown-Hill, *Cecily Neville, Mother of Richard III* (Yorkshire: Pen & Sword, 2018)

Endnotes

25. National Archives UK: https://discovery.nationalarchives.gov.uk/details/r/C4518120, https://discovery.nationalarchives.gov.uk/details/r/C4518125

26. Calendar of Patent Rolls, Henry VI, Volume V, 1446-1452, p.133

27. Lauren Johnson, *Shadow King. The Life and Death of Henry VI* (London: Head of Zeus Ltd, 2019), p.235

28. ibid

29. K. L. Clark, *The Nevills of Middleham: England's most Powerful Family in the Wars of the Roses* (Stroud: The History Press, 2016) p.97

30. 'Henry VI: November 1449', in *Parliament Rolls of Medieval England*, British History Online http://www.british-history.ac.uk/no-series/parliament-rolls-medieval/november-1449 [accessed 16 March 2021]

31. K. L. Clark, *The Nevills of Middleham: England's Most Powerful Family in the Wars of the* Roses (Stroud: The History Press, 2016) p.97

32. 'Henry VI: February 1447', in *Parliament Rolls of Medieval England*, British History Online http://www.british-history.ac.uk/no-series/parliament-rolls-medieval/february-1447 [accessed 16 March 2021]

33. See above, Chapter 6

34. 'Henry VI: February 1445', in *Parliament Rolls of Medieval England*, British History Online http://www.british-history.ac.uk/no-series/parliament-rolls-medieval/february-1445 [accessed 16 March 2021]

35. Lauren Johnson, *Shadow King. The Life and Death of Henry VI* (London: Head of Zeus Ltd, 2019) pp.210-2

36. ibid

37. Others who supposedly did are named here: 'Henry VI: November 1450', in *Parliament Rolls of Medieval England*, (2005), British History Online http://www.british-history.ac.uk/no-series/parliament-rolls-medieval/november-1450

What is Better than a Good Woman?

38. As he had been arguing with Gloucester for years.
39. 'Henry VI: February 1449', in *Parliament Rolls of Medieval England*, British History Online http://www.british-history.ac.uk/no-series/parliament-rolls-medieval/february-1449 [accessed 16 March 2021]
40. 'Henry VI: November 1449', in *Parliament Rolls of Medieval England*, British History Online http://www.british-history.ac.uk/no-series/parliament-rolls-medieval/november-1449 [accessed 16 March 2021]
41. ibid
42. ibid
43. Matthew Lewis, *Richard, Duke of York: King by Right* (Stroud: Amberley Publishing, 2016) p.141
44. 'Vatican Regesta 387: 1448', in *Calendar of Papal Registers Relating To Great Britain and Ireland: Volume 10, 1447-1455*, ed. J A Twemlow (London, 1915), pp. 22-38. British History Online http://www.british-history.ac.uk/cal-papal-registers/brit-ie/vol10/pp22-38 [accessed 16 March 2021]
45. At least, he is not mentioned in any sources to indicate he was there.

Chapter 8

1. Calendar of Patent Rolls, Henry VI, Volume V, 1446-1452
2. https://www.bl.uk/catalogues/illuminatedmanuscripts/ILLUMINBig.ASP?size=big&IllID=29350&fbclid=IwAR2vDeM3qpBwNrbxaTrYu-_OkfP3ZQIefil5KTUZMASnqxhpsW434hNoeMs
3. Testament of William de la Pole, Duke of Suffolk, quoted in: Henry Alfred Napier: *Historical Notices of the Parishes of Swyncombe and Ewelme in the County of Oxfordshire* (Oxford: James Wright, Printer to the University, 1863) p.82
4. Susan Curran: *The English Friend*. Position 992
5. Matthew Lewis, *Richard, Duke of York: King by Right* (Stroud: Amberley Publishing, 2016) p.152

Endnotes

6. Oliver, Clementine: *Murdered in the Tabloids: Billposting and the Destruction of the Duke of Suffolk in 1450*. Anales de la Universidad de Alicante. Historia Medieval, N. 19 (2015-2016): 381-402, DOI:10.14198/medieval.2015-2016.19.13

7. ibid

8. ibid

9. 'Henry VI: November 1449', in *Parliament Rolls of Medieval England*, British History Online http://www.british-history.ac.uk/no-series/parliament-rolls-medieval/november-1449 [accessed 16 March 2021]

10. ibid

11. K. L. Clark, *The Nevills of Middleham: England's Most Powerful Family in the Wars of the Roses* (Stroud: The History Press, 2016) p.97

12. Susan Curran: *The English Friend*. Position 5689

13. Oliver, Clementine. *Murdered in the Tabloids: Billposting and the Destruction of the Duke of Suffolk in 1450*. Anales de la Universidad de Alicante. Historia Medieval, N. 19 (2015-2016): 381-402, DOI:10.14198/medieval.2015-2016.19.13

14. Thomas Wright, *Political Poems and Songs Relating to English History, Composed During the Period from the Accession of Edw. III. to that of Ric. III* (London: Longman, Green Longman, and Roberts, 1859) p.345

15. ibid, p.223

16. Lauren Johnson, *Shadow King. The Life and Death of Henry VI* (London: Head of Zeus Ltd, 2019)

17. 'Henry VI: November 1449', in *Parliament Rolls of Medieval England*, British History Online http://www.british-history.ac.uk/no-series/parliament-rolls-medieval/november-1449 [accessed 16 March 2021]

18. Nicola Tallis: *Uncrowned Queen: The Fateful Life of Margaret Beaufort, Tudor Matriarch* (London: Michael O`Mara Books Limited, 2019) Position 944

What is Better than a Good Woman?

19. 'Lateran Regesta 460: 1450-1451', in *Calendar of Papal Registers Relating To Great Britain and Ireland: Volume 10, 1447-1455*, ed. J A Twemlow (London, 1915), pp. 471-474. British History Online http://www.british-history.ac.uk/cal-papal-registers/brit-ie/vol10/pp471-474 [accessed 16 March 2021]

20. ibid

21. John FIsher, *Mornyng Remembrance*, p.2

22. 'Henry VI: November 1449', in *Parliament Rolls of Medieval England*, British History Online http://www.british-history.ac.uk/no-series/parliament-rolls-medieval/november-1449 [accessed 16 March 2021]

23. ibid

24. 'Lateran Regesta 460: 1450-1451', in *Calendar of Papal Registers Relating To Great Britain and Ireland: Volume 10, 1447-1455*, ed. J A Twemlow (London, 1915), pp. 471-474. British History Online http://www.british-history.ac.uk/cal-papal-registers/brit-ie/vol10/pp471-474 [accessed 16 March 2021]

25. 'Henry VI: November 1449', in *Parliament Rolls of Medieval England*, British History Online http://www.british-history.ac.uk/no-series/parliament-rolls-medieval/november-1449 [accessed 16 March 2021]

26. Ibid

Chapter 9

1. ibid

2. Thomas Wright, *Political Poems and Songs Relating to English History, Composed During the Period from the Accession of Edw. III. to that of Ric. III* (London: Longman, Green Longman, and Roberts, 1859) pp.224-5

3. 'Henry VI: November 1449', in *Parliament Rolls of Medieval England*, British History Online http://www.british-history.ac.uk/no-series/parliament-rolls-medieval/november-1449 [accessed 8 March 2021]

Endnotes

4. ibid

5. ibid

6. Lauren Johnson, *Shadow King. The Life and Death of Henry VI* (London: Head of Zeus Ltd, 2019) p.194

7. 'Henry VI: November 1449', in *Parliament Rolls of Medieval England*, British History Online http://www.british-history.ac.uk/no-series/parliament-rolls-medieval/november-1449 [accessed 8 March 2021]

8. ibid

9. ibid

10. 'Henry VI: November 1449', in *Parliament Rolls of Medieval England*, British History Online http://www.british-history.ac.uk/no-series/parliament-rolls-medieval/november-1449 [accessed 8 March 2021]

11. Susan Curran: *The English Friend.* Position 5689

12. 'Henry VI: November 1449', in *Parliament Rolls of Medieval England*, British History Online http://www.british-history.ac.uk/no-series/parliament-rolls-medieval/november-1449 [accessed 16 March 2021]

13. Susan Curran: *The English Friend.* Positions 3134-3166

14. This usually meant that all the possessions of the condemned fell to the crown and often their widows had to live in drastically straitened circumstances.

15. 'Henry VI: November 1449', in *Parliament Rolls of Medieval England*, British History Online http://www.british-history.ac.uk/no-series/parliament-rolls-medieval/november-1449 [accessed 8 March 2021]

16. ibid

17. 'Henry VI: November 1449', in *Parliament Rolls of Medieval England*, British History Online http://www.british-history.ac.uk/no-series/parliament-rolls-medieval/november-1449 [accessed 8 March 2021]

18. ibid

What is Better than a Good Woman?

19. Matthew Lewis, *Richard, Duke of York: King by Right* (Stroud: Amberley Publishing, 2016), p.179

20. ibid

21. Henry VI: November 1449', in *Parliament Rolls of Medieval England*, British History Online http://www.british-history.ac.uk/no-series/parliament-rolls-medieval/november-1449 [accessed 8 March 2021]

22. Matthew Lewis, Richard, Duke of York: King by Right (Stroud: Amberley Publishing, 2016) p.179

23. ibid

24. Letter quoted in Henry Alfred Napier: *Historical Notices of the Parishes of Swyncombe and Ewelme in the County of Oxfordshire.* (Oxford: James Wright, Printer to the University, 1863) pp.88-9

25. ibid

26. He supposedly wrote a letter to the king before he died: James Gairdner, *The Paston Letters, AD 1422–1509. Volume I,* pp.124-5

27. James Gairdner, *The Paston Letters, AD 1422–1509. Volume I,* pp.124-6

28. Matthew Lewis, *Richard, Duke of York: King by Right* (Stroud: Amberley Publishing, 2016) Position 5393

29. James Gairdner, *The Paston Letters, AD 1422–1509. Volume I,* pp.124-5

30. For example: Matthew Lewis, *Richard, Duke of York: King by Right* (Stroud: Amberley Publishing, 2016) pp.180-2

31. For example: Nicola Tallis: *Uncrowned Queen: The Fateful Life of Margaret Beaufort, Tudor Matriarch* (London: Michael O`Mara Books Limited, 2019) Position 1024

32. Oliver, Clementine. *Murdered in the Tabloids: Billposting and the Destruction of the Duke of Suffolk in 1450.* Anales de la Universidad de Alicante. Historia Medieval, N. 19 (2015-2016): 381-402, DOI:10.14198/medieval.2015-2016.19.13

Endnotes

33. 'Henry VI: February 1449', in *Parliament Rolls of Medieval England*, British History Online http://www.british-history.ac.uk/no-series/parliament-rolls-medieval/february-1449 [accessed 17 March 2021]

34. Matthew Lewis, *Richard, Duke of York: King by Right* (Stroud: Amberley Publishing, 2016) p.182

35. https://sourcebooks.fordham.edu/source/1450jackcade.asp

36. James Gairdner, *The Paston Letters, AD 1422–1509. Volume I*, pp.124-126

37. Matthew Lewis, *Richard, Duke of York: King by Right* (Stroud: Amberley Publishing, 2016) p.182

38. ibid

39. Oliver, Clementine. *Murdered in the Tabloids: Billposting and the Destruction of the Duke of Suffolk in 1450.* Anales de la Universidad de Alicante. Historia Medieval, N. 19 (2015-2016): 381-402, DOI:10.14198/medieval.2015-2016.19.13

40. See below, Chapter 11

41. James Gairdner, *The Paston Letters, AD 1422–1509. Volume I*, pp.124-5

42. ibid

43. ibid

44. Most notably, Henry IV, who supposedly died in a chamber called the Jerusalem chamber, after being assured he would not die before being in Jerusalem.

45. Henry Alfred Napier, pp.103-4

46. Nicola Tallis: *Uncrowned Queen: The Fateful Life of Margaret Beaufort, Tudor Matriarch* (London: Michael O`Mara Books Limited, 2019) Positions 990-1004

47. Alice`s son John would live there with his family for large parts of his adult life.

48. Henry Alfred Napier, p.96

49. 'Henry VI: November 1449', in *Parliament Rolls of Medieval England*, British History Online http://www.british-history.

What is Better than a Good Woman?

ac.uk/no-series/parliament-rolls-medieval/november-1449 [accessed 17 March 2021]

50. Thomas Wright, *Political Poems and Songs Relating to English History, Composed During the Period from the Accession of Edw. III. to that of Ric. III* (London: Longman, Green Longman, and Roberts, 1859) pp.232-4

51. 'Henry VI: November 1450', in *Parliament Rolls of Medieval England*, British History Online http://www.british-history. ac.uk/no-series/parliament-rolls-medieval/november-1450 [accessed 17 March 2021]

52. https://sourcebooks.fordham.edu/source/1450jackcade.asp

53. See below, Chapter 11

54. Notably, during the Peasants` Revolt in Richard II`s reign.

55. 'Henry VI: November 1450', in *Parliament Rolls of Medieval England*, British History Online http://www.british-history. ac.uk/no-series/parliament-rolls-medieval/november-1450 [accessed 17 March 2021]

56. 'Henry VI: November 1449', in *Parliament Rolls of Medieval England*, British History Online http://www.british-history. ac.uk/no-series/parliament-rolls-medieval/november-1449 [accessed 8 March 2021]

57. Ibid

Chapter 10

1. Lauren Johnson, *Shadow King. The Life and Death of Henry VI* (London: Head of Zeus Ltd, 2019) pp.253-63

2. Matthew Lewis, Richard, *Duke of York: King by Right* (Stroud: Amberley Publishing, 2016) pp.185-92

3. https://sourcebooks.fordham.edu/source/1450jackcade.asp

4. 'Henry VI: November 1450', in *Parliament Rolls of Medieval England*, British History Online http://www.british-history. ac.uk/no-series/parliament-rolls-medieval/november-1450 [accessed 17 March 2021]

Endnotes

5. ibid
6. ibid
7. Calendar of Papal Registers, X, pp. 471-4
8. ibid
9. 'Henry VI: November 1450', in *Parliament Rolls of Medieval England*, British History Online http://www.british-history.ac.uk/no-series/parliament-rolls-medieval/november-1450 [accessed 8 March 2021]
10. ibid
11. Ibid

Chapter 11

1. Henry Alfred Napier, p.112
2. Karen K. Jambeck, *The Library of Alice Chaucer, Duchess of Suffolk: A Fifteenth-Century Owner of a 'Boke of le Citee de Dames'* (Western Connecticut State University) p.113
3. The Ewelme Inventory, quoted in Henry Alfred Napier: *Historical Notices of the Parishes of Swyncombe and Ewelme in the County of Oxfordshire.* (Oxford: James Wright, Printer to the University, 1863) pp.125-129
4. Rachel M. Delman, *Gendered viewing, childbirth and female authority in the residence of Alice Chaucer...*
5. ibid
6. Paul Murray Kendall, *Richard the Third* (London: George Allen & Unwin, 1955–1956) p.51
7. Calendar of Patent Rolls, Henry VI, Volume IV, 1441-1446, p.319
8. Albert C. Baugh, *Kirk's Life Records of Thomas Chaucer*, PMLA Vol. 47, No. 2 (Jun., 1932), pp.461-515
9. 'Henry VI: November 1449', in *Parliament Rolls of Medieval England*, British History Online http://www.british-history.ac.uk/no-series/parliament-rolls-medieval/november-1449 [accessed 17 March 2021]
10. Henry Alfred Napier, p.103

What is Better than a Good Woman?

11. James Gairdner, *The Paston Letters, AD 1422–1509*.

12. ibid

13. Marjorie Anderson, *Alice Chaucer and Her Husbands*, PMLA Vol. 60, No. 1 (Mar., 1945), pp. 24-47, p.41

14. Rowena E. Archer, 'Alice Chaucer, Duchess of Suffolk (d.1475), And Her East Anglian Estates', in: Peter Bloore, Edward A. Martin: *Wingfield College and Its Patrons: Piety and Patronage in Medieval Suffolk* (Woodbridge: The Boydell Press, 2015) p.188

15. Nicola Tallis, *Uncrowned Queen: The Fateful Life of Margaret Beaufort, Tudor Matriarch* (London: Michael O`Mara Books Limited, 2019) Position 1703

16. Lauren Johnson, *Shadow King. The Life and Death of Henry VI* (London: Head of Zeus Ltd, 2019)

17. Matthew Lewis, *Richard, Duke of York: King by Right* (Stroud: Amberley Publishing, 2016) Position 3311

18. Nicola Tallis, *Uncrowned Queen: The Fateful Life of Margaret Beaufort, Tudor Matriarch* (London: Michael O`Mara Books Limited, 2019) Position 1703

19. John Fisher, *Mornyng Remembrance*, p.2

20. Oliver, Clementine. *Murdered in the Tabloids: Billposting and the Destruction of the Duke of Suffolk in 1450*. Anales de la Universidad de Alicante. Historia Medieval, N. 19 (2015-2016): 381-402, DOI:10.14198/medieval.2015-2016.19.13

21. Lauren Johnson, *Shadow King. The Life and Death of Henry VI* (London: Head of Zeus Ltd, 2019) pp.190-2

22. Joseph Hunter, *Three Catalogues, Describing the Contents of the Red Book of the Exchequer of the Dodsworth Manuscripts in the Bodleian Library, and of the Manuscripts in the Library of the Honourable Society of Lincoln`s Inn* (London: Pickering, 1838) pp.277-8

23. He was definitely next in line, though in recent years it has been claimed Henry VI intended to make his half-brother Edmund Tudor and his youthful wife Margaret Beaufort his

Endnotes

heirs. There is no evidence for this and the idea may be born of hindsight, their son becoming king through usurpation.

24. He was involved in Margaret's churching ceremony: Joseph Hunter, *Three Catalogues, Describing the Contents of the Red Book of the Exchequer of the Dodsworth Manuscripts in the Bodleian Library, and of the Manuscripst in the Library of the Honourable Society of Lincoln's Inn* (London: Pickering, 1838) p.277-8

25. ibid

26. Lauren Johnson, *Shadow King. The Life and Death of Henry VI* (London: Head of Zeus Ltd, 2019) p.31

27. Matthew Lewis, *Richard, Duke of York: King by Right* (Stroud: Amberley Publishing, 2016) p.212

28. ibid, p.277

29. ibid

30. Deeds: A.6301-A.6400, *in A Descriptive Catalogue of Ancient Deeds: Volume 4*, ed. H C Maxwell Lyte (London, 1902), pp. 22-34. British History Online http://www.british-history.ac.uk/ancient-deeds/vol4/pp22-34 [accessed 8 March 2021]

31. Henry Alfred Napier, p.95

32. Deeds: A.6301-A.6400, in *A Descriptive Catalogue of Ancient Deeds: Volume 4*, ed. H C Maxwell Lyte (London, 1902), pp. 22-34. British History Online http://www.british-history.ac.uk/ancient-deeds/vol4/pp22-34 [accessed 8 March 2021]

33. ibid

34. James Gairdner, *The Paston Letters, AD 1422–1509. Volume III*, p.226

35. Rachel M. Delman: *Gendered viewing, childbirth and female authority in the residence of Alice Chaucer...*

36. The Ewelme Inventory, quoted in Henry Alfred Napier: *Historical Notices of the Parishes of Swyncombe and Ewelme in the County of Oxfordshire* (Oxford: James Wright, Printer to the University, 1863) pp.125-129

37. ibid

What is Better than a Good Woman?

38. ibid
39. John Ashdown-Hill, *Cecily Neville, Mother of Richard III* (Yorkshire: Pen & Sword, 2018) Position 622-630
40. Ed Alison Hanham, *John Benet's Chronicle, 1399-1462 An English Translation with New Introduction* (New York: Palgrave Macmillian, 2018)
41. In fact, there are several instances of him being addressed as Duke in that time, such as Calendar of Patent Rolls, Henry VI, Volume VI, 1452-1460
42. James Gairdner, *The Paston Letters, AD 1422–1509. Volume III*, p.226
43. ibid
44. Calendar of Patent Rolls, Henry VI, Volume VI, 1452-1460
45. Ed. John Silvester Davies, *An English chronicle of the reigns of Richard II, Henry IV, Henry V, and Henry VI written before the year 1471...* pp.101-4
46. ibid pp. 94/5
47. James Gairdner, *The Paston Letters, AD 1422–1509. Volume III*. p.226
48. ibid
49. Michael Hicks, 'Pole, John de la, second duke of Suffolk', *Oxford Dictionary of National Biography* (Oxford University Press, 2004)
50. Henry Alfred Napier, p.100
51. Matthew Lewis, *Richard, Duke of York: King by Right* (Stroud: Amberley Publishing, 2016) pp.326-7
52. ibid, pp.329-33
53. Ed. John Silvester Davies, *An English chronicle of the reigns of Richard II, Henry IV, Henry V, and Henry VI written before the year 1471...*
54. ibid
55. James Gairdner, *The Paston Letters, AD 1422–1509. Volume III*, pp.227-30

Endnotes

56. Ed. John Silvester Davies, *An English chronicle of the reigns of Richard II, Henry IV, Henry V, and Henry VI written before the year 1471* ...

57. Henry Alfred Napier: *Historical Notices of the Parishes of Swyncombe and Ewelme in the County of Oxfordshire.* (Oxford: James Wright, Printer to the University, 1863)

58. ibid, p.101

59. 'Brief notes of occurrences under Henry VI and Edward IV', in *Three Fifteenth-Century Chronicles with Historical Memoranda by John Stowe*, ed. James Gairdner (London, 1880), pp. 148-163. British History Online http://www.british-history.ac.uk/camden-record-soc/vol28/pp148-163 [accessed 19 March 2021]

60. James Gairdner, *The Paston Letters, AD 1422–1509. Volume VI*, p.72

61. Rachel M Delman: *Gendered viewing, childbirth and female authority in the residence of Alice Chaucer* https://www.tandfonline.com/doi/full/10.1080/03044181.2019.1593619?fbclid=IwAR3zANh8h84dUUpkqdX6R6_qz4DJ8v1TrljoQn22_vr_ffyFz43MqeGVdCw

62. Such as him not being invited to Parliament in late 1482.

63. Letter quoted in: Henry Alfred Napier: *Historical Notices of the Parishes of Swyncombe and Ewelme in the County of Oxfordshire.* (Oxford: James Wright, Printer to the University, 1863) p.99

64. ibid

65. ibid

66. 'Rowland's Historical and Genealogical Account of the noble family of Neville', quoted in: Henry Alfred Napier: *Historical Notices of the Parishes of Swyncombe and Ewelme in the County of Oxfordshire.* (Oxford: James Wright, Printer to the University, 1863.) pp. 110-112

67. ibid

What is Better than a Good Woman?

68. ibid

69. See above, Chapter 12

70. Curiously, this is not actually recorded in the Calendar of Patent Rolls; we know only from John`s actions that he had been granted this permission.

71. Mary Clive: *This Son of York. A biography of Edward IV* (London: Macmillan London Ltd, 1973) pp.89-99

72. ibid

73. James Gairdner, *The Paston Letters, AD 1422–1509. Volume VI*, pp-105-107

74. Ed. Charles Lethbridge Kingsford, *The Stonor letters and papers, 1290–1483, Volume I* (London: Offices of the Society, 1919), pp.116-7

75. Mary Clive: *This Son of York. A biography of Edward IV* (London: Macmillan London Ltd, 1973) p.102

76. ibid, p.106

77. Annette Carson, Richard III, *The Maligned King* (Stroud: The History Press, 2008) p.24; 'Milan: 1465', in *Calendar of State Papers and Manuscripts in the Archives and Collections of Milan 1385-1618*, ed. Allen B Hinds (London, 1912), pp. 115-117; British History Online http://www.british-history.ac.uk/cal-state-papers/milan/1385-1618/pp115-117 [accessed 19 March 2021].

Chapter 12

1. James Gairdner, *The Paston Letters, AD 1422–1509. Volume VI*, pp.136-181

2. ibid

3. The Ewelme Inventory, quoted in Henry Alfred Napier: *Historical Notices of the Parishes of Swyncombe and Ewelme in the County of Oxfordshire.* (Oxford: James Wright, Printer to the University, 1863.) pp.125-129

4. ibid

Endnotes

5. For example: Rachel M Delman: *Gendered viewing, childbirth and female authority in the residence of Alice Chaucer...*

6. The Ewelme Inventory, quoted in Henry Alfred Napier: *Historical Notices of the Parishes of Swyncombe and Ewelme in the County of Oxfordshire.* (Oxford: James Wright, Printer to the University, 1863), pp.125-129

7. Such as: Marjorie Anderson, *Alice Chaucer and Her Husbands*, PMLA Vol. 60, No. 1 (Mar., 1945), pp. 24-47, and also Henry Alfred Napier: *Historical Notices of the Parishes of Swyncombe and Ewelme in the County of Oxfordshire*

8. Ute Gerhard: *Geschlechterstreit und Aufklärung. In: dies. (Hrsg.): Frauenbewegung und Feminismus. Eine Geschichte seit 1789.* 2. Auflage. (München: C.H.Beck, 2012) p. 11

9. Christine de Pizan. *Das Buch von der Stadt der Frauen* (München: Deutscher Taschenbuch Verlag, 1995)

10. The Ewelme Inventory, quoted in Henry Alfred Napier: *Historical Notices of the Parishes of Swyncombe and Ewelme in the County of Oxfordshire*, pp.125-129

11. Rachel M Delman: *Gendered viewing, childbirth and female authority in the residence of Alice Chaucer...*

12. ibid

13. ibid

14. See, for example: James Gairdner, *The Paston Letters, AD 1422–1509. Volume VI*, pp.136-181

15. Henry Alfred Napier, pp. 120-124

16. Calendar of Patent Rolls, Edward IV, Henry VI, Richard III, Volume I, AD 1461-1485, Volume II, p.96

17. James Gairdner, *The Paston Letters, AD 1422–1509. Volume IV*, pp.297-8

18. Ibid, pp.10-12

19. Ibid, pp.162-4

20. ibid, pp.220-22

21. ibid, pp.126-220

What is Better than a Good Woman?

22. James Gairdner, *The Paston Letters, AD 1422–1509. Volume IV.*

23. For example: Marjorie Anderson, *Alice Chaucer and Her Husbands*, PMLA Vol. 60, No. 1 (Mar., 1945), pp. 24-47, p.42

24. P. W. Hammond, *The Battles of Barnet and Tewkesbury* (Gloucester: Alan Sutton, 1990) pp.8-11

25. Charles Ross, *Edward IV* (New Haven and London: Yale University Press, 1974), p.93

26. P. W. Hammond, *The Battles of Barnet and Tewkesbury* (Gloucester: Alan Sutton, 1990) pp.8-11

27. James Gairdner, *The Paston Letters, AD 1422–1509. Volume VI*, p.207

28. P. W. Hammond, *The Battles of Barnet and Tewkesbury* (Gloucester: Alan Sutton, 1990) p.8-10

29. John Ashdown-Hill, *The Third Plantagenet* (Stroud: The History Press, 2014) pp.99-112

30. P. W. Hammond, *The Battles of Barnet and Tewkesbury* (Gloucester: Alan Sutton, 1990) p.11

31. A. P. R. Obermann, H. Schoorl, '*Koning Edward IV van Engeland op Texel*', Holland, Volume 13 (1981) p.13

32. ibid

33. Ed. John Bruce, *Historie of the Arrivall of Edward IV in England and the Finall Recouerye of his Kingdomes from Henry VI AD M.CCCC.LXXI* (London: John Bower Nichols and Son, 1838) p.10

34. ibid

35. The Duke of Exeter

36. Charles Ross, *Edward IV* (New Haven and London: Yale University Press, 1974) p.161

37. Ed. John Bruce, *Historie of the Arrivall of Edward IV in England and the Finall Recouerye of his Kingdomes from Henry VI AD M.CCCC.LXXI* (London: John Bower Nichols and Son, 1838) p.11

38. ibid. pp. 18-19

Endnotes

39. ibid, p.20

40. Charles Ross, *Richard III* (York: Eyre Methuen Ltd, 1981), p. 28 and Henry Alfred Napier: *Historical Notices of the Parishes of Swyncombe and Ewelme in the County of Oxfordshire.* (Oxford: James Wright, Printer to the University, 1863)

41. James Gairdner, *The Paston Letters, AD 1422–1509. Volume V*, p.131

42. Henry Alfred Napier, pp.101-2

43. James Gairdner, *The Paston Letters, AD 1422–1509. Volume V*, p.131

44. P.R.O Warrants for Issues, E404/75/2

45. Calendar of Patent Rolls, Edward IV, Henry VI. 1467-1477 p.261

46. Michèle Schindler, *Lovell Our Dogge. The Life of Viscount Lovell, Closest Friend of Richard III and Failed Regicide* (Stroud: Amberley Publishing, 2019) pp.43 ff

47. ibid, pp.59-68

48. 'Deed A. 11118', in *A Descriptive Catalogue of Ancient Deeds in the Public Record Office*, vol. 5, ed. H.C. Maxwell Lyte (London: His Majesty's Stationery Office, 1906), 93–108

Chapter 13

1. Calendar of Close Rolls, Edward IV: Volume 2, 1468-1476, ed. W H B Bird and K H Ledward (London, 1953), British History Online http://www.british-history.ac.uk/cal-close-rolls/edw4/vol2 [accessed 15 June 2020]

2. 'Lateran Regesta 770: 1472-1475', in *Calendar of Papal Registers Relating To Great Britain and Ireland: Volume 13, 1471-1484*, ed. J A Twemlow (London, 1955), pp. 547-551. British History Online http://www.british-history.ac.uk/cal-papal-registers/brit-ie/vol13/pp547-551 [accessed 20 March 2021]

3. Calendar of Patent Rolls, Edward IV, Henry VI. 1467-1477, p.603

What is Better than a Good Woman?

4. Ed. Charles Lethbridge Kingsford, *The Stonor letters and papers, 1290–1483 Vol. I* (London: Offices of the Society, 1919) p.154
5. ibid
6. Calendar of Close Rolls, Edward IV: Volume 2, 1468-1476, ed. W H B Bird and K H Ledward (London, 1953), British History Online http://www.british-history.ac.uk/cal-close-rolls/edw4/vol2 [accessed 20 March 2021].
7. ibid
8. W. C. Metcalf, *A Book of Knights* (London, 1885)

Chapter 14

1. See above, Chapter 6
2. Who was still living in Wallingford Castle, and was technically Alice`s prisoner until Alice`s death.

BIBLIOGRAPHY

Primary sources

A Descriptive Catalogue of Ancient Deeds: Volume 5, ed. H C Maxwell Lyte (London, 1906), British History Online http://www.british-history.ac.uk/ancient-deeds/vol5 [accessed 18 March 2021].

Ed. Thomas Basin and Charles Samaran, *Histoire de Charles VII: Tome Premier, 1407-1444.* (Paris: Les Classiques de l'Histoire de France Au Moyen Age. Volume 15, 1933)

Ed. W. H. Black, *Illustrations of Ancient State & Chivalry from the manuscripts preserved in the Ashmolean Museum* (London: Roxburghe Club, 1840) https://www.bl.uk/catalogues/illuminatedmanuscripts/ILLUMINBig.ASP?size=big&IllID=29350&fbclid=IwAR2vDeM3qpBwNrbxaTrYu-_OkfP3ZQIefil5KTUZMASnqxhpsW434hNoeMs

Ed. Edward A Bond, *Thomas de Burton, Chronica Monasterii de Melsa, a Fundatione Usque ad Annum 1396, Auctore Thoma de Burton, Abbate. Accedit Continuatio ad Annum 1406.* (London: Longmans, Green, Reader and Dyer, 1868.)

Ed. Paul Brand, Anne Curry, Chris Given-Wilson, Rosemary Horrox, Geoffrey Martin, Mark Ormrod, Henry VI: November 1459, in Parliament Rolls of Medieval England (Woodbridge, Boydell, 2005)

What is Better than a Good Woman?

'Brief notes of occurrences under Henry VI and Edward IV', in *Three Fifteenth-Century Chronicles with Historical Memoranda* by John Stowe, ed. James Gairdner (London, 1880), pp. 148-163. British History Online http://www.british-history.ac.uk/camden-record-soc/vol28/pp148-163 [accessed 11 June 2020]

https://www.british-history.ac.uk/no-series/parliament-rolls-medieval/october-1407

https://www.british-history.ac.uk/no-series/parliament-rolls-medieval/november-1411

https://www.british-history.ac.uk/inquis-post-mortem/vol20/pp109-123

https://www.british-history.ac.uk/inquis-post-mortem/vol20/pp109-123

https://www.british-history.ac.uk/no-series/parliament-rolls-medieval/january-1401

https://www.british-history.ac.uk/no-series/parliament-rolls-medieval/september-1429

https://www.british-history.ac.uk/no-series/parliament-rolls-medieval/november-1450

Ed. John Bruce, *Historie of the Arrivall of Edward IV in England and the Finall Recouerye of his Kingdomes from Henry VI AD M.CCCC.LXXI* (London: John Bower Nichols and Son, 1838)

Calendar of Close Rolls, Edward IV: Volume 1, 1461-1468, ed. W H B Bird and K H Ledward (London, 1949), British History Online http://www.british-history.ac.uk/cal-close-rolls/edw4/vol1 [accessed 19 March 2021].

Calendar of Close Rolls, Edward IV: Volume 2, 1468-1476, ed. W H B Bird and K H Ledward (London, 1953), British History Online http://www.british-history.ac.uk/cal-close-rolls/edw4/vol2 [accessed 19 March 2021]

Calendar of Fine Rolls, Henry VI, AD 1452–1461

Calendar of Papal Registers, X

Calendar of Patent Rolls, Richard II, Volume VI, AD 1396-1399

Bibliography

Calendar of Patent Rolls, Henry IV, Volume II, AD 1401-405

Calendar of Patent Rolls, Henry VI, Volume II

Calendar of Patent Rolls, Henry VI, Volume III, AD 1436-1441

Calendar of Patent Rolls, Henry VI, Volume V, AD 1441-1446

Calendar of Patent Rolls, Henry VI, Volume V, AD 1446–1452

Calendar of Patent Rolls, Henry VI, Volume VI, AD 1452-1461

Calendar of Patent Rolls, Edward IV, AD 1461-1467

Calendar of Patent Rolls, Edward IV, Henry VI. AD 1467-1477

Calendar of Patent Rolls, Edward IV, Henry VI, Richard III, Volume I, AD 1461-1485

Chancery Inquisitions Post Mortem, Henry VI, File 70, No.35

'Chronological Arrangement of Vatican Regesta Documents', in *Calendar of Papal Registers Relating To Great Britain and Ireland: Volume 8, 1427-1447*, ed. J A Twemlow (London, 1909), pp. xv-xxxviii. British History Online http://www.british-history.ac.uk/cal-papal-registers/brit-ie/vol8/xv-xxxviii [accessed 12 March 2021].

British History Online http://www.british-history.ac.uk/cal-papal-registers/brit-ie/vol9/pp1-13 [accessed 13 March 2021].

Ed. G. E. C. Cokayne, *The Complete Peerage* (London, Cokayne, 1932)

Ed. John Silvester Davies, *An English chronicle of the reigns of Richard II, Henry IV, Henry V, and Henry VI written before the year 1471; with an appendix, containing the 18th and 19th years of Richard II and the Parliament at Bury St. Edmund's, 25th Henry VI and supplementary additions from the Cotton. ms. chronicle called 'Eulogium'* (London: Camden Society, 1856)

'Deeds: A.6301-A.6400', in: *A Descriptive Catalogue of Ancient Deeds Volume 4*, ed. H C Maxwell Lyte (London, 1902), pp. 22-34. British History Online http://www.british-history.ac.uk/ancient-deeds/vol4/pp22-34 [accessed 20 March 2021]

'Deed A. 11118', in *A Descriptive Catalogue of Ancient Deeds in the Public Record Office, vol. 5*, edn. H.C. Maxwell Lyte (London: His Majesty's Stationery Office, 1906), 93-108

What is Better than a Good Woman?

F. Devon, *Issues of the Exchequer* (London: John Murray, 1837) https://discovery.nationalarchives.gov.uk/details/r/C49449 19?fbclid=IwAR10WgchjUqNEUlTCKxIuW6skCUE3cID 6nawK-x6kpWLdX1_gTStHRISgoc

https://discovery.nationalarchives.gov.uk/details/r/ C4513109?fbclid=IwAR2ROk3DwqXq-xLXTjcS2W9TVpjZfZ YO3sMott3OfN1HtNJMJ9IciT1hyyA

https://discovery.nationalarchives.gov.uk/details/r/C4518120

https://discovery.nationalarchives.gov.uk/details/r/C4518125

Document from the National Archives, C138/13/42

'Edward IV: November 1461', in *Parliament Rolls of Medieval England*, ed. Chris Given-Wilson, Paul Brand, Seymour Phillips, Mark Ormrod, Geoffrey Martin, Anne Curry and Rosemary Horrox (Woodbridge, 2005), British History Online http:// www.british-history.ac.uk/no-series/parliament-rolls-medieval/ november-1461 [accessed 11 June 2020].

'Edward IV: October 1472', in Parliament Rolls of Medieval England... [accessed 15 June 2020]

Piers de Fenin, *Mémoires de Pierre de Fenin comprenant le récit des événements: qui se sont passés en France et en Bourgogne sous les règnes de Charles VI et Charles VII, 1407-1427* (Histoire)

John Fisher, *Mornyng Remembrance*

Ed. James Gairdner, *Letters and Papers Illustrative of the Reigns of Richard III and Henry VII Volume I* (London: Longman, Green, Longman, Roberts, and Green, 1863)

Ed. James Gairdner, *The Paston Letters, AD 1422–1509*. Volumes I-VI, New Complete Library Edition (London: Chatto & Windus, Exeter: James G. Commin, 1904)

Edward Hall, *The Union Of The Two Noble And Illustre Famelies Lancastre & Yorke Beeyng Long In Continual Discension For The Croune Of This Noble Realme With All The Actes Done In Bothe The Tymes Of The Princes, Bothe Of The One Linage And Of The Other, Beginnyng At The Tyme Of Kyng*

Bibliography

Henry The Fowerth, The First Aucthor Of This Deuision, And So Successiuely Proceadyng To The Reigne Of The High And Prudent Prince Kyng Henry The Eight, the Undubitate Flower And Very Heire Of Both The Sayd Linages (1548)

Ed Alison Hanham, *John Benet's Chronicle, 1399-1462 An English Translation with New Introduction* (New York: Palgrave Macmillian, 2018)

'Henry V: November 1414', in Parliament Rolls of Medieval England, ed. Chris Given-Wilson, Paul Brand, Seymour Phillips, Mark Ormrod, Geoffrey Martin, Anne Curry and Rosemary Horrox (Woodbridge, 2005), British History Online http://www.british-history.ac.uk/no-series/parliament-rolls-medieval/november-1414 [accessed 17 March 2021].

'Henry V: November 1415', in Parliament Rolls of Medieval England...

'Henry VI: October 1435', in Parliament Rolls of Medieval England...

'Henry VI: January 1442', in Parliament Rolls of Medieval England...

'Henry VI: February 1445', in Parliament Rolls of Medieval England...

'Henry VI: February 1447', in Parliament Rolls of Medieval England...

'Henry VI: November 1449', in Parliament Rolls of Medieval England...

'Henry VI: November 1450', in Parliament Rolls of Medieval England...

Raphael Holinshed, *Chronicles of England, Scotland and Ireland* (1577)

Joseph Hunter, *Three Catalogues, Describing the Contents of the Red Book of the Exchequer of the Dodsworth Manuscripts in the Bodleians Library, and of the Manuscripts in the Library of the Honourable Society of Lincoln's Inn* (London: Pickering, 1838)

http://www.inquisitionspostmortem.ac.uk/view/inquisition/21-648/651A

http://www.inquisitionspostmortem.ac.uk/view/inquisition/24-346/349

http://www.inquisitionspostmortem.ac.uk/view/inquisition/24-680/681

http://www.inquisitionspostmortem.ac.uk/view/inquisition/23-262/282

http://www.inquisitionspostmortem.ac.uk/view/inquisition/
24-680/686

Inquisitions Post Mortem on William Lovell, Lord Morley,
National Archives, C140/47/64

Translated by Thomas Johnes, Esq: *The chronicles of Enguerrand
de Monstrelet; containing an account of the cruel civil wars
between the houses of Orleans and Burgundy; of the possession
of Paris and Normandy by the English; their expulsion thence;
and of other memorable events that happened in the kingdom
of France, as well as in other countries. Beginning at the year
MCCCC., where that of Sir John Froissart finishes, and ending
at the year MCCCCLXXVII., and continued by others to the
year MDXVI* (London, William Smith, 1845)

Ed. Charles Lethbridge Kingsford, *The Stonor letters and papers,
1290–1483,* Volumes I and III (London: Offices of the Society, 1919)

Ed. J. L. Kirby, Janet Stevenson, *Calendar of Inquisitions
Post-Mortem and other Analogous Documents preserved in
the Public Record Office XXI:6 – 10 Henry V (1418-1422)*
(Woodbridge: Boydell Press, 2002)

J. L. Kirby, 'Inquisitions Post Mortem, Henry V, Entries 800-851',
in Calendar of Inquisitions Post Mortem: Volume 20, Henry V
(London, 1995), pp. 248-272. British History Online http://www.
british-history.ac.uk/inquis-post-mortem/vol20/pp248-272
[accessed 7 June 2020]

L. G. Wickham Legg, *English Coronation Records* (Edinburgh:
Archibald Constable & Co., 1901)

'Lateran Regesta 260: 1425-1426', in *Calendar of Papal Registers
Relating To Great Britain and Ireland: Volume 7, 1417-1431,* ed. J
A Twemlow (London, 1906), pp. 439-451. *British History Online*
http://www.british-history.ac.uk/cal-papal-registers/brit-ie/vol7/
pp439-451 [accessed 10 March 2021]

'Lateran Regesta 770: 1472-1475', in *Calendar of Papal Registers
Relating To Great Britain and Ireland: Volume 13, 1471-1484,* ed.

Bibliography

J A Twemlow (London, 1955), pp. 547-551. *British History Online* http://www.british-history.ac.uk/cal-papal-registers/brit-ie/vol13/pp547-551 [accessed 20 March 2021]

Leland's Collectana, Volume VI (London: 1770)

Life Records of Chaucer (London: Kegan Paul, Trench, Trübner &Co, 1900)

'Milan: 1458', in *Calendar of State Papers and Manuscripts in the Archives and Collections of Milan 1385-1618*, ed. Allen B Hinds (London, 1912). British History Online http://www.british-history.ac.uk/cal-state-papers/milan/1385-1618/pp18-19 [accessed 16 March 2021]

'Milan: 1465', in *Calendar of State Papers and Manuscripts in the Archives and Collections of Milan 1385-1618...* [accessed 19 March 2021]

Ed. Cecil Monro, *Letters of Queen Margaret of Anjou and Bishop Beckington and Others. Written in the Reigns of Henry V and Henry VI. From a manuscript found at Emral in Flintshire* (London: Camden Society. 1863)

www.nationalarchives.gov.uk/pathways/citizenship/citizen_subject/transcripts/will_neville.htm

Nicholas Harris Nicolas, *Testamenta Vetusta: Being Illustrations From Wills Of Manners, Customs & c. As Well As The Descents And Possessions From Many Distinguished Families. From the Reign Of Henry The Second To The Accession Of Queen Elizabeth. Volume I* (London: Nicols And Son, 1826) pp.215-7

A. P. R. Obermann, H. Schoorl, *'Koning Edward IV van Engeland op Texel'*, Holland, Volume 13 (1981)

Christine de Pizan, *Das Buch von der Stadt der Frauen* (München: Deutscher Taschenbuch Verlag, 1995)

PCC 43 Marche An edition of wills proved in the Prerogative Court of Canterbury, 4-31 November

https://www.poetrynook.com/poem/departing-thomas-chaucer

What is Better than a Good Woman?

P.R.O.   DL28/3/2http://www.inquisitionspostmortem.ac.uk/view/
inquisition/25-527/

P.R.O. Warrants for Issues, E404/75/2

H. T. Riley, *Ingulph's Chronicle of the Abbey of Croyland* (London: George Bell and Sons, 1908)

Rotuli Parliamentorum, ut et petitiones, et placita in Parliamento, Ab Anno Duodecimo R. Edwardi IV. ad Finem eiusdem Regni Volume VI (London, 1777)

Rowland's Historical and Genealogical Account of the noble family of Neville

Sequitur generacio illustrissimi principis Ricardi, Ducis Eboraci & c ex serenissima principissa, uxore sua, Caecilia. T. Hearne, Liber Niger Scaccarii nec non Wilhelmi Worcestrii Annales Rerum Angelicarum, Volume 2 (London: 1774)

Reginald R. Sharpe, *London and the kingdom: a history derived mainly from the archives at Guildhall in the custody of the corporation of the city of London, vol. III* (London: Longmans, Green & Co., 1895)

Ed. Lucy Toulmin Smith, John Leland, *The itinerary of John Leland in or about the years 1535-1543*

https://sourcebooks.fordham.edu/source/1420troyes.asp

https://sourcebooks.fordham.edu/source/1450jackcade.asp

Ed. Thomas Stapleton FSA, *Plumpton Correspondence: A Series of Letters, Chiefly Domestick, written in the reigns of Edward IV, Richard III, Henry VII and Henry VIII* (London: John Bowyer and Son, 1839)

The Worthies of the United Kingdom; Or Biographical Accounts of the Lives of the Most Illustrious Men, in Arts, Arms, Literature and Science, Connected with Great Britain. With Numerous Portraits, Etc (London: Knight & Lacey, 1828)

https://www.vaticannews.va/en/saints/02/06.html

'Vatican Regesta 677: 1476-1484', in *Calendar of Papal Registers Relating To Great Britain and Ireland: Volume 13, 1471-1484*, ed.

Bibliography

J A Twemlow (London, 1955), pp. 274-277. British History Online http://www.british-history.ac.uk/cal-papal-registers/brit-ie/vol13/pp274-277 [accessed 14 June 2020]

'Vatican Regesta 387: 1448', in *Calendar of Papal Registers Relating To Great Britain and Ireland: Volume 10, 1447-1455*, ed. J A Twemlow (London, 1915), pp. 22-38. British History Online http://www.british-history.ac.uk/cal-papal-registers/brit-ie/vol10/pp22-38 [accessed 16 March 2021]

Polydore Vergil, Anglica Historia (1534) http://www.philological.bham.ac.uk/polverg/26eng.html

Thomas Wright, *Political Poems and Songs Relating to English History, Composed During the Period from the Accession of Edw. III. to that of Ric. III* (London: Longman, Green Longman, and Roberts, 1859) p.345

Secondary Sources

Jacob Abbot, *Margaret of Anjou. Makers of History.* (Glasgow: Good Press, 2019) Original Publication: 1861

Nathen Amin, *The House of Beaufort. The Bastard Line that Captured the Crown.* (Stroud: Amberley Publishing, 2017)

Marjorie Anderson, *Alice Chaucer and Her Husbands*, PMLA Vol. 60, No. 1 (Mar., 1945), pp. 24-47

Rowena E. Archer, 'Alice Chaucer, Duchess of Suffolk (d.1475), And Her East Anglian Estates', in: Peter Bloore, Edward A. Martin: *Wingfield College and Its Patrons: Piety and Patronage in Medieval Suffolk* (Woodbridge: The Boydell Press, 2015)

John Ashdown-Hill, *The Third Plantagenet* (Stroud: The History Press, 2014)

John Ashdown-Hill, *Cecily Neville, Mother of Richard III* (Barnsley: Pen & Sword, 2018)

John Ashdown Hill, *Elizabeth Widville, Lady Grey: Edward IV's Chief Mistress and the 'Pink Queen'* (Barnsley: Pen & Sword, 2019)

David Baldwin, *Elizabeth Woodville: Mother of the Princes in the Tower* (Stroud: Sutton Publishing Limited, 2002)

Albert C. Baugh, *Kirk's Life Records of Thomas Chaucer*, PMLA Vol. 47, No. 2 (Jun., 1932)

George Frederick Beltz, *Memorials of the Order of the Garter, from its foundation to the present time. Including the history of the order; biographical notices of the knights in the reigns of Edward III. and Richard II., the chronological succession of the members.* (London: W. Pickering, 1841)

Alex Brayson, *Deficit Finance During the Early Majority of Henry VI of England, 1436-1444. The "Crisis" of the Medieval English "Tax State".* (2019)

Annette Carson, *Richard III, The Maligned King.* (Stroud: The History Press, 2008)

Helen Castor, *Joan of Arc. A History.* (London: Faber and Faber Ltd, 2014)

Pierre Champion, *'La Dame Anglaise de Charles D'Orleans'.* (Romania, XLIV, 1923)

K. L. Clark, *The Nevills of Middleham: England's Most Powerful Family in the Wars of the Roses* (Stroud: The History Press, 2016)

Mary Clive: *This Son of York. A Biography of Edward IV.* (London: Macmillan London Ltd, 1973).

Susan Curran, *The English Friend.* (Norwich: Lasse Press, 2011)

Anne Curry, *Guide to the Hundred Years' War.* (New York: Palgrave Macmillan, 2003)

Anne Crawford, *The Yorkists: The History of a Dynasty* (London: Continuum Books, 2007)

Rachel M. Delman, *Gendered viewing, childbirth and female authority in the residence of Alice Chaucer, duchess of Suffolk, at Ewelme, Oxfordshire.* (2019) https://www.tandfonline.com/doi/full/10.1080/03044181.2019.1593619

Ed. Gwilym Dodd, Douglas Biggs: *Henry IV, The Establishment of the Regime, 1399-1406.* (York: York Medieval Press, 2003)

Bibliography

Ed. Gwilym Dodd, Douglas Biggs, *The Reign of Henry IV: Rebellion and Survival, 1403-1413.* (York: York Medieval Press, 2008)

James Gairdner, *History of the Life and Reign of Richard the Third, to which is added the story of Perkin Warbeck: from original documents.* (Cambridge: Cambridge University Press, 1898)

Ute Gerhard: *Geschlechterstreit und Aufklärung. In: dies. (Hrsg.): Frauenbewegung und Feminismus. Eine Geschichte seit 1789. 2. Auflage.* (München: C.H.Beck, 2012)

Chris Given-Wilson, *Henry IV.* (New Haven and London: Yale University Press, 2016)

Nancy Goldstone, *The Maid and the Queen: The Secret History of Joan of Arc.* (London: Phoenix Paperbacks, 2013)

John Goodall: *God's House at Ewelme: Life, Devotion and Architecture in a Fifteenth-Century Almshouse.* (London: Taylor & Francis, 2017)

P. W. Hammond, *The Battles of Barnet and Tewkesbury.* (Gloucester: Alan Sutton, 1990)

Michael Hicks, 'Pole, John de la, second duke of Suffolk', *Oxford Dictionary of National Biography.* (Oxford University Press, 2004)

Luc Hommel, *Marguerite D'York ou La Duchesse Junon.* (Paris: Librairie Hachette, 1959)

William Hunt, 'Chaucer, Thomas', *Dictionary of National Biography*, 1885-1900, Volume 10

William Hunt, 'Montacute, Thomas de', *Dictionary of National Biography*, 1885-1900, Volume 38

Karen K. Jambeck, *The Library of Alice Chaucer, Duchess of Suffolk: A Fifteenth-Century Owner of a 'Boke of le Citee de Dames'.* (Western Connecticut State University)

Lauren Johnson, *Shadow King. The Life and Death of Henry VI.* (London: Head of Zeus Ltd, 2019)

Michael K. Jones, Malcolm G. Underwood, *The King's Mother. Lady Margaret Beaufort, Countess of Richmond and Derby.* (New York: Cambridge University Press, 1992)

What is Better than a Good Woman?

Terry Jones, *Who Murdered Chaucer?* (London, Methuen Publishing Limited, 2013)

Sheila Kant, *Alice, Duchess of Suffolk.* (2000)

Paul Murray Kendall, *Richard the Third.* (London: George Allen & Unwin, 1955-1956)

Henry Murray Lane, *The Royal Daughters of England, and their representatives: together with genealogical tables of the Royal Family from the Conquest to the present time; v. 2* (London, Constable & Co.,1911)

J. L. Laynesmith, *Cecily, Duchess of York.* (London, New York: Bloomsbury Academic, 2017)

Matthew Lewis, *Richard, Duke of York: King by Right.* (Stroud: Amberley Publishing, 2016)

Henry Noble MacCracken, *An English Friend of Charles of Orléans*, PMLA Vol. 26, No. 1 (1911), pp. 142-180

W. C. Metcalf, *A Book of Knights.* (London, 1885)

Wendy A. E. Moorhen, 'The Career of John de la Pole, Earl of Lincoln'. (*The Ricardian*, Volume 13, 2003, pp.341-358)

Wendy E. A. Moorhen, 'Such was his Renown in Warfare', *Ricardian Bulletin* (2004) http://www.richardiii.net/2_3_0_riii_leadership.php#military

Henry Morley, *English Writers: An Attempt Towards a History of English Literature, Volume 5.* (London, Paris & Melbourne: Cassel and Company Limited, 1890)

Ian Mortimer, *1415: Henry V's Year of Glory.* (London: Random House, 2009)

Ian Mortimer, *Henry V, The Warrior King of 1415.* (New York City: RosettaBooks, 2009, 2013)

Henry Alfred Napier: *Historical Notices of the Parishes of Swyncombe and Ewelme in the County of Oxfordshire.* (Oxford: James Wright, Printer to the University, 1863)

Clementine Oliver. *Murdered in the Tabloids: Billposting and the Destruction of the Duke of Suffolk in 1450.* Anales de la

Bibliography

Universidad de Alicante. Historia Medieval, N. 19 (2015-2016): 381-402, DOI:10.14198/medieval.2015-2016.19.13

Nicholas Orme, *Medieval Children* (New Haven and London: Yale University Press, 2001)

Anthony J. Pollard, *Lord FitzHugh's Rising in 1470* (Bulletin of the Institute of Historical Research, 1979)

Thomas A. Prendergast, Stephanie Trigg: *30 Great Myths about Chaucer* (Hoboken, New
Jersey: John Wiley & Sons, 2020)

J. S. Roskell, '*Thomas Chaucer of Ewelme*', in Parl. and Pol. in Late Med. Eng. iii. 151-91

Charles Ross, *Edward IV.* (New Haven and London: Yale University Press, 1974)

Charles Ross, *Richard III.* (York: Eyre Methuen Ltd, 1981)

Martin B. Ruud, *Thomas Chaucer*, University of Minnesota Studies of Language and Literature, No. 9 (Minneapolis, 1926)

Larry Scanlon and James Simpson, *John Lydgate: Poetry, Culture, and Lancastrian England.* (Indiana: University of Notre Dame Press, 2006)

Michèle Schindler, *Lovell Our Dogge. The Life of Viscount Lovell, Closest Friend of Richard III and Failed Regicide.* (Stroud: Amberley Publishing, 2019)

Peter Spring: *Sir John Tiptoft: 'Butcher of England': Earl of Worcester, Edward IV's Enforcer and Humanist Scholar.* (Barnsley: Pen & Sword, 2018)

Ed. Thomas Stapleton, *De Antiquis Legibus Liber. Cronica Maiorum et Vicecomitum Londoniarum et quedam, que contigebant temporibis illis ab anno MCLXXVIII; cum appendice.* (London: Camden Society, 1846)

Nicola Tallis: *Uncrowned Queen: The Fateful Life of Margaret Beaufort, Tudor Matriarch.* (London: Michael O'Mara Books Limited, 2019)

What is Better than a Good Woman?

J. A. F. Thomson, 'John De La Pole, Duke of Suffolk', *Speculum* (1979)

Marion Turner, *Chaucer: A European Life.* (Woodstock: Princeton University Press, 2019)

https://twitter.com/SylviaBSo/status/1301813823079436288?s=20&fbclid=IwAR1-FtbKu63Cfp23ZLdJQNFxFceg4mPeGEUm9Y6UWx45EtGQjI-opPU2qUA

Roger Virgoe, *The Death Of William De La Pole, Duke Of Suffolk.* https://www.jstor.org/stable/community.28211836

Kathryn Warner, *Edward II's Nieces: The Clare Sisters. Powerful Pawns of the Crown.* (Barnsley: Pen & Sword, 2020)

Stanley Weintraub, *Uncrowned King. The Life of Prince Albert.* (New York: Free Press, 1997)

Josephine Wilkinson, *Richard the Young King to Be.* (Stroud: Amberley Publishing, 2014)

Bertram Wolffe, *Henry VI.* (New Haven and London: Yale University Press, 1981)

INDEX

Ailmer, Thomas 122
Anjou, Margaret of, Queen
  Consort of England
  (1446–1461, 1470–471)
  119, 132-3, 135-7, 143-56,
  159-61, 163-4, 180,
  199-200, 207-8, 215-18,
  223, 225, 248, 250-51, 258

Battles:
  Agincourt 27, 31, 75, 86
  Barnet 250
  Hexham 235-6, 248
  St Alban's 201, 218-9
  St Alban's, Second Battle of
    226
  Tewkesbury 250
  Towton 226
  Wakefield 225
Beaufort, Cardinal Henry 30,
  32, 47, 68, 78, 93, 160, 161,
  213

Beaumont, Elizabeth, neé Phelip,
  Viscountess Beaumont 128
Beaumont, John, 1st Viscount
  Beaumont 180
Beaumont, Katherine, neé
  Neville, Viscountess
  Beaumont 246
Burgersh, Matilda 7, 10, 11, 12,
  13, 14, 15, 17, 23, 32, 92,
  94, 108
Bylton, William 229, 230, 231,
  232

Cade, Jack 201, 203
Cade, Jack, rebellion 201, 202,
  203, 204, 205, 206
Charles, Duke of Orléans 68,
  86-91, 115
Chaucer, Alice
  birth 14
  first engagement 18, 21

What is Better than a Good Woman?

marriage to Sir John Phelip
22-5
death of Sir John 25-7
adolescence 29-31
marriage to Sir Thomas
Montacute 33*ff*
wedding 34-5, 37
attempted seduction by Philip,
Duke of Burgundy 41-2, 46
possible child by Thomas
48-9, 58-61, 107
second widowhood 53
and William, Earl of Suffolk
64*ff*
protects her rights in the
marriage settlement 70-71
connections to the Nevilles 78,
224
made a Lady of the Order of
the Garter 84
accused of greed 101
wardship of Henry VI's
half-brothers 111
possible miscarriages 49, 113,
115, 117-18, 129, 163
birth of son John 129
wardship of Margaret Beaufort
138-43
and Margaret of Anjou
150-53, 155, 157-64 passim,
207-8, 215-6, 250-51
wardship of Anne Beauchamp
156-9
illness 162-4, 167
becomes a duchess 165

death of Anne Beauchamp 171
charges against her 203
loses wardship of Margaret
Beaufort 213-5
arrangement of son's marriage
219-23
her will 253-4
death 256-8
and passim
Chaucer, Geoffrey 7-9, 13, 30,
94
Chaucer, Thomas 7-17, 18,
19-24, 27, 30-377, 62,
63, 70, 76, 78, 89, 91-9,
100-101, 107-8, 125, 211
Clifford, John, 9th Lord Clifford
226

Ewelme 12, 14, 16, 17, 19, 29,
35, 40, 77, 95, 107-110,
117, 127, 128, 130, 145,
158, 166, 171, 180, 185,
229, 231, 234-7, 239, 240,
241, 246, 248, 256-8

FitzHugh, Alice 251
Foix, Jean de, 1st Earl of Kendall
141

Hastings, William, 1st Baron
Hastings 248
Henry IV, King of England
(1399–1413) 12, 13, 18, 19,
20, 24, 39, 124

Index

Henry V, King of England (1413–1422) 20-21, 23-4, 26-7, 29, 30-31, 35-7, 39, 42, 48, 51, 64, 86-7

Henry VI, King of England (1422–1461, 1470–1471)
coronation 65
makes Alice a Lady of the Order of the Garter 84
mother dies 110
half-siblings 111
negotiations for marriage 132-7
gives William and Alice wardship of Margaret Beaufort 138-42
uncle Humphrey, Duke of Gloucester accused of treason 159
elevates William to a dukedom 165
exiles William 184
rescinds Alice's wardship of Margaret Beaufort 214
'gone mad' 217-8
banishes Richard, Duke of York from court 218
released from prison 248
captured 250
and passim

Henry VII, King of England (1485–1509) 142, 227

Holland, Anne, neé Plantagenet, Duchess of Exeter 249

Humphrey, Duke of Gloucester 123, 159, 160, 169

Lovell, Francis, 9th Baron Lovell, 1st Viscount Lovell 251, 252

Lovell, Henry, Lord Morley 256

Lovell, John, 8th Baron Lovell 251

Montacute, Alice, Countess of Salisbury 33, 34, 38, 48, 53, 54, 56, 58, 59, 60, 78, 79, 98, 99, 106, 121, 125, 219, 224, 232, 233, 234

Montacute, Thomas, Earl of Salisbury 30, 33, 34, 35, 36, 37, 39, 40, 41, 42, 43, 44, 45, 46, 47, 48, 49, 50, 51, 52, 53, 54, 55, 57, 58, 59, 60, 61, 62, 63, 66, 74, 75, 77, 78, 84, 96, 98, 100, 103, 104, 105, 106, 107,108, 113, 118, 120, 121, 125, 207, 219, 234, 242, 243

Neville, Anne, née Beauchamp, Countess of Warwick 104, 105

Neville, Cecily, Duchess of York 121, 145, 151, 249

Neville, Isabel, Duchess of Clarence 247

Neville, John, Marquis of Montacute 235

315

Neville, Ralph, Lord Neville 34, 78

Neville, Richard, Earl of Salisbury 34, 38, 58, 59, 60, 61, 62, 63, 78, 84, 98, 103, 104, 105, 106, 120, 121, 219, 224, 234, 235

Neville, Richard, Earl of Warwick 103, 104, 219, 224, 235, 247

Paston, John 194, 195, 223, 228, 236, 244, 245, 246, 151

Paston, Margaret 236, 237, 239, 244, 245, 246, 251

Phelip, Joan, neé Bardolph, Lady Bardolph 21

Phelip, John 21, 22, 23, 24, 25, 26, 27, 28, 31, 33, 46, 49, 52, 54, 234, 242

Phelip, William, Lord Bardolph 21, 28, 79, 125, 126, 127, 128

Plantagenet, Edmund, Earl of Rutland 224, 225, 226

Plantagenet, Edward, Edward IV 224, 225, 226, 227, 228, 232, 235, 237, 243, 246, 247, 248, 249, 250, 251, 257

Plantagenet, George, Duke of Clarence 247, 248, 249, 250

Plantagenet, Margaret, Duchess of Burgundy 243, 249, 250

Plantagenet, Richard, Duke of York 26, 121, 145, 161, 169, 170, 193, 194, 203, 204, 214, 215, 216, 218, 219, 220, 222, 225, 227

Pole, Elizabeth de la, neé Plantagenet 116, 211, 220, 221, 222, 227, 228, 229, 232, 236, 237, 239, 240, 241, 242, 243, 244, 245,246, 247, 248, 249, 250, 251, 252, 254, 255, 256, 257, 258

Pole, Humphrey de la 256

Pole, John de la, Duke of Suffolk (1442–1492)

birth 128-9

related to Margaret Beaufort 139

bequest from his father 168

protection by his mother 172-3, 186, 197-8, 200, 223

marriage to Margaret Beaufort 175-6, 204-5

letter from his father 187-9

a scholar 209

marriage to Elizabeth Plantagenet 211, 219-21

perennially short of money 211-12

annulment of marriage to Margaret Beaufort 213-4

does not fight for his father-in-law 225

Index

sides with Edward, Earl of
March 226
injured at the Battle of
Hexham 235-6
moves to Ewelme 239
possible influence on his
mother 243
granted wardship of Francis,
Lord Lovell 251
arranges marriage for Joan
Lovell
and passim
Pole, John de la, Earl of Lincoln
228, 232, 243, 257
Pole, William de la, Duke of
Suffolk
second in command at Orléans
52-3, 62, 64
imprisonment in France 65-73
marriage arrangements 66-74
re-establishes himself back in
England 75-7
illness 79-81
rise in Henry VI`s government
76, 78, 84-90, 153-161
and Charles d`Orléans 87- 91,
102-3
illegitimate daughter Jane
95-99
death of possible stepdaughter
103-107
almshouse at Ewelme 107-110
wardship of Henry VI`s
half-brothers 111

hopes for children 113, 115,
117-18, 129
birth of son John 129
negotiation of Henry VI`s
marriage 132-136
acting as Henry VI`s proxy
136-8
relationship with Margaret of
Anjou 149-52
wardship of Margaret Beaufort
138-43
wardship of Anne Beauchamp
156-8
Alice`s illness 162-164
elevation to Dukedom 165
writes a will 166-69
smear campaign against
170-75, 193-5
trial 178-87
last letter to son John 188-9
murder 189-90
reaction to his murder
191-200
supposed murderers executed
215
posthumous reputation 230,
233-5, 242-3
and passim

Ravenspurn 249
Richard II, King of England
(1377–1399) 12-13, 24, 34,
39, 124, 203

What is Better than a Good Woman?

Richard III, King of England (1483–1485) 113, 227, 247, 248

Stanley, Margaret, née Beaufort, Countess of Derby 138-43, 157-8, 175-6, 183, 204-5, 213-15
Stonor, Jane 96-7, 100, 183, 256
Stonor, Thomas 96-7, 99
Stonor, William 97, 256

Tudor, Edmund 110-112, 211, 213-14
Tudor, Jasper, Duke of Bedford 110-112, 211, 213-14, 250

Westminster 228, 237
Wingfield Castle 196-7, 227, 229, 235-7, 239, 241
Woodville, Anthony, Earl Rivers 248
Woodville, Elizabeth 237

Also available from Amberley Publishing

MARGARET OF ANJOU
SHE-WOLF OF FRANCE, TWICE QUEEN OF ENGLAND

JOANNA ARMAN

Available from all good bookshops or to order direct
Please call **01453-847-800**
www.amberley-books.com